Dajjal
the
Antichrist

Revised Edition

Ahmad Thomson

© Sha'ban 1443/April 2022 Ahmad Thomson

First Edition published by Ta-Ha Publishers Ltd in 1986
Reprinted in 1993 and 1995

Revised Edition published in 1997
Reprinted in 1998, 2000, 2001, 2004, 2007, 2011, 2015

Second Revised Edition published in 2022
Reprinted in 2024

Ta-Ha Publishers Ltd
Unit 4, The Windsor Centre
Windsor Grove, West Norwood
London SE27 9NT, United Kingdom

URL: www.tahapublishers.com
Email: support@tahapublishers.com

Revised and typeset by Ahmad Thomson

All rights reserved. No part of this publication may be reproduced, stored in any retrieval system, or transmitted in any form or by any means, electronic or otherwise, without written permission of the publishers.

A catalogue record of this book is available from the British Library

ISBN-13: 978-1-84200-144-8

Printed by IMAK Ofset, Türkiye

Contents

Pre Script iv

Preface to the Revised Edition v

Dajjal – the king who has no clothes 1

Glossary of Arabic Terms 195

Post Script 215

Bibliography 217

This book is a work of fiction. Any resemblance between what is described and what you see is entirely coincidental. It is only a dream of a dreamer in the dream of

Allah

Acknowledgements

This book could not and would not have been written had it not been for the inspiration of Shaykh Dr 'Abd'al-Qadir as-Sufi ad-Darqawi al-Murabit, alayhi rahma • Ma sha Allah wa la hawla wa la quwwata ila bi'llah – What Allah wants happens and there is no power and no strength except from Allah •

Many thanks to all those who have taught me, to those who taught me knowing they were doing so, and to those who taught me without knowing they were doing so • Al-hamdulillahi wa shukrulillah – Praise belongs to Allah and thanks belongs to Allah •

Pre Script

During the time which has passed since this revised edition was first published in 1997, events have shaped the world and how its inhabitants experience existence profoundly: the destruction of the twin towers in New York in 2001; the invasion and pulverisation, in harmony with Oded Yinon's *Strategy for Israel* published in 1982, of nearly all of the countries which surround occupied Palestine; the introduction of the corona virus in 2019 in a manner reminiscent of the film *V for Vendetta* accompanied by mass indoctrination and enhanced social control via the media; the fine tuning of the systems and techniques utilised by the unelected international financial elite to enslave the peoples of the world by making dependence on worthless digital fiat currencies and their associated spiralling debt traps an apparently inescapable daily fact of life; the exponential destruction and pollution of the natural environment at such a pace that climate change is now an undeniable reality – and underpinning all of this, the development of the internet and its associated social media platforms, none of which were publicly available when the first and revised editions of this book were originally published. As the leading hologram in the film *THX1138* observes, "It all happened so quickly, hardly anyone noticed."

During these end times, safety and sanity are to be found in worshipping Allah and living in accordance with the guidance of Islam as established by the Prophet Muhammad, may Allah bless him and grant him peace, while it continues to become increasingly apparent that the meaning of past, present and future events in the Middle East can only really be fully understood within the context of recognising what is entailed in attempts to achieve the publicly proclaimed Zionist dream of establishing a Greater Eretz from the Nile to the Euphrates.

It is this chain of events, catalysed by the unrelenting oppression of the Palestinians and the attempted destruction of Al-Aqsa Mosque and re-construction of the third Temple of Solomon in its place, which will inevitably culminate in the final confrontation prophesied both in the Old Testament and by the Prophet Muhammad: the arrival of the Dajjal and the Mahdi; the final conflict between them and their armies; the return of Jesus, peace be on him, and the annihilation of the Dajjal and his people; followed by a brief interim of peace and abundant blessings before this world ends and the next unfolds.

Ahmad Thomson – Rajab 1443 / February 2022

Preface
to the
Revised Edition

Dajjal, the king who has no clothes was originally written in 1980. Major events that have taken place since then have tended to confirm the overview contained in the original work:

On the one hand, these have included the 'official' dismantling of communism – in reality the 'siamese twin' of capitalism which rather than having been surgically dissected from its counterpart has in fact become totally united and at one with it – as well as the Gulf War, the Bosnian war, the wars waged by Russia on the Muslims to the south, the containing of the Muslims in Palestine, the continuing offensive against Muslims in North Africa, the strengthening of the hold of the international banking network over all people, and of course the declaration that the 'new world order' is now in place, with the accompanying view that any opposition to this 'order' is by definition anarchistic and terrorist in nature.

On the other hand, the resurgence of Islam throughout the world during the same period has continued to grow steadily, and although efforts to redefine the teachings of Islam continue – so as to reduce it to just another state religion which does not threaten the foundations of the new world order in any way, but rather is one of its control mechanisms – the signs are that the desire amongst the main body of Muslims to live in accordance with the original living deen of Islam – and accordingly their ability to distinguish between the real thing and the official version – has not diminished in the least. If anything it has grown in depth and intensity.

Accordingly, the revised version of this book is not very different to the original – other than having been expanded slightly – although I have tried to reduce the frequency with which the word 'kafir' was used in the first edition. The reason for such abundant use was that it was only as the book was originally being written that I realised how much of what I had been brought up and educated to regard as 'normal' was in fact only 'normal' for the kafirun – but, when viewed from a Qur'anic perspective, extremely 'abnormal' for the muminun.

I accordingly used the adjective 'kafir' so frequently in the first edition not only in order to remind myself, but also so as to shake and awake the reader out of any complacency that he or she might have.

It is interesting to note in passing that when *Dajjal, the king who has no clothes* was originally written, the term 'new world order' had not yet been overtly introduced into common parlance through the media, although it had already been in circulation in its Latin form – novus ordo seclorum – on the American one dollar bill for many years, as well as being sparingly referred to by both President Wilson and President Roosevelt, inter alia, when plunging America into the two 'world' wars.

President Wilson told American Congress on the 2nd April 1917 that the purpose of the war was 'to set up a new international order' – and once the first 'world' war was over the League of Nations was duly established, in 1920. Similarly, President Roosevelt allegedly drafted 'a plan to preserve peace' which he named 'The United Nations' – the name given to the organisation which replaced the League of Nations shortly after the end of the second 'world' war, in 1946.

It is only since the conclusion of the Gulf War in 1991 – which effectively ensured the virtual bankruptcy of all the previously 'oil-rich' Muslim Middle East states – however, that the term 'new world order' has been openly used on the media, accompanied by the corresponding deployment of United Nations 'forces' in the name of 'peace' to politically destabilise even further the countries which, it is claimed, they have been sent to 'protect'.

Thus, to give but one example, the Bosnian Muslims in former Yugoslavia were 'protected' by having a United Nations arms embargo imposed on them, while the Serbian aggressors – who were simultaneously granted almost unlimited access to arms and military supplies – were only 'deterred', or rather delayed, from wiping out the defenceless Bosnian Muslims altogether by the setting up of 'safe zones' and 'protected areas' and the occasional token NATO practice airstrike. Having collected large numbers of Muslims in these safe areas and having persuaded them to surrender their arms, the UN forces then systematically abandoned them to their fate – which for the men often meant death and a mass grave, for the women rape and life as a refugee, and for the children scars which will never be healed.

The Prophet Muhammad, may Allah bless him and grant him peace, said that kufr is one system, and I accordingly tried to write the first edition in a very general manner, without referring to too many specific examples, so that it would be like a mirror which would reflect life wherever the book might happen to be read – whether in Sydney, or Southampton, or Singapore, or Santander, or Shiraz, or Santiago, or Seattle, or Saskatoon, or San Francisco, or Srinagar, or Strasbourg, or Sokoto, or Soweto, or Shanghai, or Sharjah, or Sofia, or Seville, or Sinkiang, or Stuttgart, or Swansea, to name but a few. I have attempted to maintain this approach in this revised edition, and for the same reason.

Some people have also observed that perhaps the book would have been clearer and easier to read if it had been divided up into chapters. One of the points that I was trying to make in the book, however, was that everything is known by its opposite, and in existence the opposites are for ever interacting. Although they meet, they do not mix – and although they do not mix, they are never entirely separate from each other. The two sides of the coin are opposite each other – but they are part of a whole, and even if you try to physically divide the coin into two 'halves', each 'half' will still have two sides to it.

I therefore had one long 'chapter' in which I tried to present a kaleidoscope effect with words – a mental hologram – which showed one picture at one moment and then another, its opposite, the next, in order to indicate what appeared to be some of the main patternings in existence, and knowing full well that it could not be done! Again, I have retained this approach in this revised edition, and for the same reason, still knowing full well that it is impossible, for example, to convey what the taste of honey and the taste of a lychee pip are really like by means of the printed word alone.

When the original book was first written, I took it as read that the reader would already be familiar with the hadith which describe the Dajjal, and which are accordingly only referred to but not extensively quoted in the text. Of course this has not always been the case, and accordingly any reader who is not familiar with these hadith should resort to the main and trustworthy collections of hadith. The reader would also benefit from referring to *The Signs Before the Day of Judgement* of Ibn Kathir, translated by Huda Khattab and published by Dar al-Taqwa Ltd, which contains many of the relevant hadith.

During the last fifteen years, many people have asked about the reason for the sub-title which appeared in the first edition – 'the king who has no clothes' – and which has been exchanged for 'the AntiChrist' in this revised edition.

The sub-title used for the first edition was primarily a reference to the well-known children's story about the tailors who deceived a king, making him think that they had made the finest clothes in the land for him, when in fact all that they had done was to make believe and take his money. Everyone pretended that 'everything was all right' and that the king was fully clothed in the finest garments – until a child destroyed the illusion by simply speaking the truth, and asking why the king was completely naked!

The sub-title used for the first edition also refers indirectly to the Prophet Muhammad, may Allah bless him and grant him peace, who was the wisest and most human being that has ever lived among men – a king in the true sense of the word – and yet who possessed very little and avoided the pomp and circumstance and finery which envelops most so-called kings.

It has been related by sayyedina 'Umar, may Allah be pleased with him, that once when he visited the Prophet Muhammad, may Allah bless him and grant him peace, who was lying on a mat in his small room, he was moved to tears when he saw how little the Prophet possessed.

When the Prophet asked him why he was crying, sayyedina 'Umar replied, 'O Messenger of Allah, how can I not cry? This mat has left marks on your sides and I can only see what I have seen of your stores. Caesar and Chosroes are leading their lives of plenty, while you are the Messenger of Allah, His Chosen One – and look what you have!'

'Ibn al-Khattab,' he answered, 'isn't it enough for you that for us there is the next world, and for them there is this world?'

This has always been the case as regards the empire builders on the one hand, and the true followers of the Prophets, on the other, may the blessings and peace of Allah be on them and on their families and companions and followers in every age.

The sub-title used for the first edition also refers to Allah, the Lord of the worlds, the King of the Creation, the King Who is over all kings – and yet Who has no clothes!

Needless to say, the reason for changing the sub-title to 'the Anti-

Christ' should be obvious. People in general – especially non-Muslims – are more familiar with this term and have at least some idea of what it refers to, even in an age where secular education has ensured that the general population is even less aware of what is in the Bible than in the past! Those non-Muslims who have read the Bible, or who have received some religious education, however, will no doubt be as fascinated and curious as I was when reading about and reflecting on the prophecies contained in it which concern the AntiChrist, and Gog and Magog, and the second coming of Jesus, peace be on him.

They will probably also be as equally unaware as I was about the detailed knowledge of these matters concerning the last days which the Muslims possess, and it is for people such as these – for people who know that they do not really know, but who want to know – that this book is primarily intended, not as a conclusive statement of how things are I hasten to add, but rather as a means of whetting the appetite to find out more, for ultimately real knowledge is not found in books – it is transmitted by those who have been given wisdom.

Many people have also asked why the following statement occurred at the front of the first edition – 'This book is a work of fiction. Any resemblance between what is described and what you see is entirely coincidental. It is only a dream of a dreamer in the dream of Allah.' – when, as they are quick to point out, the book often appears to be carefully describing at least some of what is currently going on in the world.

The answer is that when the book was completed, I was only too well-aware that in terms of its being a description of life, the contents of the book were incomplete, over-simplified, and inevitably coloured by my own limited personal experience, perceptions and understanding – and accordingly it was not a completely true depiction of life as it actually is. However much we know, we only know a little.

Furthermore, I was also only too well aware of Ibn al-Arabi's well-known words: 'Know that the whole creation is an imagination (khayal), and that you are an imagination in that imagination, and that whatever you think is an imagination, in that imagination, in that imagination.'

How then can anyone with any sense give reality to a khayal, to an imagination, and not to the source of that imagination – Allah, the Real?

No one has created Allah – although some of today's 'experts' in their white coats and pinstripes would have us think this, that we have imagined a God in order to try and make sense of existence, or to turn to in times of trouble.

The truth of the matter is that it is we who have been 'imagined' by Allah. It is Allah Who has given us reality, not the other way around. It is Allah Who has created us. Everything in creation has a beginning and comes to an end and ceases to exist. Allah has no beginning and no end. He has never not existed and He will never not exist. He is as He was before the Creation was brought into existence, and He will remain as He is after the Creation has ceased to exist. Surely everything in creation comes from Allah and surely to Him everything in creation returns.

Allah is the Real. Allah is True. Everything other than Allah is a fiction. It, whatever 'it' is, may appear to exist, but it will inevitably melt away like a fading dream – including 'you', and 'me', and 'them', and 'it', and any 'thing' else you may care to mention.

To conclude, when the first edition of this book was first being written, I was only too well aware that it is impossible to summarise and encapsulate life in its totality on the printed page. The most that could be achieved was to project a combination of 'headlines' and 'images' which, it was hoped, would indicate some of the main characteristics of the world as it is today. This remains the case today and it will always be so, and, if anything, I am now even more aware than ever before that the innumerable variations and forms in life defy detailed description and categorisation: We all try to 'make sense' of life and of what happens in it – both to ourselves and to others – but ultimately, if we are not foolish enough to think that we know it all, we are driven to realise that Allah knows and we do not know, and so to humbly place our foreheads on the ground in complete and unconditional surrender before our Lord.

Allah

Ahmad Thomson
London 1417/1997

In the Name of Allah
the Merciful the Compassionate

And when the magicians came, Moses said to them, 'Throw what you are going to throw!'

And when they had thrown, Moses said, 'What you have produced is magic. Surely Allah will destroy it! Surely Allah does not protect the work of mischief makers.'

And Allah will vindicate the truth by His words, however much the guilty detest it.

(*Qur'an: Surah Yunus* – 10.80-82)

The Companions of the Fire and the Companions of the Garden are not the same. It is the Companions of the Garden who are the victors.

(*Qur'an: Surat'al-Hashr* – 59.20)

In the country of the blind
the one eyed man
is king

Dajjal

There are three aspects of the Dajjal. There is Dajjal the individual. There is Dajjal as a world wide social and cultural phenomenon. There is Dajjal as an unseen force.

✿ ✿ ✿ ✿ ✿

Although the word 'Dajjal' – which comes from the Arabic word meaning 'to deceive', 'to cheat', 'to smear with tar' – does not appear in the *Qur'an*, the Dajjal is described in considerable detail in all the major collections of the *Hadith*, including the two well-known Sahih collections of Imam al-Bukhari and Imam Muslim, especially in the sections which are concerned with 'the last days', the period of time immediately preceding the end of the world, as well as in many other compilations of *Hadith* such as *Al-Mishkat Al-Masabih*, *The Gardens of the Righteous*, and *Al-Muwatta'* of Imam Malik:

From 'Abdullah ibn 'Umar, may Allah be pleased with him:

> The Prophet Muhammad, may Allah bless him and grant him peace, stood up to speak to his people and after praising Allah as He should be praised, may He be Exalted and Glorified, he spoke about the Dajjal, saying, 'I warn you against him, and there is no Prophet who has not warned his people against him – even Noah warned his people against him. But I will tell you something which no other Prophet has told his people. You must know that the Dajjal is one-eyed, and Allah is not one-eyed.' (It was related by Muslim)

From Abu'l-Dira, may Allah be pleased with him:

> The Prophet Muhammad, may Allah bless him and grant him peace, said, 'Whoever memorises the first ten ayat of Surat'al-Kahf will be protected from the Dajjal.' (It was related by Abu Da'ud and by Muslim)

From 'Abdullah ibn 'Abbas, may Allah be pleased with him:

> The Messenger of Allah, may Allah bless him and grant him peace, used to teach this du'a in the same way that he would teach them a surah of the *Qur'an*:

'Allahumma inniy a'udhu bika min adhabi jahannama, wa a'udhu bika min adhabi'l-qabri, wa a'udhu bika min fitnati'l-Masihi'd-Dajjal, wa a'udhu bika min fitnati'l-mahya wa'l-mamati.'

'O Allah, I seek refuge in You from the torment of Hell, and I seek refuge in You from the torment of the grave, and I seek refuge in You from the trial of the Dajjal, and I seek refuge in You from the trial of life and death.' (It was related by Malik)

'Al-Masih ad-Dajjal' literally means 'the False Messiah', in other words, 'the Anti-Christ' – as opposed to 'Al-Masih ibn Maryam', meaning 'the Messiah son of Mary', in other words, the Prophet Jesus Christ, peace be on him:

From 'Abdullah ibn 'Umar, may Allah be pleased with him:

The Prophet Muhammad, may Allah bless him and grant him peace, said, 'I dreamt at night that I was at the Ka'ba, and I saw a dark man like the most handsome of dark men you have ever seen. He had hair reaching to between his ears and his shoulders like the most excellent of such hair that you have seen. He had combed his hair, and water was dripping from it. He was leaning on two men or on the shoulders of two men doing tawaf around Ka'ba. I asked, "Who is this?" It was said, "Al-Masih ibn Maryam." Then we were with a man with wiry hair and blind in his right eye, as if it was a floating grape. I asked, "Who is this?" It was said to me, "This is Al-Masih ad-Dajjal."' (It was related by Malik).

◦　◦　◦　◦　◦

At some point between now and the end of the world the Dajjal will most certainly appear.

The Prophet Muhammad, may the blessings and peace of Allah be on him, was sitting with a group of his companions, may Allah be pleased with all of them, one day during the late afternoon. The disc of the sun was just about to begin to disappear behind a wall. The Prophet said that the time between their sitting there that afternoon and the end of the world, was as short as the distance between the bottom of the sun and the top of the wall at that moment. This was fourteen hundred years ago.

Allah confirms in the Qur'an that the person who is asked about the end of the world – that is, the Hour – knows as much about it as the person who asks the question. Allah also says that mankind has only been given a little knowledge concerning the Hour. No-one knows exactly when it will be, but Allah indicates in the Qur'an that perhaps it is closer than you think. As far as you are concerned, the world ends for you when you die.

From Abu Hurayra, may Allah be pleased with him:

> The Prophet Muhammad, may Allah bless him and grant him peace, said, 'There are five things which nobody knows except Allah.' Then he recited:
>
> **Truly knowledge of the Hour is with Allah – and it is He Who sends down rain, and it is He Who knows what is in the wombs – and no self knows what it will earn tomorrow, and no self knows in what land it will die. Truly Allah is All-Knowing, Aware.** (*Qur'an: Surah Luqman* – 31.34)
>
> (It was related by Muslim)

Many of the signs of the end of the world are clearly indicated in the *Hadith* collections, and whoever is awake and aware of the signs in the self and on the horizon, knows about these signs and recognises them when they appear. Virtually all the signs of the end of the world are now apparent, except for the last four major signs, and it would appear that even these are now imminent.

Amongst the signs already apparent are: that the poor and the destitute build tall buildings in which people glorify themselves; that the slave girl gives birth to her mistress, one meaning of which is that a mother who is enslaved by her work situation has children who grow up to be uncontrollable and who dominate and tyrannise the family situation; that women greatly outnumber men; that there are many women who no longer give birth to children; that everyone is concerned with working so that not only the men but also the women go out to work; that family ties are neglected or abandoned; that there is an abundance of food, much of which has no blessing; that when a person is offered food it is refused; that time is short; that there are many people who are hard-hearted and mean; that there are many people who bear false witness; that the truthful are disbelieved and the liars are believed; that the strong devour the weak; that few are wise and many are ignorant; that the leader of a people is the worst of them; that a people fear a tyrant so much that they dare not even tell him that he is a tyrant; that there is much fighting and killing of people; that the ones who do the killing do not know who is being killed, and that the ones who are killed do not know why they have been killed; that there are people who behave like animals; that there are women who wear their clothes like a second skin so that they appear naked even though they are clothed; that many people drink alcohol; that adultery and fornication are common; that men lie with men, and women with women; that men wear silk; that female singers and musical instruments are popular; that usury is so widespread that even those who are not directly involved in it are affected by it; that there are few people who are trustworthy in their business transactions; that people distrust those who are honest and trust those who are dishonest; that writing is widespread; that attempts are made to make the deserts green; that there are people who attempt to change the balance of nature and who interfere with and interrupt the basic cycles and processes of existence; that earthquakes and other natural disasters increase in frequency and intensity; that people wish they were out of this world and in their graves; that people believe in the stars rather than trusting in God; that there are many false prophets, each claiming to be a messenger of God; that voices are raised in anger in places of worship; that many of the Muslims become extremely wealthy; that the Muslims are numerous but powerless – because of their love for this world and their fear of death – and unable to stop the nations of the world from invading and plundering them; and finally that the sun rises in the west, one meaning of which is that the life transaction of Islam is adopted by people living in the western world – although it is clear from the *Hadith* collections that this is also an event which is destined to literally take place:

From 'Abdullah ibn 'Amr, may Allah be pleased with him:

> The Prophet Muhammad, may Allah bless him and grant him peace, said, 'The first of the signs (of the Hour) to appear will be the rising of the sun from the West and the appearance of the Beast before the people in the forenoon.

Whichever of these two events happens first, the other will follow immediately. (It was related by Muslim).

Commenting on this hadith, Ibn Kathir states that the emergence of the Beast – either in or near Makka – will be the first of the earthly signs, just as the rising of the sun from the West will be the first of the heavenly signs. In summarising what the *Qur'an* and the *Hadith* say about the Beast Ibn Kathir states in his book *Al-Bidayah wa'n-Nihayah*, meaning 'The Beginning and the End', as follows:

> Among the signs of the Hour will be the emergence of a beast from the earth. It will be very strange in appearance, and extremely huge; one cannot even imagine what it will look like. It will emerge from the earth and shake the dust from its head. It will have with it the ring of Solomon and the rod of Moses. People will be terrified of it and will try to run away, but they will not be able to escape, because such will be the decree of Allah. It will destroy the nose of every unbeliever with the rod, and write the word 'kafir' on his forehead; it will adorn the face of every believer and write the word 'mumin' on his forehead, and it will speak to people.

As well as the rising of the sun from the West and the emergence of the Beast from the earth, the *Hadith* also refer to other major signs which have yet to take place, including the Smoke – which will drive people from the east to the west; the destruction of Madina al-Munawarra; the destruction of the Ka'ba in Makka by an Abyssinian called Dhu'l-Suwayqatayn; and three major landslides – one in the East, one in the West, and one in Arabia – at the end of which fire will burst forth from the direction of Aden in the Yemen, and drive people to the place of their final assembly.

According to most of the commentators, these events will probably take place after the last four major signs of the end of the world have occurred – and these are: the appearance of Dajjal the individual; the appearance of the Mahdi, the rightly guided leader of the Muslims who will fight the Dajjal; the re-appearance of the Prophet Jesus, on him be peace, who as well as breaking all the crosses, killing all the pigs, marrying and having children and praying with the Muslims, will also kill the Dajjal; and the appearance of Yajuj wa Majuj, or Gog and Magog, a tribe of people who will scatter across the world, creating destruction.

o   o   o   o   o

There are three aspects of the Dajjal. There is Dajjal the individual. There is Dajjal as a world wide social and cultural phenomenon. There is Dajjal as an unseen force.

❂   ❂   ❂   ❂   ❂

It is clear that before Dajjal the individual appears on earth, there must already be present and established the system, and the people running that system, which and who will support and follow him when he does appear. Evidence of that system, and the people running that system, is evidence of Dajjal as a world wide social and cultural phenomenon, and Dajjal as an unseen force. The signs of these broader aspects of Dajjal, that is what Dajjal the individual will epitomise, are very apparent today, which would indicate that Dajjal the individual is soon to appear.

❂   ❂   ❂   ❂   ❂

Amongst the descriptions of the Dajjal in the *Hadith* collections we find the following: Dajjal has one eye, like a floating grape. Dajjal can be heard all over the world at the same time. Dajjal will show you fire, but it will not burn you. Dajjal will show you water, but you will not be able to drink it. Dajjal will talk of the Garden, and make it seem like the Fire. Dajjal will talk of the Fire, and make it seem like the Garden. These descriptions all fit the characteristics of today's media systems and communications technology, and especially the manner in which they are largely used.

The Dajjal is also described in the *Hadith* as having many eyes on both sides, and travelling about the world in large hops. This description fits the characteristics of today's means of mass transport. Dajjal is also described as having the letters KFR written on the forehead. Some of the jets in the Israeli airforce have these letters painted on their noses.

The letters KFR are the basic root letters of the Arabic word kufr, or kafir. Kufr is to cover up and to reject. The kafir is the one who covers up the true nature of existence – that is, that there is no god only Allah – and who rejects the messengers who are sent by Allah to show people how to live in harmony with what is within them and with what is without them, and to worship and have knowledge of Allah.

When the Prophet Muhammad, may the blessings and peace of Allah be on him, said that you should seek knowledge as far as China, he was talking about knowledge of Allah, or at the very least knowledge which leads to knowledge of Allah. If your knowledge does not come from fear of Allah, you have been deceived. Fear Allah, and Allah will give you knowledge. The kafir rejects this. The kafir is thus diametrically opposed to the mumin.

The mumin is the muslim who openly affirms the true nature of existence, and who accepts and follows the example and teachings of the Prophet Muhammad, may the blessings and peace of Allah be on him, the last of the Prophets to have been sent by Allah before the end of the world.

○   ○   ○   ○   ○

It should already be clear that the kafir system, and the kafirun who control and believe in that system, are none other than the manifestation of Dajjal as a world wide social and cultural phenomenon and Dajjal as an unseen force. Dajjal the individual will be the epitome of the kafir system, the ultimate kafir, and therefore inevitably to be chosen as the leader of that system by the kafirun who are running that system, when he appears. The Prophet Muhammad said that kufr is one system. The kafir system is Dajjal. The three aspects of Dajjal are in fact interlinked and indivisible. Dajjal.

In the same way the Mahdi will be, when he appears, the epitome of Islam, the way of the Prophet Muhammad, although it must be said immediately that he will be like a drop compared to the ocean of the Prophet Muhammad, may the blessings and peace of Allah be on him. It follows that the Mahdi will be the one who is inevitably recognised and accepted by all true Muslims as their leader. The Prophet Muhammad said that the Muslims are one body.

Kufr is at war with Islam. Islam is at war with Kufr. It is clear from the *Hadith* that the Dajjal will fight the Mahdi. The Mahdi will fight the Dajjal. The Prophet Jesus, who was not crucified, but taken by Allah out of this world into the Unseen – and another who looked like him crucified in his place – the Prophet Jesus, on him be peace, having returned to this world, will kill the Dajjal together with all his followers.

○   ○   ○   ○   ○

The Dajjal has been the subject of much writing in the past. Prophecies relating to the Dajjal are to be found, for example, in the *Bible*, in the *Book of Revelations* by John, and in the writings of Nostrodamus. Many people have repeatedly attempted to interpret these prophecies anew in the light of events taking place during their own particular lifetimes. The Dajjal is usually referred to as 'the AntiChrist' in these prophecies and the commentaries on them – as also, more recently, in the loose interpretations which have been placed on them in various films and videos.

It is not known how reliable or accurate either these prophecies, or the commentaries on them, or the later interpretations of them, are. It is quite probable that at least some of them came by way of the jinn.

The jinn are made of smokeless fire. They can see us. Only some of us can see them. Human beings are made of water and clay. Angels are made of pure light. They are incapable of wrong action. They do not eat or sleep or procreate. They praise Allah continuously. They are the means by which the creational process operates. The jinn, like us, are capable of right action and wrong action. Some of them are muslim, some are kafir, and some are munafiq, that is hypocrites who say they are muslim when in truth they are kafir. The jinn often communicate with people, and from their knowledge of the unseen tell of events which lie in the future. They are often used by magicians and fortune-tellers.

Clearly, if the writings of John and Nostrodamus came by way of, or were influenced by, bad or mischievous jinn, then they are not entirely reliable, since, as is the case with many of the jinn who are the familiars of those who practice magic, or who communicate with mediums, for every truth that is told, several half-truths and outright lies are also added. Given this element of possible uncertainty and error, the only way that the prophecies of John and Nostrodamus can be shown to be reliable is when what has been said corresponds to what eventually happens.

As far as the written word is concerned, therefore, the *Hadith* contain the most reliable descriptions of the Dajjal and of the events which are to take place both before and after the appearance of the Dajjal – wherever, that is, there is a reliable isnad, that is a reliable chain of transmission from the one who heard or saw what was actually said or done by the Prophet Muhammad himself, to the ones who remembered by heart what that person remembered by heart, to the one who recorded what they remembered in writing.

The *Hadith* which were recorded in writing were only accepted after both their contents and their isnads had been scrupulously checked and authenticated by the scholars who collected them – unlike today's versions of the *Bible*, all of whose contents are incapable of being authenticated in this manner, and much of which may therefore originate from unreliable sources and cannot definitely be attributed to the Prophets whose words and actions the *Bible* purports to record.

Allah says in the *Qur'an* – which, being a direct revelation from God to Muhammad via the Angel Jibril which was both memorised by heart and recorded in writing as it was revealed, is even more reliable than the fully authenticated *Hadith* – Allah says in the *Qur'an* that the Jews and the Christians have changed and altered the original teaching of their respective Prophets, peace be on them, and the numerous contradictions and discrepancies which now exist within the *Bible* bear eloquent witness to this fact.

The Prophet Muhammad did say, however, may the blessings and peace of Allah be on him, that knowledge is the lost property of the mumin, who may pick it up wherever he or she finds it. The mumin is the muslim who not only believes in Allah, but who also actually and actively trusts in Allah in the course of his or her every-day affairs. The muslim may believe in Allah whilst still relying on his or her own actions. The mumin relies on Allah for success. The muhsin is the muslim who knows that there is only Allah, and that accordingly reliance on other than Allah is an impossibility. The muslim, the mumin and the muhsin are all Muslims, but they possess different degrees of knowledge of Allah. Those who fear Allah the most are the ones who have the greatest knowledge of Allah, because such fear only comes with such knowledge. The Prophet Muhammad said that no other being feared Allah as much as he.

Knowledge comes to the one who purifies the heart by the grace of Allah. As the heart becomes clear and calm, the knowledge of the heart increases. This knowledge begins where the written word ends. For those whose hearts are purified, so that the signs in the self and on the horizon – and they are the same – are recognisable and understood, the signs of Dajjal as a world wide social and cultural phenomenon and Dajjal as an unseen force are plain to see, and what they experience is a confirmation and amplification of the information which the written word contains.

The mumin is the muslim who trusts in Allah. Part of this trust is to trust others, and to trust one's self, and one's experience of life, and one's interpretation of the signs in the self and on the horizon. This trust is complete when the person knows his or her self, for whoever knows their self knows their Lord, and whoever knows their Lord knows what comes from their Lord, which is creation, the universe and everything in it – and no form tangible or intangible, actual or conceptual, can be associated with Allah. Whoever has this trust and this knowledge is muhsin.

Reading is not the same as seeing. The seeing is a much stronger confirmation of what has been read. Books can only remind you of what has already been tasted and of what is yet to be tasted or of what is capable of being tasted. It is the tasting which is important, not the record of the tasting, whether that record be audio or visual, or on paper or plastic, or on metal or celluloid. To see is to know, but there are different seeings and different knowings.

o   o   o   o   o

Considering Dajjal as an unseen force, the presence of this force is indicated by the arrival of beings from another world who take possession of human beings in the same way as the jinn sometimes possess humans and animals. It may well be that Dajjal as an unseen force can, like the jinn, actually manifest as humans and animals without actually having to possess them, that is by taking on their likeness rather than by taking them over. It may well be that Dajjal as an unseen force is none other than a horde of kafir jinn, as opposed to being beings of some other kind. It is not known from which world they come. It is known that there are many worlds. Allah is described in the *Qur'an*, in *Surat'al-Fatiha*, as 'Lord of the Worlds'. Ibn al-'Arabi visited some of these worlds in vision, and describes these experiences in his book *The Makkan Revelations*. He names vast cities possessing technologies far superior to the ones of which some people on this earth boast today.

The sign that this possession has taken place is that you see large numbers or groups of people all acting as one body, apparently possessing no individual identity. Although they look like human beings they simply do not behave like human beings, but more like robots. The large numbers of books and films which deal with this phenomenon are not mere figments of the imagination. They point to the reality of what has already occurred and continues to occur, as, for example, in the film *The Man who Fell to Earth*.

Since this aspect of Dajjal as an unseen force is in the Unseen, direct knowledge of it is only available to those who have been given access to the Unseen. Although the Prophet Muhammad, may Allah bless him and grant him peace, was given such access, he was not hungry for it.

The desire for such knowledge is an obstacle to the one who desires direct knowledge of Allah.

The evidence in the phenomenal world, that is the world which is apprehended by the senses, however, that this takeover has taken and is taking place is to be found by observing the manner in which the social and cultural conditions in our world have changed, especially in this century, and by examining how life is conducted today. In other words, it is possible to ascertain the characteristics of Dajjal as an unseen force by examining Dajjal as a world wide social and cultural phenomenon.

○　　○　　○　　○　　○

Considering Dajjal as a world wide social and cultural phenomenon, we see that the takeover is well under way, and that the time would appear to be soon approaching when it will be time for Dajjal the individual to appear, simply because the systems and the people running those systems, that is the kafir system, that is the Dajjal system, have apparently gained sufficient world wide control to be able to instate him as the leader they have all been waiting for, once he has been recognised and acclaimed as such.

Dramatic changes have taken place on the face of this earth in the last hundred years. The social groupings which used to be prevalent throughout the world, most of them based on the village pattern, a community of families who all knew and helped each other and which interacted with other village communities, have been rapidly eroded and de-personalised. In the large cities of today, the individual has become increasingly alienated from his or her self, and from others, and from knowledge of Allah – a cog in the consumer producer process who, when not at work or asleep, is often trapped in an infantile and unfulfilled search for illusory self-gratification, which ensures that there is usually very little time left to reflect and to consider where he or she is going, and no time to actually do something about breaking out of the recurring behaviour pattern in which he or she is trapped.

Even where the social grouping of today is limited in size to the village number, the actual social transaction between its members is far less intimate and cohesive than in the past. There is less time to meet together and more time to watch television. There is less time spent working together and more time spent working alone. For those who have been born into this state of affairs, this change in social conditions is not always apparent. It is assumed that things have always been the way they are, as, for example, in the film *THX 1138*.

Perhaps the only way of appreciating how dramatic the change has been is to observe what happens when a multi-national corporation decides to exploit the natural resources of a hitherto inaccessible region of the world. In a relatively brief period of time, the activities of the people controlling the corporation have not only disrupted the way of life of the people living in that area, but have also eliminated their traditional sources of livelihood and thereby ensured that there is cheap labour available to carry out the work being generated by the corporation's activities. Suddenly everyone has a number and wants this thing called money, and the social harmony which existed before the mine, or the oil-field, or the timber-felling operation, or the factory assembly plant, or the hydro-electric power scheme, or whatever, became a reality, is gone.

All this is done in the name of progress, and civilising the backward, and improving the quality of life, but in reality the new lifestyle which is inevitably linked with the new technology, and with the mockery of real knowledge which the kafir calls literacy and education, is the sign of the erosion or end of a truly human transaction in that area, as those who cannot be utilised are either deliberately driven away, or eliminated by the introduction of new illnesses and viruses to which they have no natural resistance.

Another significant change in social activity, which is clearly linked with the degree of automation in any particular social grouping, is that whereas in the past a community used to be united by its worship of God, nowadays this basic and unifying element is often lacking in people's lives. In the western world this pattern of worship used to be predominantly that of the Christian religion – a peculiar amalgam of Paul's own ideas, Greek philosophy, the innovations of a priesthood, which itself was an innovation, in its attempts to compromise by all means with kafir rulers, and finally a few traces of the original teaching of the Prophet Jesus, peace be on him.

Since this pattern of worship was not and is not the same as that which was originally embodied by Jesus and his followers, it follows that it did not, and can not and never will, affirm the true nature of existence or lead to direct knowledge of Allah. It was and is accordingly inevitable that people would constantly abandon this pattern of worship – the kafir because he or she had no desire to worship Allah in the first place, and the true believer because he or she realised that the brand of Christianity which was being advertised had little to do with the original teaching of Jesus, and was not based on the behavioural pattern of him and his community, and would not lead to knowledge of Allah.

It was the fragmentation of western society by the advent of the mechanised way of life, the so-called 'industrial revolution' which made it easier for people to break free of the Christian pattern of worship. No worship was preferable to a pattern of worship which although performed in the name of Jesus did not conform to the pattern of worship which Jesus had in fact brought – and which has in fact been long lost for ever.

It is interesting to note that there are some writers who have equated the Official Trinitarian Church, in all its different manifestations, with the AntiChrist, since so many of its basic doctrines are not only invented by man but also openly contradict what Jesus himself taught, may the peace of Allah be on him, and since so many of its rituals derive from sources other than the lifestyle of Jesus and his community.

This view is reinforced by the fact that it was the champions of the Official Trinitarian Church, both Roman Catholic and then also Protestant, who in past centuries waged war on and eliminated all those Unitarian Christians – including the Nazarenes, the Ebionites, the Donatists, the Arians, the Adoptionists, the Paulicians, the Illumnists, the Catharii and many of the Goths – who sought to follow the original teaching of Jesus and the way of life embodied by him. Once the last of these Unitarian Christians had been eliminated by the Mediaeval Inquisition and its successor the Spanish Inquisition – along with a great many of the Unitarian Jews living in Europe – the Official Trinitarian Church then concentrated on attempting to eliminate all the Unitarian followers of the Prophet Muhammad, the Muslims, and despite its lack of success in this project continues in these attempts even today.

The degree of success which was achieved by the Official Trinitarian Church in these attempts, both in the past and in the present, was, and is, only made possible by the fact that it has always worked hand in glove with the kafir system, that is the Dajjal system, which of course was, and is, also committed to subverting and destroying the practice of a living and dynamic Islam.

In the light of this, it is clear that any apparent conflict between 'Science' and Trinitarian Christianity is largely illusory and certainly only skin deep, since they both depend on and support the same system. However it is equally clear that a distinction must be drawn between those Trinitarian Christians who are perfectly well aware that the way they follow is not the way of Jesus, and those people who in all sincerity wish to worship God and who have been misled into believing that the brand of Christianity which they follow is synonymous with what Jesus originally taught, and who up to now have had no chance of access to the living life transaction of Islam – which is the Prophetic lifestyle for this age, and which naturally bears a striking resemblance to the lifestyle once embodied by Jesus and his original followers, may Allah be pleased with them.

What has just been said about the Christians also applies to the Jews. Many of those who today call themselves Jews clearly do not follow the way of Moses, may the peace of Allah be on him, and indeed a great number of them do not even claim to be descended from the original Tribe of Israel for whom both Moses and Jesus were specifically sent, but freely admit that they are descended from other forbears. Perhaps one of the most significant origins of these non-jewish Jews is the people known as the Khazars, who were originally a small nation living in what is now Turkey and southern Russia, in the area between the Black Sea and the Caspian Sea. Their leader, King Joseph, adopted Judaism out of political expediency during the eighth century AD so as to avoid being conquered either by the Christians who were approaching his kingdom from the north, or by the Muslims who were coming up from the south. He was perfectly well aware that this move would ensure a limited protection from those who also worshipped God.

The descendants of the Khazars, who are usually referred to as the Ashkenazim, noted for their ability and expertise both in the arts and in their business and financial transactions, are now spread throughout the earth. The way of life which they follow is not the way of life which Moses and his community followed, may Allah be pleased with them. That way of life had already been lost when Jesus first appeared on earth. Jesus, it will be remembered, came to re-establish the way of Moses amongst the Tribe of Israel and not to change it one jot or tittle. The fact that the scribes and pharisees, the self-appointed priesthood of what had become the Jewish religion, did not even recognise who Jesus was shows how far astray they were from the original way of Moses even then, and that was twenty centuries ago.

Sometimes described as 'the thirteenth tribe' of Israel, the descendants of the Khazars are linked by some historians with one of the last four major signs of the end of the world, that is the appearance of Yajuj wa Majuj, or Gog and Magog, since they are in reality 'Jews but not Jews', and since King Joseph confirmed, in about 960 AD (in the famous *Khazar Correspondence* between himself and Hasdai ibn Shaprut, the Sephardhic Jewish foreign minister of the Andalusian Khalif, 'Abdu'r-Rahman III), that the Khazars are descended from Togarma, the grandson of Japheth, son of Noah – and according to *Genesis 10: 2-3*, the uncle of Togarma was Magog. If this be true, then we see that they are intimately linked with the appearance of the Dajjal, since many of them today are in high positions of control in the various interlinking systems which together make up the kafir system, that is the Dajjal system.

There are those who are only too eager to point out that what has been said about the Christians and the Jews also applies to the Muslims, and that there are many people alive today who call themselves 'Muslims' but who are not following the way of the Prophet Muhammad and his community. This is quite true, and it is partially a measure of the success enjoyed by the Christians and the Jews in their attempts to subvert and destroy those who have sought or who seek to follow the way of Muhammad and his community, may the blessings and peace of Allah be on him and them.

One of the chief methods used by the kafir system, that is the Dajjal system, to erase living Islam is to introduce the kafir way of life into the Muslim countries, whilst disguising this ploy by describing it in 'islamic' terminology. Nearly all the traditional Muslim lands are today controlled and governed in accordance with the precepts of the kafir system, and not according to what is in the *Qur'an* and the *Sunnah*. Although the Prophet Muhammad, may Allah bless him and grant him peace, said that some Muslims would follow the example of their predecessors – meaning the Christians and the Jews – just like a lizard making for its hole, he also said that not all of his community would go astray. There are still many Muslims who today follow the same pattern of life as that which was followed by the Prophet Muhammad and the first Muslim community which formed around him. The point is, that although there are people who say they are Muslims but who do not follow the way of Muhammad, at least the way of Muhammad is still available for those who do wish to follow it, and at least there are people who still do follow it. The main difference between the Jews, the Christians and the Muslims is that the Jews no longer know or do the prayer which Moses did, the Christians no longer know or do the prayer which Jesus did, and the Muslims still know and do the prayer which Muhammad did.

The way of Moses and the way of Jesus have been lost. The religions of Judaism and Christianity have been developed and introduced instead. These religions are an integral part of the kafir system, that is the Dajjal system. The Dajjal system is the complete antithesis of the Prophetic way of life, as embodied not only by Moses, Jesus and Muhammad, but also by all the Prophets as far back as Adam, may the blessings and peace of Allah be on all one hundred and twenty four thousand of them.

❂   ❂   ❂   ❂   ❂

There are three basic patterns of social grouping in the world. There is the simple community which lives in fitra, that is in simple harmony with existence but without following the Prophetic pattern of worship of Allah. There is the muslim community which as well as living in harmony with existence also worships Allah in the manner indicated by Allah through the Prophet Muhammad, may Allah bless him and grant him peace. Finally there is the kafir society which neither lives in harmony with existence nor consciously worships Allah. In Reality of course every single atom is in its place and the overall harmony of existence eloquently proclaims the Majesty and Beauty of the Bringer into Existence and the Bringer out of Existence and the Only Existent, Allah.

We have seen how the pattern of life followed by the small community living in fitra and by the muslim community has been considerably eroded and destroyed, especially in the last century, by the spread of the kafir system, that is the Dajjal system. In order to appreciate the characteristics of this system, which is outwardly the expression of Dajjal as a world wide social and cultural phenomenon and inwardly the manifestation of Dajjal as an unseen force, it is necessary to examine the system in greater detail.

❂   ❂   ❂   ❂   ❂

The way in which today's kafir state is managed and controlled is by means of a highly centralised and increasingly computerised government. The advance of technology, especially in the realms of communication and travel, together with the use of complex computerised information storage and retrieval systems, has made widespread control from one place a reality. Most kafir states are police states. Compared with the situation a hundred years ago, the degree of surveillance and control exercised by the rulers over the ruled is staggering. Much of this control is made possible by the form which work takes in today's industrial society.

It is significant that the most common form of business concern today is the large corporation, whether privately or state owned, which often not only has branches all over any one particular country, but also all over any one particular land-mass, and even all over the world. Everyone who works within a particular corporation structure is controlled by the manner in which that corporation operates. People are increasingly obliged to put the rules of the corporation above the application of common sense and humanity in the conduct of their everyday lives. Even the individual concern or the small business is highly regulated in what it may or may not do. Everyone is always told that these rules are for their own good, but they are never given the chance to see what life would be like without them.

It comes as no surprise to find that those who control the government of a kafir state usually control the large corporations too. The elite of the kafir controllers control the kafir legal system, which is used to control all the other interlinking sub-systems in the kafir system, that is the Dajjal system, by determining what form they may take and what the people who work within them may or must not do. This means that life in a kafir state is highly institutionalised, standardised and regularised. The most common social grouping today is centred around the work nexus. It is pyramidical in form. The manner of its control is pharaonic. This enables the few to enslave and control the many, often without the many realising just how great the degree of control being exercised over them is. All kafir institutions are run as a business concern, whether it be the legal system, the government system, the factory system, the university system, the hospital system or the media system, to name but a few.

All these institutions are geared to enable the effective running of the producer consumer process, which is today's predominant religion, enthralling the many with its myriad rules and controlled by its priesthood of experts. The consumer producer process is promoted as the ideal way of life by all those who at present control the kafir states of the so-called modern world. This is not surprising, since it is they who benefit most from that process and gather most of its financial rewards.

When establishing the consumer producer process in what is called the third world or the under-developed countries, the colonisers, as has already been noted, have always disrupted the way of life which was being followed by the indigenous population prior to the colonisers' arrival. The basic approach has always been to persuade people to produce more than they need. To do this they have to be persuaded to work longer hours than before, and the women have to be persuaded that they will be free if they go and work in the factory all day. In order to make the work an attractive proposition, the people are offered money, but only enough to ensure that once they are dependant on it they will have to keep on working to have it, because they have not earned enough to save up. In order to make the money seem worth anything, the people are persuaded to want products which they never wanted before and many of which they simply do not need. Once you have the people wanting the products, they have to obtain the money to buy the products, which means they have to work to obtain the money. Thus in a very short period of time a large number of people can be persuaded to abandon their former way of life, in order to manufacture the products which they have been persuaded they want, and so get paid to buy them.

This pattern is reinforced by introducing the debt-mechanism. Everyone is encouraged to 'need' – in fact, to 'want' – more money than they are actually earning, and to borrow the difference. Once in debt, then they are hooked and usually trapped. For the majority of people, 'have it now, pay for it later' usually means, 'once you're in debt, you'll be trying to pay it off for the rest of your life.' The compound interest trap is a particularly vicious one.

Naturally there are those who, although they have been persuaded to want the goods and the money to buy them, either cannot obtain work or cannot be bothered to obtain work. Instead they turn to crime. This provides the ideal excuse for the kafir controllers to introduce their legal system to protect those who are working and at the same time to increase their control over the working population. This also means the creation of more jobs for those who are needed to make the kafir legal system work, including not only the bureaucrats and office staff, but also the people who have to build the offices to house them, and the courts and prisons to deal with the people who will not play the consumer producer game. Naturally the fines collected in the courts do not provide a sufficiently large income to pay for all these buildings to be erected and to supply the people working in them with a decent salary. Accordingly additional taxes have to be levied. This necessitates more office space and creates more jobs for the tax collectors. It means people have to work harder to maintain their spending capacity. It means people try to avoid paying the taxes, which means the people in the legal system are given more work. As the taxes are increased and as the accepted value of money diminishes, because prices are put up to gather additional income without having to do any additional work, the work force becomes disgruntled. It attempts to organise and alter the status quo. As a result more laws are passed to control their activities. This means more work for the people in the legal system. In no time at all the consumer producer process has been firmly established. The working population is enmeshed in a bureaucratic system of organised disorder, in which their attention has been directed away from their Sustainer and concentrated on their sustenance – on their economic viability and their daily bread.

As activity within the consumer producer state becomes ever more complexified and diverse, and as human society becomes correspondingly alienated and fragmented, there inevitably comes the stage which we are now witnessing in those countries in which the consumer producer process can be said to have originated:

Total Collapse.

It is this cycle of self-destructive activity, the kafir consumer producer process, which has all but destroyed the radical alternative to this behavioural pattern, the Prophetic lifestyle. Today millions of people are trapped in the kafir system, that is the Dajjal system, and although many of them are not happy with it, it seems unlikely that they will be able to appreciate what living Islam really is until the collapse of the consumer producer process in the High Tec North is far more advanced than at present, so well have they been programmed to believe that a life based on consuming and producing is 'civilised' and 'advanced', whilst a life based on the way of Muhammad, may Allah bless him and grant him peace, is 'primitive' and 'backward'.

The consumer producer process ensures that people are treated like children, encouraged to work hard and to enjoy their play – and not to ask awkward questions. The ignorance of the people who control that process and of the people who are controlled by them is displayed by the fact that they are unaware of the true nature of existence, and of what happens to you after you die. They take existence for granted, pretend that they are not going to die in the foreseeable future, and think that when they do eventually die, they will simply become dust or ashes.

Those who follow the Prophetic life pattern, which is based on a revealed message from Allah and not on the speculation and experimentation of the so-called 'expert', know that everything comes from Allah and returns to Allah. They know that they are on a journey from Allah to Allah. They know what happens after death: the questioning in the grave, the period of waiting until the end of the world, the being brought back to life on the Last Day, the Balance being set up, the weighing of one's actions and intentions, the decision being made as to whether you are for the Fire or the Garden, and finally your going to one or the other, for ever.

Those who follow the Prophetic life pattern not only know what lies on the other side of death, they also appreciate how short life is, and they act accordingly. Clearly for the one whose sights are fixed on the Garden, or only on Allah, the exploitation of others in order to build up wealth and power in this life is clearly a worthless and pointless proposition. It is only an attractive proposition to the kafir because he or she thinks that this life is all there is, and accordingly attempts to construct his or her notion of the Garden in this life and in this phenomenal world.

The Prophetic life pattern is grounded in the worship of Allah. The five prayers which every Muslim does each day are sometimes referred to as the five pillars of the day. They support your day and keep things in perspective. Of course it is necessary to work, for it is only in the Garden that food comes to you whenever you want it, but the mumin is not subservient to his or her work situation, only to Allah. It is much more difficult for a mumin to be anxious about his or her provision, because he or she knows that Allah is the Provider, and that whoever remembers Allah is remembered by Allah, and that whoever praises Allah is fed by Allah.

Muslim economics is not based on the creation of debts. It is based on the voluntary sharing of wealth by the rich with the poor. What the kafir state seeks to achieve by means of heavy taxation enforced by repressive measures, the muslim community achieves by voluntary sharing. Voluntary sharing is only possible where the true nature of existence is known. The one who has been given wealth knows firstly, that it is from Allah, secondly, that if he or she shares it as he or she has been commanded by Allah this will help take him or her to the Garden, and thirdly, that if he or she does not share it then such greed may take him or her to the Fire. The one who wishes to see the face of Allah also knows that he or she must give out of what Allah has given to him or her.

The Prophet Muhammad, may Allah bless him and grant him peace, said to Abu Dharr in the shadow of the Ka'ba one day that those who are in most danger of going to the Fire are the very rich unless they spend in every direction. He also said that giving out is a shield from the Fire. The reason why a muslim community has no need of a police force, or of prisons, or of a repressive legal system, is that the prospect of the Fire provides a far greater deterrent to committing antisocial or selfish actions, and the prospect of the Garden provides a far greater incentive to do right and generous actions, than the deterrents and incentives needed in a kafir state by people who think that the Fire and the Garden are imaginary places dreamed up by the Christians in the past so that corrupt priests could blackmail simple people into parting with their wealth.

The truth is that although the heaven and hell conceived of by the Christians – who no longer have access to the original teaching of Jesus, peace be on him – may not bear any actual resemblance to the Fire and Garden, and although corrupt Christians in the past have used the threat of their hell and the promise of their heaven to make money out of people who feared God, nevertheless the Fire and Garden are real and you will be going to one or the other. There is no third alternative or easy option. It should be quite clear to anyone who reads the descriptions of the Fire and the Garden in the *Qur'an* that no one in their right mind would have invented the life after this one in order to make this life more bearable, since the possibility of going to the Fire is a horrifying one – and no one can be certain which of these two abodes will be his or her destination in the next life.

Giving out and being generous is the basis of Muslim commerce and of increasing wealth, since whatever you give in the Name of Allah is given back to you by Allah at least ten times over. Thus the mumin is only indebted to Allah. The kafir attempts to make money out of nothing by charging interest, and when the interest rates go too high there comes a time when paper and plastic currency is seen to be what it is, numbers printed on paper or stored in a computer, absolutely worthless. The mumin gives out and leaves the rest up to Allah. The kafir has to be ruthless to become a millionaire, whilst the mumin has to be generous to achieve the same object. Whereas the mark of a kafir state is vast taxation and the accumulation of capital, the mark of a muslim community is minimal taxation supplemented by voluntary giving out and with no accumulation of capital. Money – gold and silver, not paper and plastic – is kept on the move and in circulation.

The Prophet Muhammad, may the blessings and peace of Allah be on him, once said that if he was given a mountain of gold the size of Mount Uhud, he would be ashamed if it had not been disposed of within three days. Indeed it was his customary practice never to keep any money overnight. Whatever he happened to have at the end of the day was given away

The kafir state attempts to systematise and orchestrate the distribution of wealth, to the annoyance of all except its ruling elite who benefit from the manner in which that distribution operates, whilst in a muslim community the distribution of wealth takes place naturally, spontaneously and unexpectedly, to the delight of all who trust in Allah.

The people in a muslim community find their meaning in the worship of Allah. Allah says in the *Qur'an*, '**I did not create man and jinn except to glorify Me.**' Allah also said on the lips of the Prophet Muhammad in a hadith qudsi, 'I was a hidden treasure and I wished to make Myself known, so I created the Universe.' The knower, the known and the knowledge are one. The people who are trapped in the kafir system, that is the Dajjal system, do not know this. They have been conditioned to find their meaning in the consumer producer process and to accept and submit to the system which enslaves them.

o o o o o

It has already been stated that the kafir system, that is the Dajjal system, is formed of interlinking systems. In order to understand how the interlink operates, it is necessary to look at some of the more influential systems more closely. It must be emphasised and remembered that it is the systems and structures which are being examined, and not necessarily the people in them.

It often happens that people are born and brought up within the kafir system, that is the Dajjal system, but they do not believe in it. Indeed it is because of their direct experience of it that their understanding of its extent and nature is often more piercing and penetrating than that of those who have been born and brought up either in a simple community living in fitra, or in a traditional muslim community.

The opposite is also true: A person born and brought up within a Muslim community may also end up rejecting it. Nothing in life is fixed. Everything is in change. See how many children born of kafir parents are embracing Islam, and see how many children born of muslim parents are embracing kufr. Everything is in its opposite.

o   o   o   o   o

It is an old cliché, but there is an element of truth in it: whereas some people work in order to live, many now live in order to work. The kafir factory system is an inhuman and degrading system. It treats people as a necessary yet expendable part of the consumer producer process. Increased automation means that the people who man the machines are increasingly subservient to the machines. They are obliged to keep pace with the machines. In a factory which produces twenty-four hours every day, the people have to be highly regulated in order to ensure that the machines do not have to be stopped and the flow of production obstructed. Births, marriages and deaths tend to be viewed not as major events in a life-time, but rather as potential inconveniences which threaten to disrupt the continuity of the production process. Any sense of job security is undermined by the practice of only offering short-term contracts and the threat of being replaced, thereby facilitating motivation through fear. The only way to survive in such an environment is either to act like a robot, or to be one.

Success in the factory system is measured by the degree of control which you exercise over others, and by the degree of control which is not exercised over you, and by the amount of money which you make in the process. The more products you can afford, the more successful you are. The more you embody the illusory ideal of the perfect consumer producer as depicted in the media – and there is more than one ideal in order to have as many profitable markets as possible – the greater is your reputation for success in the consumer producer game.

o   o   o   o   o

In a kafir society people are educated primarily in order to work, not in order to understand themselves or the nature of existence. The kafir educational establishments are themselves like factories, only the end product is not merely a product, but a person who will help to make products either directly by working in the factories, or indirectly by managing the factories or by working in one of the interlinking sub-systems which ensure that the final product can be successfully advertised, distributed, sold and consumed. Whether an individual is going to work in the public sector, or in the private sector, or in the services sector, the educational system ensures that he or she has been programmed to look at the world largely in terms of the cost of living, the number of unemployed and the gross national product. The kafir media system maintains this economic perspective in conjunction with the kafir educational system.

The only way to keep people enslaved in the consumer producer system is to keep them in ignorance. Accordingly they are given selected information during their so-called education and by the media, and not real knowledge. They are conditioned to desire the bits of paper and the know-how which will give them the best positions possible in the producer consumer hierarchy. If the conditioning is not successful, it is almost inevitable that the kafir legal system will be called into play in order to implant the basic ideal of the consumer producer process more vigorously upon the person in question. The individual who has a good work record and a job waiting for him or her is usually dealt with more leniently in the courts of so-called justice. Some people are so impervious to the educational conditioning process that they end up spending a great deal of their lives in prison. The result is the same, an individual who has been rendered ineffective by means of institutionalisation.

The great majority of people who teach in the educational system do not have real knowledge, that is knowledge of the Real, that is Allah, or they would not allow themselves to be part of that system and accordingly part of the producer consumer process which, as we have already seen, only appears to be an attractive proposition when Allah and the Last Day and the Fire and the Garden are firmly forgotten. Furthermore, real knowledge is free. As soon as a fee is charged, you can be sure that you will only be receiving information for your money, most of it useless. Useful information is any information which leads to real knowledge. The opposite of that is useless information.

Those who have real knowledge, and share it, do not charge money for it, because they know that it is not their knowledge to sell, and because they know that their knowledge is a gift from Allah which has only been given to them because they wanted it and Allah wanted it, and not because they could pay for it. The only kind of payment which is necessary in order to acquire real knowledge is worship of Allah and fear of Allah and having a good expectation of Allah. Ultimately it is only given by the grace of Allah if that is what Allah wants. You will not acquire this knowledge by seeking it, but only if you seek it will you acquire it. Allah says in the *Qur'an*, 'Fear Me and I will give you knowledge,' and 'Remember Me and I will remember you,' and 'Ask and I will answer.' Allah is the Rich, and not in need of what appears to be other than Him. All that appears to be other than Him is in need of Allah.

Allah is Al-'Alim, the Knowing, and Al-Khabir, the Knower of every separate thing that befalls us, Al-Latif, the All-Pervading. Allah gives knowledge to whom He pleases, and His outpouring is vast. The producer consumer system is designed to stop you from finding out.

o   o   o   o   o

The kafir university system as we know it today, the apex of the educational conditioning system, is big business. It not only completes the conditioning process for those who are eventually going to be given control of the consumer producer process and the systems which regulate and define its functions and make its existence possible, but it also ensures that a handsome profit is made whilst so doing. It also ensures that the future controllers of those countries which have been successfully colonised by the originators of the consumer producer process can be suitably programmed to uphold that process and to protect the colonisers' interests, long after these countries have been granted so-called independence and apparent release from the control of their former colonial masters. This conjuring trick, whereby the colonisers appear to relinquish control whilst in reality still retaining it, is sometimes called neo-colonialism.

Fifty years ago there were hardly any universities. Those which did exist had a relatively small number of students whose primary objective was knowledge, although admittedly these universities did cater primarily for the offspring of the then ruling elite who were educated in order to take over control as and when their relatives died. As the new universities began to materialise, they at first retained the character and aims of the older universities, or at least tried to imitate them. Within ten years of the end of the second kafir world war, however, a marked change in policy had become apparent. Whereas in the past the acquisition of knowledge – which is always a hopeless proposition anyway in any institution whose teachers have no access to a living and intact Prophetic guidance – had been the main consideration, now two fresh objectives emerged. The first objective was to expand as quickly as possible so as to have as many fee-paying students as possible, despite the fact that this would mean that a close and meaningful relationship between the teacher and the taught would no longer be possible. The second objective was to channel more people into 'the sciences', and to lay less emphasis on 'the arts'.

Of course these objectives were dressed up in suitable terminology such as, 'everyone has a right to a decent education', and, 'in the interests of national safety and livelihood research must go on'. In reality the so-called education was far from decent, whilst the very methodology used by these educational institutions often ensured that what was being searched for would not be found. Useless research is encouraged in the kafir university because it keeps people busy and provides the fortunate few with an opportunity to build up a reputation and a sizeable income out of nothing.

What lay behind this change in policy, which clearly emerged after the end of the second world war, was this: The power struggle which had been taking place behind the scenes for over two centuries, between the Official Trinitarian Christian Church on one hand, and, on the other hand, those who were busy completing and building upon the foundations of the consumer producer process as we know it today – the architects of the new world order – had been concluded. The bank was now more powerful than the church, the top financier more influential than the archbishop.

The scientific movement had by now confirmed enough about the nature of existence for anyone with any intellect to realise that the Christian metaphysic, whose basis was the untenable doctrine of Trinity – which had never even been mentioned by Jesus, peace be on him, and which had not been completely formulated until about four hundred years after he had left the earth – was no more than a myth and no less than a lie. It is interesting to note in this context that, in contrast, what little knowledge the scientists have acquired through their methods of research is confirmed by what is in the *Qur'an*, which is after all the A to Z of existence as revealed by the Originator of all which appears to exist.

The primary struggle, however, in this power struggle between the Christians and the scientists, was not between those who claimed to know the nature of existence but disagreed with each other. It was between those who wanted power over the land and the people living in it. Thus the real purpose behind the new 'educational' policy was to ensure the uniform conditioning of as many people as possible. It was important that there was only one predominant version of the meaning of life available for public consumption, with only one predominant way of life to go with it. The fact that the Christian version could be 'scientifically disproved' meant that the scientific version gained more credibility and acceptance. As a result life-styles began to change. Churches began to empty. Sports stadiums began to fill up.

Although many people still believed in God, they did not have the means at their disposal – that is, a living and intact Prophetic guidance – to integrate that belief with the scientific 'facts' with which they were now being presented. Thus although the scientific version was clearly not the whole truth, it could not, on the face of it, be disputed – and in the meantime that magical word, 'research', could be invoked to show not only that whatever was not yet known was in the process of being discovered, but also that 'research' was accordingly necessary to make these discoveries.

It was on this basis – that the scientists were able to provide answers to all the questions which the Christians could no longer avoid by telling people 'this is a mystery', or 'this is not important as long as you have faith' – that the scientific version of existence, plagued as it is with speculation and theory, came to be widely accepted in the High Tec North. Whereas the Christians know that God exists, but cannot explain the nature of existence, the scientists have some inkling of the nature of existence but cannot relate it to God.

Once the scientific version of the nature of existence and the scientific approach to existence had become widely accepted, the people who championed this version and this approach, inevitably gained control of the educational system. The research which they in fact encouraged was orientated largely towards the development of the producer consumer system. This development depended on there being a uniform conditioning of as many people as possible. Only as a result of effective and widespread conditioning could overall control of the general population be ensured. It was necessary to imbue the people with the notion that the meaning of life was to be found in producing and consuming.

As the numbers of students increased, dramatically after the end of the second world war, the people who taught at and controlled the universities changed. The old school either retired or died, and those who replaced them were either dedicated to the producer consumer process and its ideals, or else they were 'free thinkers', unaware of what that process was, and where its development was leading. The few who were aware of the change of approach to life which was being engineered by means of the so-called educational system, and who objected to it, could not afford to object too strenuously or to attempt to change the trend as long as they wished to retain their position, and its accompanying reputation and salary, in the educational hierarchy.

There was nothing they could do to change the system from within that system, and even less if they left it. The interlinking systems which together form the kafir system, that is the Dajjal system, supported the educational system too effectively for anyone to be able to change it merely by opposing it. Severing a head or two from the many-headed beast does not kill the beast. Indeed those who control the system encourage a certain amount of dissent, since it is easier to rule a people when they are divided against each other, and also those who are not easily placated by minor cosmetic changes to the system – which do not in fact disturb the status quo – usually end up exhausted and ineffective if they try to change the system single-handed.

Of course if too many people try to change the system together, and look like succeeding, then they can usually be dealt with by means of the kafir legal system. All that is needed is a law making their group 'illegal', and then anyone who persists ends up in jail. In Algeria, for example, the banner of 'democracy' was held up high until it became clear that the vast majority of the people were about to vote for a Muslim government – whereupon a military regime backed principally by France was hastily installed to 'protect the minority' and to tyrannise the Muslims who had so nearly upset their 'former' colonisers' political control mechanism by using democratic means.

As the numbers of students at the universities increased, it became necessary to provide the buildings in which to house and teach them.

The erection of these buildings, or the acquisition of buildings already standing, provided a good source of income for many people, and of course helped to establish the producer consumer process more firmly in the process.

As the university system expanded, it took on the usual characteristics which typify the kafir institution. Gradually the university system, together with the sub-stratum of polytechnics and colleges which had grown up below it, became increasingly impersonal and meaningless – until it had become what it is today, just another production line in the kafir system, that is the Dajjal system.

The relationship between the teacher and the taught was such, and the academic environment in which that relationship functioned was such, that the transmission of real knowledge, even if the teachers had had it in the first place, was an impossibility. The numbers were such and the systems were such that the only transaction which could take place was the systematic and impersonal provision of vast quantities of structured information, much of which was and is utterly useless. The better a parrot a person was, the more clever he or she was considered. Wisdom was reduced to a word with a devalued meaning. The takeover, not only as far as the university system was concerned but also the rest of the educational system which prepared people for that university system, was completed, and continues to function today.

Although life at university is usually depicted as a time of freedom and experimentation – that first release from the restrictions of school and the parental nest – it is in fact highly structured and regulated, other than in the realm of 'private' relationships and 'personal' morality. Students at today's universities are encouraged to indulge in university politics and thereby to play a largely non-influential part in the running of the university – and woe betide any group of Muslim students who appear to be too well organised – to work and to play so that they can let off steam whilst still submitting to their conditioning, and finally to seek promising jobs in the consumer producer process once they have been duly awarded their pieces of paper which are commonly called degrees, and which are nothing to do with the degrees of knowledge to which the *Qur'an* refers.

The majority of students do not even know that they are being conditioned, or what the nature of their conditioning is. The few who do realise what is going on either nevertheless choose to go along with it, or else they drop out. Of those who drop out a few can overcome the inertia to wake up and look beyond the kafir conditioning process for real knowledge. Indeed it is one of the characteristics of the kafir system, that is the Dajjal system, that whilst you are in it – that is whilst the state of mind which its conditioning process induces, whether by education or media, continues to prevail – it is virtually impossible to even conceive of any alternative to it.

The world view, that is the version of the meaning of life, which is engendered and nurtured by the kafir educational and media systems is kufr. Only the one who is not content with this view and who has rejected the system, is in a position to cut through all the misconceptions and disinformation with which he or she has been blinded, and to see what Islam really is – is in a position to begin to understand and follow the way of the Prophet Muhammad, may the blessings and peace of Allah be on him, who once asked Allah, 'Teach me to see things as they really are.'

o o o o o

The kafir hospital system has in the last fifty years become an integral and important part of the producer consumer process. It exists to keep people in working fit condition. Many of the illnesses with which it has to deal are the direct result of the way in which people live, and are obliged to live, by virtue of the way in which the consumer producer process operates. The kafir system, that is the Dajjal system, creates its own illnesses, thereby creating work for those who are employed in the hospital system.

The hospital system is run as a business. Everyone is paid for what they do. The livelihood of a large number of people depends on other people being ill – and the way of life, which has evolved and developed as an inevitable result of the way in which the modern producer consumer state is run, ensures that there are more than enough ill people to keep the hospital system busy and in business, thereby ensuring countless others, who supply the hospitals and doctors with the tools and medicines of their trade, steady and profitable employment.

The capacity of the kafir system, that is the Dajjal system, to create unnecessary jobs and meaningless activity in any sphere of life is something almost to be marvelled at. This is in marked contrast to the situation to be found in the simple village community living in fitra, or in a balanced muslim community. Of course there is illness in such communities, for illness is the manifestation of imbalance and everyone loses balance at some time or other, but firstly, the healthy not only look after the sick, but also they know how to look after the sick, and secondly, they do not make a business out of it.

Since these two kinds of communities do live more or less in harmony with existence, and since they know what to eat and what not to eat, and since they have a balanced way of life, it inevitably follows that there is far less serious illness around than in a kafir society, simply because there is far less imbalance. If the heart is at peace, it follows that there will be no illness which is caused by nervous strain, anxiety or tension. If the correct food is eaten then the illnesses which originate from the stomach – and most illnesses do – will not arise. If people really understand and accept the way things are, and if they know where they have come from and where they are going to, then it is extremely unlikely that they are going to be on the verge of a nervous breakdown.

Life is very simple. It is simply a question of balance.

The Prophet Muhammad was once sent some costly medicines from Egypt. He returned them with the message that his way of life was its own medicine, and the best of medicines. He was so finely balanced that his only major illnesses arose when people tried to poison him, whether by means of food or magic. The Prophet Muhammad, may the blessings and peace of Allah be on him, said that if the heart was well then the body would be well, and that if the heart was ill then the body would be ill.

The heart is the centre of one's being. It is the means by which we know the self and Allah, and whoever knows their self knows Allah. All the various outward ways of doing things which together comprise the pattern of life embodied by the Prophet Muhammad have an inward and beneficial effect on the heart. The heart is not at peace unless you worship Allah. Only by the remembrance of Allah is the heart made serene. The only way to worship and remember Allah in every single lived moment is by following the way of Muhammad, may Allah bless him and grant him peace.

Like the kafir factory and educational systems, the kafir hospital system tends to be run like a production line. As automation has increased, it has become correspondingly more de-personalised. Medical staff are obliged, by the sheer number of people with whom they have to deal, not to become involved with their patients. It is easier to treat them as objects than as humans. Since most of the people who run the hospital system have usually been university conditioned, it usually follows that the vast majority of them have no real deep medical knowledge. Many of their so-called cures are only skin deep. In the same way that the university professors toy with ideas in their theoretical speculations, so the doctors experiment with drugs in their medication. Inevitably the patient can become a human guinea pig, the final test for a new drug once no more can be learnt from trying it out on animals. One of their best medicines is the loving care of the nursing staff.

Doctors are often obliged to experiment simply because they do not understand the nature of existence. Many so-called doctors today are even unaware of the basic knowledge, which is so important in the practice of medicine, that all matter is composed of varying combinations of the four elements, that is air, fire, earth and water; that these elements are respectively hot wet, hot dry, cold dry and cold wet; that the body of a human contains four humours that is blood, black bile, yellow bile and phlegm; that these humours are respectively hot wet, hot dry, cold dry and cold wet; that all foods have their own medicinal properties and, depending on the elements from which they are formed, are hot, dry, cold or wet in varying degrees and combinations. Illness occurs in the body when there is an imbalance of the humours. This imbalance can be corrected by taking the food which has the opposite qualities of whatever qualities the illness has, whilst at the same time refraining from the food which has the same qualities as the illness. The 'modern' doctor often denies this approach, dismissing it as 'primitive', and preferring to rely on twenty-first century wonder-drugs, even though they will eventually destroy his or her patients' immune systems and accordingly their natural resistance to illness.

Homeopathy, which is a complementary way of medicine to the natural way just described – in that it treats like with like rather than with its opposite – is usually treated with the same disdain by the kafir practitioner, even though he or she accepts the very same principle when it is applied in the use of vaccines. Similarly the ancient methods which are used to free the subtle energy flows in the body, such as acupuncture and shiatsu, are treated with suspicion. In reality the kafir doctors' opinions as regards these enlightened ways of treating illness only mirror the reflection of their own ignorance in the matter.

It is interesting to note that in order to ensure that the kafir medical view of treating illness predominates, the kafir legal system usually makes it illegal to practise as a doctor unless you have the appropriate kafir medical qualifications and initials after your name. It is of course necessary to protect unsuspecting people from quacks and charlatans, but there have certainly been many instances where doctors with a profound knowledge of natural medicine have been discredited as 'imposters' simply because they do not comply with the kafir norm – just as in the days of the British Raj, an Indian who could speak Arabic, Persian and Urdu fluently, and who knew the entire *Qur'an* by heart, would be classified as 'illiterate' if he or she could not read and write English!

This approach is typical of the kafir system, that is the Dajjal system, as a whole. Any view or course of action which contradicts the kafir norm is rendered ineffective and of minimal influence, by making it 'illegal' before the stage is reached where it might become effective. Once any action or approach to existence has been deemed to be against the law, then the weight of the whole kafir legal system can be used to squash it. In effect, the kafir system, that is the Dajjal system, ensures that if you disagree with it, you may criticise it but you may not actively try to change it.

As far as surgery is concerned, there can be no doubt that as a result of recent advances in technology, coupled with the discoveries made during the second world war when patients were in plentiful supply, many wonders are performed, and many lives are either saved for the time being and improved or otherwise enhanced. It is also equally clear that many of the operations carried out in the modern hospital system are unnecessary, while many of the operations which do appear necessary are needed to deal with ailments which are directly caused by the way in which people live in a kafir society. If the patients had had a balanced way of life in the first place, they would not have incurred the illness which caused them to arrive in the operating theatre. If techniques did not need to be practised and perfected, some operations would not take place. If sexual promiscuity was not an established social norm, then there would be no need for the thousands and thousands of abortions which are routinely performed every year. If ignorance about what is on the other side of death was not so prevalent, many elderly patients might choose to die a natural death at the end of their natural life-span, rather than being encouraged to opt for a major operation – in order to buy a little more time – from which they might well never fully recover anyway.

Once in the operating theatre, again many patients are no more than guinea pigs. Let us see what this will do to him. Will this new technique work? One of the descriptions of the Dajjal in the *Hadith* states that the Dajjal will cut a man in two, so that it seems that he is dead, and then put him together again, so that it seems that he is alive and well. This description aptly fits what goes on in many an operating theatre, as well as being applicable to some of the psychological disorders, such as schizophrenia, which inevitably result from a kafir way of life.

There can be no doubt, however, that good surgeons – assisted both by skilled anaesthetists and skilful theatre staff – do perform many invaluable operations, and that good doctors do heal many people, and that in the process many wonderful discoveries are made. Indeed it should be emphasised that in all the various interlinking systems that comprise the kafir system, that is the Dajjal system, there are many good people who do good – and that any criticism of the system itself should never be mistaken as a criticism of such people. Life is a learning process and whoever seeks knowledge will find it everywhere. Even the Pharaoh's wife, Asiya, was a believer.

○ ○ ○ ○ ○

The ignorance which is often displayed by the manner in which the kafir medical profession treats physiological disease is only equalled by the lack of knowledge which is evident in the way in which many psychiatrists attempt to deal with psychological disorders. Since they do not know the nature of existence, it follows that they do not know the nature of the human self. It follows that they do not know how to treat the ailments of the self. They have no unitary knowledge. They do not know how the universe and what it contains comes into being, nor how it goes out of being, nor how it appears to be in each moment between its birth and death. Since they have a fixed, as opposed to a dynamic, view of reality it follows that they have a fixed idea of what 'normal' is, and so anyone who does not fit that idea is considered 'abnormal', and accordingly is assaulted either physically or psychically in an attempt to bring them within the bounds of that definition. Since at the very best they only have a partial idea as to how the human self works, they are reduced to the barbaric practice of rendering the brain quiescent and ineffective, either by drugs and heavy sedation, or even by electric shock treatment, or lobotomy, or laser-gun bombardment.

The fact that kafir psychiatrists concentrate on the mind, that is on the contents of the head, in itself shows that they have completely missed the point, since it is the heart which requires attention. Recitation of the Qur'an is enough to still the heart and calm the mind, thereby rendering many of the kafir psychologist's approaches obsolete. The reason why many people in today's kafir societies suffer varying degrees and kinds of madness is because they try and figure out the nature of existence with their heads, when only the heart is capable of arriving at such an understanding. Some liken the heart to the sun, and the head to the moon. The moon does not generate its own light. What light it has is reflected light from the sun. Once the heart has been illuminated by the remembrance of Allah, the intellect is then illuminated, and not before.

Perhaps the greatest error of the kafir psychologist is to give reality to the illusory self, that is the self which does not really exist. They give reality to what we think we are, or to what we think others think we are. To the people of real knowledge this illusory self does not exist. It only appears to exist if an imagined reality is given to it, since what ever you imagine, is real for you. If you cease to imagine anything, existence does not cease, but rather you see existence as it really is. You see, wherever you turn, the Existent. Wherever you look, there is the face of Allah. There is no reality – only Reality.

In effect, the illusory self is nothing more than a solidification of events obscuring a light which is the true self, the light of Allah. The kafir psychologist gives reality to that solidification of events and not to the light which it obscures. That is why he or she is kafir: his or her action covers over the truth of the matter. By giving reality to what is unreal and by refusing to give reality to the Real, Allah, it follows that the kafir psychiatrist is not going to have any real success in the cures which he or she attempts to perpetrate, since whatever he or she does will almost inevitably be without reference to the true nature of existence and will accordingly be out of harmony with it. The so-called 'cure' of the kafir psychologist is imbalance piled on imbalance, darkness piled on darkness, the outward semblance of 'normality' imposed on an inward state of insanity.

The mumin doctor – and by this term we do not mean a muslim who has been subjected to the kafir educational conditioning process in the field of medicine and who has accepted that conditioning – the real mumin doctor knows that the illusory self has to be dismantled before the true self emerges. This is achieved by purification of the heart, the centre of your being. This purification is achieved by the remembrance of Allah. The transformation of the heart only occurs by the grace of Allah. This purification and this transformation of the heart in the inward can only take place if there is a corresponding purification and transformation in the outward, that is in your existential behaviour pattern.

The only way of life which today makes this inward and outward purification a possibility, and for the one who follows it a reality, is the way of Muhammad, may Allah bless him and grant him peace. This is the means by which, once the heart has been purified, one knows one's self and one's Lord, and these two knowings are the same knowing. In Reality the knower, the known and the knowledge are one. To gain this knowledge, it is necessary to stop thinking altogether – which means that the one who has this knowledge cannot be trapped by the educational and media conditioning processes, since this conditioning is only successful where the thought process has been attracted, harnessed and programmed.

There is no deep reality to the kafir psychologists' definitions of what 'normal' is. They are arbitrary definitions. Deep sanity is to affirm the reality of Allah, and this affirmation finds its fullest expression in the one who follows the Prophetic life style. This life style finds its fullest expression in the way of the Prophet Muhammad, may the blessings and peace of Allah be on him, the first and last of the Prophets in the Prophetic cycle. His way is its own proof. The one who follows it benefits from a healthy body and a peaceful heart and the tranquillity which comes with real knowledge.

The ignorance of the leaders of the kafir medical profession today is evidenced by the fact that they do not have the cures for the physiological and psychological ills which are the natural result of the consumer producer process and the lifestyle which comes with it. They concentrate more on the ailments once they have manifested, than on the original cause of their having manifested in the first place. From one view-point life is like a chemical equation: Given certain ingredients and certain conditions, the result which follows is inevitable: If you follow the kafir lifestyle you will be in turmoil, and are for the Fire. If you follow the way of the Prophets you will be at peace, and are for the Garden. The *Qur'an* is the only book on the face of the earth today which contains all the equations. It is the A to Z of existence, and in it is a guidance which shows you what to do in every situation. The Prophet Muhammad, may Allah bless him and grant him peace, said that in the *Qur'an* there is a medicine, so take what you need from it.

The one who has no *Qur'an* in his or her heart is like a ruined building, is like a dead person already in their grave. Since kafir doctors do not have access to the *Qur'an*, and indeed would refuse it even if it were offered to them, they proceed on a basis of trial and error which they describe as a path of evolution and progress – perhaps little realising that much of what forms the original basis of institutionalised medicine today was often culled from Muslims in the past, who only received their knowledge by Allah and by following what is in the *Qur'an*. The kafir doctors may discover some of what is already in the *Qur'an* by accident, but they can only have a limited knowledge of what is in the *Qur'an*, because they do not follow what is in the *Qur'an* themselves. They have no unified field of knowledge. You can only understand what is in the *Qur'an* by embodying what is in the *Qur'an*. It is possible to use the right remedy without really knowing why or how it works, but this is not wisdom.

As with the kafir factory and educational systems, the kafir medical system is often not really concerned with healing and with what is beneficial, but with money. It is big business, creating business for the vast pharmaceutical concerns which provide its drugs and equipment, and keeping thousands upon thousands of people usefully employed in patching up people, so that they too can be usefully employed. It is more common to hear the medical students of today talking about the large fees they hope to earn once they have passed the right exams and collected the right bits of paper, than the number of people whom they hope to heal, or more importantly the means by which that healing is to take place.

The kafir medical system is an integral part of the kafir consumer producer process. It promises great rewards for the fully qualified. It plays a very important role in the overall management of the kafir system, that is the Dajjal system. Closely linked with the kafir educational system and the kafir legal system, its leaders wield great influence in the kafir state. A hundred years ago the medical system as we know it today did not exist. During that relatively short period of time the takeover has been completed.

o   o   o   o   o

The system which makes the operation of the kafir factory, educational and medical systems a viable proposition, and indeed which controls the operation of all systems in the kafir system, that is the Dajjal system, is the kafir legal system. The kafir legal system makes the interlink between all the other sub-systems possible. It is thus the heart of the kafir system, that is the Dajjal system, as a whole.

The kafir legal system defines the structures of all other systems in the kafir state, regulating what they may do and what they may not do, and it ensures that any alternatives to the kafir system, that is the Dajjal system, are rendered ineffective, either by making them illegal, or at least by severely restricting them. The kafir legal system also dictates what human behaviour is permissible in the kafir state, thereby ensuring the effective control and monitoring of the majority of people living within that state. Anyone who ignores or actively opposes the legal system finds him or her self locked up in prison in a very short space of time. In effect, the kafir legal system is utilised to ensure that the consumer producer process runs as smoothly as possible.

o o o o o

The inevitable result of such a state of affairs is the police state, that is a society divided against itself, where one half preys on and feeds off the other half. The kafir police force is given wide powers and freedom of action. Basically its members can do in the name of the law what for anyone else is against the law. They are paid a lot of money to do this, even though the taxpayers who provide the money and who at times are both protected and tyrannised by the police do not always want either to pay the taxes or to have the police force. The argument used is that if there were no police force there would be chaos. The answer to this is that there would be chaos amongst those who are truly kafir, but not amongst those who are truly muslim.

The way of Islam means that those who follow it do not need a police force, because each individual is his or her own police man or woman. Instead of policing others the muslim looks to his or her own actions in the knowledge that he or she is answerable to Allah for them. Furthermore, the nature of the muslim community is such that the roots and causes of crime which are permitted to flourish in a kafir society simply do not have a place to grow in the muslim community.

As in the field of kafir medicine, so in the field of kafir laws, many of the ills and ailments which provide the legal system with work are the direct results of the way in which the kafir system, that is the Dajjal system operates, and of the lifestyle which the people working in that system are conditioned to follow. The kafir system, that is the Dajjal system, creates needless activity patterns in order to keep people occupied, and in order to make money out of that activity. Of course some of the police are helpful, but then helpful people always are.

After the kafir medical system, or rather in conjunction with it, the experts of the kafir legal system are required to undergo the most rigorous of conditioning educational processes, before they are permitted to operate. In effect, this is a screening process, whereby those who are inimical to the kafir system, that is the Dajjal system are prevented from finding out too much about its workings and are weeded out. Only those who will support and strengthen the system are permitted to qualify and eventually assume positions of responsibility within the system.

As in the kafir educational system and the kafir medical system, it is clear that there has also been a change in personnel as it were in the kafir legal system. This is evidenced especially by the fact that although God is mentioned from time to time in accordance with legal tradition – usually just before a witness is about to give evidence – many of the people who exercise control in the judicial system clearly do not either fear God or even believe in Him. If they did, they would act very differently to the way in which they do at the moment. It is interesting to note that the manner in which a typical trial is conducted is a pale imitation of the Last Day. The person who acts as judge and decides what is to be done to the person in the dock acts on many an occasion as if he or she were God, often completely oblivious of the fact that there will come a time when he or she will in turn stand alone before Allah, answerable for all that he or she has done.

By examining the changes in the legal system over the last hundred years it is clear that the takeover has taken and continues to take place. Whereas a hundred years ago the laws of most of today's kafir states were based on the remnants of the teachings of Jesus, peace be on him, and on common sense and common practice, today they are unashamedly designed to control and manipulate wherever possible. It is said that the laws have been passed to create a more just society, but in reality their effect has been to keep the majority of people firmly enmeshed in the producer consumer process. Again, that insidious doctrine, the doctrine of evolution, is invoked in order to persuade people that the legal system is progressing and getting better, which it will continue to do – until it finally collapses, brought down by its own weight.

Like the kafir medical experts, the kafir legal experts do not understand the nature of reality. They give reality to what has no reality and refuse to give reality to the Real, Allah. It follows that they do not know how to deal with reality. All their attempts at social engineering are grounded in speculation and arbitrary theories. They have no certainty. It follows that the alleged objectives of many of their laws will never in fact be realised. Thus, for example, the development of the laws designed to uphold human rights has been parallelled by a vast increase in the degradation and ill-treatment of humans throughout the world, much of that ill-treatment and degradation being caused by the infliction of laws formulated by the very same legal systems which invented human rights law in the first place. In reality these human rights laws are given publicity in order to persuade people that they have a just legal system, but not in order to actually establish a just society.

The only cure for the social fragmentation which is today everywhere in evidence, and which is being aided by the way in which the kafir legal system operates – even though that system purports to be curing that fragmentation – is Islam.

One of the results of kafir colonisation has been that the kafir system, that is the Dajjal system – and especially its kafir legal system – has been successfully implanted in nearly all the countries which, before the coming of the colonisers, were ruled in accordance with what is in the *Qur'an* and the *Sunnah*. This means that at the time of writing this, there is not one country in the world today which is free from the kafir system, that is the Dajjal system.

The study, however, of history from a Qur'anic perspective and not from the currently favoured kafir perspective, clearly demonstrates that any community, country, or group of countries, has always flourished when following Prophetic guidance, and has always suffered when its people abandoned that guidance.

The Qur'anic study of history also clearly shows that the people in any one country, during the passage of time, fluctuate between kufr and iman. There is a time when the majority of them are kafir, and there is a time when the majority of them are mumin, and there are times of transition between these two opposites. This pattern of activity is in accordance with the true nature of existence, which is the manifestation and dynamic interplay of opposites originating from one source, Allah.

Since everything lies in its opposite, and since the majority of people in the High Tec North have not been following an unadulterated Prophetic guidance for several centuries, it follows that the advent of Islam in the west is not only the cure for the sick kafir states of the High Tec North, but is also absolutely inevitable. Allah says in the *Qur'an* that there is no changing the way of Allah. Only Allah knows what is in the future, but insh'Allah the practice of Islam will grow and flourish amidst the ruins of the present kafir society once it has finally and fully collapsed.

The last fifty years has witnessed a dramatic increase in the number of new laws which have been formulated, throughout the world, as well as in the multitude of regulations which are drawn up under, and by virtue of, the so-called authority conferred by these laws. Never before in the history of mankind have humans been so regulated in what they may and may not do. People are punished for the least deviation from the legally defined norm, even in circumstances where neither person nor property has been injured or damaged or even endangered in any way. The doctrine of strict liability means that a person can be found guilty of an offence even where there is no blame, and even if, in the circumstances of his or her particular case, he or she was doing what according to common sense was most appropriate.

The more laws there are in a country the more 'offenders' there will be. The more offenders there are, the more business there is for the people who operate the legal system, and the richer they become. Even in situations where injury or damage to person or property does occur, and even if the person who caused the damage or injury has made good that damage or injury, he or she will still be subjected to the legal process as well and punished. This indicates that kafir law is not used to maintain balance, but has become an idol – which if violated must be swift in retribution. The kafir legal system is not used to maintain social harmony, but to maintain social inequality by means of oppression and repression. It favours the people who control the kafir system, that is the Dajjal system, and it is used by them to control and manipulate the people who are enslaved by that system.

Many of the laws in force today arise out of a situation and a society in which there is no trust between people. In a time when many people have become hard-hearted and mean, they seek to take advantage of others rather than to help them. Such people are described in the *Qur'an* as the mutafafifin, meaning 'the defrauders', those who demand full measure from others but who give short measure in return. Laws are passed to curtail their actions, but as quickly as these new laws are passed the defrauders find ways to evade them, which means that more laws have to be passed to stop up the loopholes as they become apparent.

Since it is often the defrauders who make the laws in the first place, it comes as no surprise to find that there are always some loopholes left open permanently for the lucky few who know about them. Although, for example, both the *Bible* and the *Qur'an* – which many witnesses hold in their right hands as they swear by God to tell the truth in courts of law – forbid usury, these very same courts not only authorise and uphold usury but at times even insist on it.

As well as the ever-growing multitude of laws, life is further complicated by the doctrine of judicial precedent which states that all past judicial decisions are binding on judges when deciding a case which has a similar fact situation. Since no situation is ever exactly repeated again in creation, and since all judicial decisions are made subject to the personal prejudices of the judges who make them, it inevitably follows that sometimes judges are obliged to reach decisions which are patently unjust because of a case which may have been decided many years ago, when life and attitudes were very different to what they are today.

The only way around the doctrine of judicial precedent is to 'distinguish' cases that would otherwise be binding by indulging in word-play and intellectual dishonesty – which ultimately causes confusion and uncertainty when a decision arrived at by these means has to be applied to yet another similar fact situation at a later stage.

The result of all these laws and all these regulations and all the past decisions which have been reached – often when the law then was very different to what it is now – is a complex web of 'do's and 'don't's which is for ever changing or being changed, so that only the legal expert who spends his or her whole life in this maze has any idea of its geography. Indeed the maze is now so large that the need to specialise in one particular area has become a necessity, until the time is reached, if it is ever reached, when all the information is stored on magnetic tapes and compact discs and we have trial by computer. It is this complexity – a complexity which is magnified by having a specialist vocabulary and complicated procedures – which ensures that the legal expert will always be needed, and will always command a good price for his or her advice and services both in and out of court.

This situation is the complete antithesis of that which arises in a muslim community. A muslim community has no need of a legal system. Everything that it needs is in the *Qur'an* and the *Hadith*. The *Qur'an* does not need to be changed because it already contains the necessary guidance as to what to do in every conceivable situation in which a person may find him or her self. It already has what more enlightened legislators have been seeking to attain for the last several hundred years. Since its contents as regards the behaviour of people within the community and the manner in which they are to conduct their affairs are simple, it follows that there is no need whatsoever for a specialist elite to set themselves up as its interpreters or to enforce it on others. The people in a real muslim community follow what is in the *Qur'an* and the *Hadith* because they do not wish to do otherwise. Provided that they fear Allah and the Last Day, and follow the way of the Prophet Muhammad and the first Muslim community which gathered round him, may the blessings and peace of Allah be on him and them, they are not a threat to anyone else and no one is a threat to them. The way of Islam is a guidance for whoever means well and fears Allah.

One of the secrets of existence is that whatever is in your heart appears before you in existence. Since a kafir has disorder in his or her heart he or she experiences disorder in existence. The kafir then tries to put existence 'in order' by changing it outwardly. If there is still disorder in the heart, however, the measures taken by the kafir have no effect, and disorder merely manifests before him or her in a different form. Since the mumin, that is the one who is at peace, has peace in the heart it follows that peace manifests before the mumin in creation – and Islam is established.

The only way to change or transform what is in your heart is to follow the way of the Prophet Muhammad and the community which first gathered around him at Madina al-Munawarra, that is, the illuminated place where the life transaction is. Madina was illuminated by a people whose hearts had been illuminated with knowledge and love of Allah and His Messenger, may the peace and blessings of Allah be on him and them, and who accordingly had no need of anything like the systems which characterise the kafir system, that is the Dajjal system – especially its legal system.

Islam is not a system. It is a way of life, and you can only be described as being a Muslim if you follow that way. Those countries which have been colonised and subjected to the kafir legal system and the kafir consumer producer process cannot be described as having 'muslim' governments, merely because a little of what is in the *Qur'an* and the *Hadith* has been incorporated into 'acts of parliament'. A truly muslim country has no need of a kafir styled parliament. The *Qur'an* is its constitution.

Allah says in the *Qur'an* that there is no compulsion in the life transaction. Once you know which way to go, you simply abandon the way which was a hindrance to you. It is not enough to be called a muslim. It is necessary to be a Muslim, that is to embody the way of Islam and to be at peace with yourself and with existence. The Prophet Muhammad, may the blessings and peace of Allah be on him, said that a Muslim is one from whose hand and whose tongue you are safe. He said that the Muslims should be like two hands washing each other, and like the rafters of a roof which support each other. He said that you are not a Muslim until you want for your companion what you want for yourself. He said that you are not a mumin until you prefer for your companion what you want for yourself. He said that if you have a full stomach and someone in the house next door has an empty stomach, then you are not a Muslim. He said that the best aspect of Islam is to greet those you know and those you do not know, and to welcome and feed the guest.

If the people in a muslim community have this approach to life and to each other, then it follows that they already are 'law-abiding' citizens, and abiding by the best of laws – the laws of God, and not the laws of men. This is only possible in a community of people whose lives are based on the worship of Allah. As has already been noted, Muslim communities in the past always disintegrated once their members abandoned the *Qur'an* and the *Sunnah* and turned away from Allah to what is other than Allah.

The majority of offences which have been formulated by the kafir legal system have not been so formulated with what happens after death in mind. This is in marked contrast to the relatively few offences against the Muslim community which are indicated in the *Qur'an*. The offences referred to in the *Qur'an* are those anti-social acts which, if freely permitted, would undermine the trust which is essential if the members of that community are to live together in harmony. Adultery, for example, is an offence not only because it involves deception and betrayal, but also because it destroys the family and therefore the community. The number of witnesses required before the offence may be punished – which, in the absence of a voluntary confession, is four – means that there can never be any doubt in the matter – while anyone who accuses someone of committing adultery but has no witnesses receives eighty lashes.

This is in marked contrast to the kafir legal system, where a person can be accused and convicted of and punished for any number of offences on the flimsiest of circumstantial evidence, and nearly always when a member of the police says that the person in the dock was either seen to do the act in question, or admitted to doing it at the police station. The police are highly skilled in incorporating into their written records of alleged interviews with the accused or of the alleged behaviour of the accused, admissions or acts which will guarantee a conviction once the matter comes to trial. Even where interviews are taped, the manner in which the transcript of that interview is subsequently edited often means that a completely different impression of the substance and tenor of the interview can be created on paper – which is often the only version of the interview which will be presented in evidence. Furthermore, it is an unwritten presumption of kafir law that where there is a conflict between the police version of events and the accused's version of events, then the police version is to be believed unless the contrary is proved. If the presumption were the other way around then there would be too many acquittals, and as a result the legal system would not be the thriving business concern that it is today.

As far as punishment is concerned, in the kafir legal system the motivation behind punishment is to make money and to render ineffective those who threaten the fabric of society. In theory the punishment is also regarded as the just retribution which is to be inflicted on the offender by the legal system on behalf of the other law-abiding members of society. The fact that a great majority of people in today's 'modern' societies do not always agree with either the law or the offender's being punished in accordance with that law is always conveniently overlooked by those who continue to administer the law in their name and allegedly on their behalf.

The punishments inflicted in a kafir society are also intended to deter others from following the example of the person who has been punished. Indeed by invoking that nebulous concept known as 'public policy' – which is never formulated by the general public but only for the general public – or 'the interests of the state' – which in reality are the interests of the ruling elite who benefit most from maintaining the status quo as it is – it is possible to punish someone far more than they deserve in order that others will be sufficiently deterred from following suit. Since the punishments are in order that the status quo can be maintained, it follows that they invariably derive from a distorted perspective.

The relatively few punishments prescribed in the *Qur'an* and the *Sunnah* are admittedly both retributive and deterrent in effect, but the primary motivation behind them is that the one who submits to a Qur'anic punishment is thereby released from his or her wrong action, and accordingly may still go to the Garden. Indeed since the mumin fears Allah and longs for the Garden and dreads the Fire, it follows that he or she is far less likely to do a major wrong action in the first place.

This perspective is entirely lacking in a kafir society, whose members usually believe that they will 'get away with it' as long as no-one either catches or sees them doing whatever 'it' may be. The kafir does not realise that every action is witnessed by the recording angels, and by Allah, and that whatever he or she does will have to be answered for on the Last Day. Given this ignorance, the kafir is far more prone to do wrong action, and if he or she is then caught, will be processed by the kafir legal system without reference to what is yet to take place on the Last Day. Allah says in the *Qur'an* that the kafir receives a double punishment, in this world and in the next.

Since the kafir legal system is not based on any divine revelation – other than those few laws which derive from the remnants of earlier Prophetic guidances, or which happen to tally with what is in the *Qur'an* by sheer coincidence – but rather is formulated in defiance of such revelation, it follows that many of the offences which have been formulated by the legal system are offences only because they have been defined as such by ignorant men, who are not acting in accordance with what Allah has indicated should be regarded as wrong action. Man-made laws are only as good – or as bad – as the people who make them. 'The Law' is neither an abstract entity, nor is it God. In reality, 'the rule of law' is the rule of whoever makes the law. The Shari'ah of Islam is the law of God.

Dajjal – the king who has no clothes   47

Many of the offences defined by the kafir legal system are not even based on common sense, and certainly do not arise from wisdom. They have come into being because the consumer producer system needs a great many rules if it is to operate efficiently, and these rules can only be enforced by punishing the people who break them. They are the result of political expediency, the necessary means for effective manipulation and population control in the kafir system, that is the Dajjal system. It will be remembered that the definition of an ignorant person is the one who thinks he or she knows, when in reality he or she does not.

Just as the kafir medical experts have an illusory definition of what 'normal' is, so too do the kafir legal experts. In effect, if you fulfil the functions of an obedient robot in the producer consumer system, then you fall fully within the legal definition of what is considered 'normal', provided of course that you abide by the rules. Anyone who falls outside the legal norm of the kafir system, that is the Dajjal system, soon finds him or her self in trouble with the legal system. As the police state becomes more and more of a reality, and more and more oppressive, it becomes increasingly more difficult to follow any human way of life which is a viable alternative to that norm, without experiencing greater and greater harassment from the legal system.

The legal experts who frame the laws which make the system work are skilled in defining laws which will enable the controllers of that system to take whatever steps are necessary to protect their interests and to maintain the status quo. Anyone whose actions fall within the legal definition of an offence is automatically considered a criminal, and can be punished accordingly. It follows that any pattern of activity which threatens the continued existence of the kafir system, that is the Dajjal system, can be 'legally' destroyed or disrupted merely by passing a law which makes that pattern of activity 'illegal'.

The kafir media system is then used to justify and promote that law by using the appropriate emotive adjectives to describe the pattern of activity which has just been outlawed – such as 'anarchistic', 'fanatical', 'terrorist' – and by using the appropriate platitudes to make the law seem necessary – such as 'in the public interest', 'in the interests of the state', 'for the protection of society'. The ease with which such laws can be passed is eloquent proof of the fact that the ruling elite of the kafir system, that is the Dajjal system, are not only established at the head of all the interlinking systems which form the kafir system, but also by virtue of that fact are able to work in close conjunction with each other.

The law-making body in any kafir state is also the body which administers those laws, is also the body which governs in purported accordance with those laws, no matter how many carefully worded theories concerning the doctrine of the separation of powers there are, which seek to create the impression that the legislators, the judiciary and the executive are independent of each other, and therefore by implication incorruptible. In reality the opposite of this doctrine is true of the typical kafir state, and that is why it is possible to 'legally' silence anyone who is too manifestly opposed to the kafir system, that is the Dajjal system, with ease.

As well as ensuring that the kafir norm and status quo are upheld and maintained, the legal system, like the medical system, is big business. It is for this reason that so many prosecutions, which otherwise would be completely pointless and unnecessary, are pursued. The outcome of the prosecution is not important. Whether the person accused is convicted or acquitted is quite irrelevant. What matters, as far as the people working in the legal system are concerned, is that they are kept occupied. If they had a just society they would be out of a job, and that is why the controllers of the kafir state ensure that they do not have a just society.

As is the case with every system in the kafir system, that is the Dajjal system, the legal system ensures its continued and profitable existence by creating work for itself. Of all the systems it is the most cannibalistic, for in effect it feeds off human beings. Even a simple motoring 'offence' by one person, for example, is a potential source of income for the police who deal with him or her, the solicitor, the barrister, the prosecutor, the judiciary, and of course all those who fill the bureaucratic positions which are necessary to enable the cumbersome machinery of the legal system to grind on its way. It is one of the surprises of creation that there are people who can view such a system with pride and love, but then every created being loves something. The fly loves shit, while the bee loves honey – and of course there are times when the system does function well, when the lawyers are skilled, and the truth does emerge, and the judge is impartial, and the outcome is just.

Again, as with the hospital system, it must be emphasised that within the legal system too there are good people, men and women endowed with intelligence and integrity whose desire is to see that justice is done, and who more often than not ensure that justice is done – but often in spite of the system and not because of it!

Given the way the system is set up, it is not surprising that the police are forced by the very nature of the kafir system, that is the Dajjal system, to hunt for and prosecute even the most trivial of so-called offences and offenders. Given the presence of all the various legal entities in the legal system, it follows that they must have work to justify their existence. The vast amounts of money which are gathered by means of fines imposed in the courts each day are used to supplement the money gathered by means of taxes, in order to cover the running costs of the legal system. These costs are vast. The police force is continually increasing in size, and not only must its members receive their above average pay, but also they must have all the latest equipment.

Since kafir legal procedure and kafir laws are complex, and expressed in a specialist vocabulary, most people who find themselves accused of anything usually have to obtain assistance from lawyers if they are to stand any chance of acquittal in court at all. Since not all the victims of the legal system are rich, and indeed most of them come from among the helpless and the poor, provision has to be made for the lawyers who represent them. The legal aid scheme ensures that the lawyers will still get paid, even when their client has no money. Naturally the handsome income of the judiciary, and the not so handsome income of the people filling the bureaucratic posts in the legal system, is also safely guaranteed, but adds a great deal to the annual cost of running the legal system.

Finally there is the upkeep of the buildings in which the people who operate the legal system enact their daily dramas, as well as the need to erect more buildings in what is after all a profitable and expanding business. As any society disintegrates, more prisons are always needed. All this expense, most of it unnecessary – in the sense that if a different approach to 'crime' were used, much of the expense at present incurred could be avoided – has to be met by the people enslaved in the producer consumer process.

o o o o o

It is not only the criminal law but also the civil law which is a potential source of handsome reward for those involved in the legal system. The dependence of people on the civil law process is achieved by ensuring that even the simplest of transactions needs to be evidenced in writing if it is to be regarded as 'valid'. When you are born, your birth must be registered, as must eventually your death. Marriage must be registered and if it does not work out, it is only by means of the civil law that it can be legally dissolved, and financial provision and division of shared assets be legally made. When you die your property cannot be distributed according to your wishes without your personal representatives, or their legal representatives first going to court to obtain probate.

Thus all the main milestones along the journey of life, that is birth, marriage and death, are in a kafir society only regarded as real and valid and legal and right and proper, if they have been endorsed by usually quite unnecessary paper work. Further reliance on the civil legal process is also ensured by the fact that in a situation where people do not trust each other, and are suspicious of each other's motives – and this is the natural condition of the kafir mind – they usually tend to place more reliance on courts of law to obtain for them what they want. What this means is that the kafir has to be confronted with the threat of impending punishment before he or she will keep his or her word when it does not seem expedient so to do. Whoever does not fear God, or fear the Fire, or long for the Garden, inevitably has to be threatened with a big stick!

Everyone is motivated by hope and fear – but what a difference between those whose hope and fear are dictated by their attitude towards the creation, and those whose hope and fear are directed by their attitude towards the Creator.

By far the greatest volume of work for the kafir civil courts derives from the consumer producer process itself. Since that process is based on competition and exploitation, it follows that there will always be people who are trying to get something for nothing, and this can usually only be achieved by clever word play which achieves the desired result without infringing the law. The guidance of a legal expert is needed in such matters. Similarly, such dishonest activity can usually only be prevented by taking or threatening to take the matter before the courts. Allah says in the *Qur'an* that the kafirun appear to be one body, but they are divided against each other. It is this division, which is characterised by lack of trust and by the willingness to take advantage of others, which ensures that the civil courts and lawyers are kept in business.

Furthermore, because the kafir system, that is the Dajjal system, needs so many rules and regulations in order to function, this means not only that there will always be constant breaches of these rules occurring, but also that experts will be needed to interpret these rules both in their application and when dealing with any breaches thereof. Further dependence on the civil judicial process is also ensured by the fact that these rules and procedures are for ever changing, which means not only that the publishers of legal text books are given continued and lucrative work, but also that it is only the legal expert who has even the slightest idea of what the legal position probably is in any given situation, at any particular point in time.

When anything goes wrong in a kafir transaction, the only way to ensure that things are put right is by employing the people who know how to deal with the paperwork, and who have some idea of how all the relevant laws – which govern the validity of what the paper in question records – operate. Amongst people who trust each other, neither these laws, nor the courts which administer them, nor the experts who interpret them, are needed.

The involvement of the kafir banking, insurance, hire purchase, building society and other finance systems in the producer consumer system, and indeed in all aspects of people's lives lived in the context of that system, also help to ensure that the kafir civil judicial process is kept busy. All these kafir financial institutions deal in sophisticated magic, in that they create money out of nothing by charging interest, an activity which Allah expressly prohibits in the *Qur'an*, saying that those who indulge in it are for the Fire. They all work on the understanding that anyone who has been adequately programmed to desire the products of the consumer producer process will be willing to pay extra if he or she can have immediate possession of the product in question. The 'extra' is calculated in terms of interest.

Since all these finance institutions only exist to make money out of people, they are usually merciless in commencing legal proceedings whenever a customer falls behind in payment, especially now that decisions are increasingly being made by computers rather than by human beings. The overriding criterion no longer appears to be whether or not someone who needs help is trustworthy, but whether or not he or she is a good investment – that is, whether or not enough money can be made out of him or her.

If someone, for example – who under a mortgage agreement has agreed to pay over three times the amount that would have been payable if he or she had been able to pay for the house in full at the time of agreeing to buy the house – falls behind on the mortgage repayments after having conscientiously paid them for twenty years – and after he or she has already in fact paid twice the original value of the house – then under the terms of the mortgage agreement, the house will usually be repossessed and sold, and if the proceeds of sale do not cover the outstanding debt, then its former owner will be pursued for the balance. In effect, the end result will be that after having paid for the house three times over, he or she will end up without the house and without any money!

There can be no doubt whatsoever that usury, in whatever form it takes – and charging interest on bank overdrafts or loans is only one of these forms – is legalised theft.

This situation is the complete opposite of that in which one Muslim lends money to another Muslim, and is quite prepared to wait long beyond the agreed time of repayment, and if necessary relieve the debtor of having to repay the loan altogether, firm in the knowledge that Allah will repay the debt for him or her ten times over. Indeed there are some Muslims who refuse to lend money, but will only give it away, on the principle and in the knowledge that if they lend money they only stand to regain the sum lent, whereas if they give it away they will recover ten times that amount, in accordance with the promise and by the generous outpouring of Allah.

This knowledge is entirely lacking in the typical kafir financial institution which, because of its size and the manner in which it is run, can be utterly ruthless with the most deserving of people, simply because the individual who is borrowing the money never meets the individual who is lending it. The representative of the financial institution is always in a position to say that if he or she could help then he or she would, but unfortunately rules are rules, and he or she is bound by the rules of the company and his or her contract of employment. Most of the transactions are conducted via computer, and, since most computers have not been programmed to be compassionate, for their programmers are not compassionate, accordingly legal proceedings can be initiated automatically and without deliberation or compassion.

Although the insurance companies are concerned primarily with safeguarding products once they have been acquired, by agreeing to pay out money to the owner if the product is lost or damaged in certain specified circumstances, and provided that the owner agrees to pay a specified premium to the insurance company throughout the period of insurance, they also play a large role in the context of personal injury and fatal accident claims. Since they are in the insurance trade solely for purposes of business, the amounts they are prepared to pay out on the various claims have already been carefully calculated, so that after they have been paid out the company will be left with an overall profit. If they can get away with paying less on a claim than they expect they will have to pay, then they will do so. This means that many claims become the subject of litigation, for it is only when experts' reports have been prepared, and lawyers employed to bargain by correspondence and advise the respective parties as to what sum the judge would be likely to award if the matter went to court, that it may become clear as to how much the claim is really worth. This pattern of activity is another clear example of how the kafir system, that is the Dajjal system, creates activity in order that money can be made out of it.

The kafir civil legal process is like the kafir criminal legal process: It makes money out of other people's misfortunes. A person who breaks an arm at work because, for example, he was given a faulty ladder to use, will not receive any financial compensation for his injury until after the insurance company has been involved, solicitors and barristers have been involved, medical experts have been involved, and, if agreement cannot be reached, until the matter has been finally settled in court. In a simple case like this the costs of all these different entities being involved will be greatly in excess of the sum which is finally recovered by the victim of the accident. The truth of the matter is that this pattern of activity is not really for the benefit of the victim. It is more for the benefit of the so-called experts without whose help the victim can recover nothing.

This is the key to the kafir system, that is the Dajjal system. Once the experts who control that system have persuaded the majority of the population to rely on their services, then the position and income of the experts, and therefore the continued existence of that system, is assured.

The muslim community has no need of these so-called experts. In the case of unexpected damage to property or injury to life and limb, the members of the community help each other out. Where appropriate, money can be distributed from the bayt al-mal, that is the fund into which the members of the community pay the minimal taxes required by the *Qur'an*.

The only taxes which a Muslim is obliged by Allah to pay are the zakat which is a tax of two and a half per cent of any capital or income above a certain amount which has been accumulated and not used for at least a year – in other words, wealth which is over and above what its owner actually needs in order to live; and a tax of two and a half per cent on merchandise above a certain amount which has remained in stock for at least a year; and a tax of ten per cent on naturally watered crops, or five per cent on artificially watered crops, which is to be paid in the form of one tenth or one twentieth of what has actually been harvested; and a tax of a small proportion of any herd of livestock over a certain size; and a tax of two and a half per cent of the value of all mineral and subterranean resources which are mined.

There is also the zakat al-fitr, which is four both-hands-cupped-fulls of a local staple food, usually grain or dried fruit, payable by or on behalf of every Muslim in the community at the end of Ramadan, which is the lunar month during which every adult Muslim in good health fasts between dawn and sunset. Finally, if a Muslim finds buried treasure, he or she must pay a tax on it of twenty per cent. All these taxes are paid into the bayt al-mal.

Since the way of Islam is based on giving out, a real muslim community ensures that the contents of this central fund are immediately distributed to those in need – as defined in the *Qur'an* and the *Sunnah* – as quickly as it fills up. Since the taxes are gathered in at different times of the year, it follows that the bayt al-mal is continually being filled, expended and replenished. The taxes are so simple that they can be understood by someone who is illiterate. There is thus no need for the expert to interpret and administer them.

There are two other taxes, payable by non-muslims, which are equally simple: The jizya tax, which is paid by all adult males of the ahlu'l-dhimma, that is any non-muslims living under Muslim rule and protection. The amount per head, which can be reduced in cases of real poverty, is four dinars of gold or forty dirhams of silver each year. This is approximately the equivalent, at the time of writing this, of £200-00 English, or $300 American. By virtue of paying the jizya tax, the ahl'ul-dhimma do not have to fight if the Muslim community is attacked, and are entitled to protection by the Muslims during such an attack. The other tax is ten per cent on imports into Muslim territory from other countries, which is levied on traders who are not muslim.

The absolute simplicity of the muslim taxes means that they can be gathered with ease. There is thus none of the unnecessary activity which is engendered by the kafir tax laws, which are so complex and so oppressive that they create the demand for legal experts to interpret them and find ways of evading and avoiding them, and for a complex bureaucratic system to collect them – and of course provide the authorities with the work of catching tax offenders and the kafir legal system with more business in dealing with them. Since muslim taxes are so low, virtually everyone can afford to pay them, especially since they are only payable out of what a person actually possesses, and not on what someone may have earned during the year. A Muslim, for example, who has an annual income of a million pounds or dollars would not have to pay any zakat on this amount if none of it had been accumulated for at least a year or more.

○   ○   ○   ○   ○

It is quite evident that, after the regulation of society, the main concern of many kafir legal system is making money and creating situations from which money can be made – not justice. It follows that the outcome of a good many cases depends not on the facts or the merits of the case, but on who is going to have to pay the costs. This means that there are two laws, one for the rich and one for the poor. This means that the kafir legal system favours those who control the kafir system, that is the Dajjal system, at the expense of those who are enslaved by that system. The profits involved are increased by the fact that since the kafir legal machine involves much bureaucracy there is much delay. This delay is a disadvantage to the accused or to the litigant as the case may be, since when events are no longer fresh in people's minds the outcome of the case becomes more uncertain. As far as the people involved with the conduct of the case are concerned, however, any delay means more pay.

The kafir legal system, the heart of the kafir system, that is the Dajjal system, creates work for itself and is provided with work by virtue of the way in which the producer consumer system operates, and it makes vast sums of money out of that work, whilst at the same time maintaining the status quo which ensures that work continues to be made available.

Only those who know how the kafir system that is the Dajjal system works, and who help to control it, share in the profits which arise from the way in which it operates. Everyone else loses out, in monetary terms at any rate. Of course in the final analysis success or failure can only be measured in terms of whether you end up in the Garden or in the Fire in the life after this one. If one looks at the kafir system, that is the Dajjal system, from this Qur'anic perspective, then it is clear that the kafir controllers, who imagine that they have got it made in this world, are in for a big shock in the next one.

It follows that the following excerpt from a letter from the London branch of the banking firm of Rothschild Brothers, dated the 25th of June 1863 and addressed to the New York bank of Ickleheimer, Morton and Van der Gould – which was quoted by Ezra Pound in his writings, and which gives some indication of both the nature and the identity of the iceberg of institutionalised usury which has so deeply affected the characteristics and quality of life in the twentieth and twenty-first centuries – is only of limited accuracy when viewed from a kafir perspective, and of none when viewed from a Qur'anic perspective:

> 'The few who understand the system ... will either be so interested in its profits, or so dependant on its favours, that there will be no opposition from that class, while, on the other hand, the great body of people, mentally incapable of comprehending the tremendous advantages that Capital derives from the system, will bear its burden without complaint, and perhaps without even suspecting that the system is inimical to their interests ...'

It must be emphasised that the Prophetic mode of existence is the complete opposite of the kafir system that is the Dajjal system. Kufr creates complexity. Islam embodies simplicity. In the muslim community there is a complete absence of institutions and bodies of experts whose livelihood and continued existence depends on creating work for themselves, by feeding off other people's misfortunes. The Prophet Muhammad, may the blessings and peace of Allah be on him, said, 'We are an illiterate community. We do not write and we do not calculate.' Human transactions in a muslim community are conducted on the basis of mutual trust, and not on the basis of a spurious legal validity which necessitates paper work. The *Qur'an* and the *Sunnah* contain all the guidance an individual human being or group of people needs.

Where disputes arise, they can be settled by reference to what is in the *Qur'an* and the *Hadith*, and not necessarily by reference to other people's decisions in similar fact situations in the past, or to complex, arbitrary and for ever changing laws and rules.

It is true that there are those who have attempted to make a legal system, based on one or more kafir legal systems, out of some of the teachings of Islam, but they cannot be regarded as muslims and must be ignored. They are merely the fulfilment of the Prophet Muhammad's prophecy, may Allah bless him and grant him peace, that there would be those who, in the name of Islam, would follow the example of their predecessors, meaning the Jews and the Christians, just like a lizard making for its hole, that is by compromising and abandoning the guidance which their Prophet had brought.

The nature of the real muslim community is such, that there can be no consumer producer process, because the Muslims know that they were not created for that purpose; that there can be no educational system such as is operated by the kafir system, that is the Dajjal system, because the Muslims do not need to be conditioned to be exploited – because the basis of a muslim community is the worship of Allah and not the exploitation of others, and because the knowledge which the true Muslims have is certain knowledge, derived from the *Qur'an* and the *Hadith*, directly from Allah and His Messenger, and not the often useless or irrelevant speculative information in which the kafir educational system largely traffics; that there can be no medical system, because the Muslim by virtue of his or her way of life is basically healthy – and when sick, uses a different form of healing to that employed by the kafir medical system; that there can be no legal system, because the guidance in the *Qur'an* and the *Hadith* is complete and does not need to be changed or amended, and because anyone can follow it without the necessity of experts to interpret it, and because it can only be followed if it is accepted voluntarily and not if it is imposed by or on others; that there can be no financial systems which operate on the basis of charging interest, because not only are these forbidden by Allah, but also because muslim commerce is based on generosity and giving out, and not on being mean and retention.

In a real muslim society there are no faceless institutions, there are no banks as we know banks today, there are no prisons and no law courts, and there is no police force, or standing army for that matter. The ruler is the person whom everyone has accepted as their ruler, and who follows what is in the *Qur'an* and the *Sunnah*. Since there is no ruling elite – for the way of Muhammad expressly forbids dynastic rule and whoever adopts dynastic rule does so in defiance of the guidance sent by Allah – it follows that there is no body of people who, because they wish to exploit the rest of the population, need to have both the means of oppression and the means which are used to disguise the nature of that oppression.

Whenever anyone in a muslim community goes beyond the limits of Allah, as indicated in the *Qur'an* and the *Hadith*, in a manner which harms someone else or the community as a whole, then that person is dealt with, in accordance with what is in the *Qur'an* and the *Hadith*, by the community through its leader and on the spot without delay. No one in a muslim community should be deprived of their liberty for more than three days, no matter what they may have done. Everyone inclines to wrong action at some time or other. The compassionate way in which the Prophet Muhammad, may Allah bless him and grant him peace, dealt with those who had gone beyond the limits set by Allah provides a clear example of how to rule, for all those who have been chosen to rule. He directed rulers not to reach a conclusion until they had heard both sides of the story, and not to sit in judgement if they were angry or constipated. He never built a prison.

The fact that anything which occurs in a muslim community and which requires a decision is dealt with on the spot means that there is no room for bureaucracy or bureaucrats or paper work. In a muslim community justice is not a matter of who pays the costs, because there are no costs of the kind which the operation of kafir legal systems engenders to pay.

Anyone in a muslim community who has taken upon him or her self the obligations of the Shari'ah, that is the road to Allah, which are simply stated in the *Qur'an* and the *Hadith*, and who fears Allah and the Last Day, is solely by virtue of the way in which he or she has chosen to live neither a threat to others nor to his or her own self. To follow the Prophetic life style is to live in harmony with one's self and with others, and in order to achieve this balance there is no need whatsoever for a body of people who have appointed themselves as the judges of others' actions and as the enforcers of this way of life. Indeed whenever this group appears, and there is always a time when it does, it is a sign of disintegration, a sign of the first inclination away from Islam towards Kufr.

The whole point of the way of Islam is that it cannot be successfully imposed on anyone who does not wish to follow it. It can only be voluntarily adopted by the one who wishes to live in that way. Allah says in the *Qur'an* that there is no compulsion in the life transaction. Only a fool tries to force people to live in a certain manner, for the reality of existence is that every atom is in its place, and everything that takes place is intended by Allah. If you look at creation you can find no fault in it. It is perfect. If you are a mumin it is no good trying to be a kafir. If you are a kafir it is no good trying to be a mumin. You can only be who you are and allow others to be who they are. There is no power and no strength except from Allah.

o o o o o

Reference has been made to the ruling elite of the kafir system that is the Dajjal system, and to the fact that they now control all the sub-systems which together make up that system. Up to now this group of kafir controllers has not been positively identified. It is now necessary to take a closer look at who they are. Co-ordinated control of the apparently separate albeit interlinking sub-systems which together form the kafir system, that is the Dajjal system, is made possible by the existence of the ruling elite's secret organisations, the various lodges of the freemasons. The ruling elite of the kafir system, that is the Dajjal system, are the freemasons. Their activities are masked by the popular misconception that the freemasons are no more than a fraternity who help each other in the business world and do charitable work. This is true, but the extent of that mutual assistance, and the high degree of influence and control which they exercise, is hidden from public knowledge. The hierarchy within these lodges, as is typical of all kafir systems, is pyramidical in form. One of their symbols is the pyramid with the 'all-seeing' eye, the eye of the Dajjal. The freemasons are the magicians of the twentieth and twenty-first centuries. All magic is concerned with a formal manipulation of existence which is conducted in such a way that the method used to achieve the desired result is not apparent to the onlooker. This accurately describes the nature of freemasonic activity in the sphere of the kafir producer consumer system, that is the Dajjal system, even to the point where governments are subverted and wars engineered in order that debts may be created, by supplying so-called advisers and arms at a cost, which are further inflated by charging interest on the debts thereby incurred. The freemasons are today's equivalent of Pharaoh's magicians, many of whom, as we know from the Qur'an, supported the kafir manipulation control system of the Pharaoh who opposed Moses and his teaching, and who eventually brought about his own downfall by so doing. The story of the transaction between Moses and Pharaoh is related in great detail and more than once in the Qur'an. It demonstrates with great clarity that when a man of Allah, who knows that he is completely helpless in the hands of Allah, meets a man of kufr, who relies on the magic which Allah has given him without his knowing it, then it is the man of Allah to whom victory is given by Allah. There is no strength and no power except from Allah.

○   ○   ○   ○   ○

The transaction which occurred between Moses and Pharaoh is the same as the transaction which occurred between Noah and the kafir ruler of his time, is the same as the transaction which occurred between Abraham and Nimrod, is the same as the transaction which occurred between Jesus and the Roman Emperor, is the same as the transaction which occurred between Muhammad and Abu Jahl, is the same as the transaction which today occurs between iman and kufr, and which will find its final expression in the confrontation between the Mahdi and Dajjal.

Looking at history from the Qur'anic perspective, we see that there has only ever been one major transaction between people on the face of this earth, that is the transaction between those who accept Allah and His Prophets and those who reject Allah and His Prophets.

Allah is as He was before the creation of the Universe and continues to be. Allah is as He will be. Allah cannot be conceived of, and everything other than Allah which appears to be is the conception of Allah. Vision cannot contain Him, but He contains vision, and he is the All-Pervading, the Knower of every separate thing that befalls us. Allah is One. Allah is independent of what appears to be other than Him. He was not born from anything and nothing is born from Him and there is nothing like Him. There is no god only Allah. There is only Allah.

All the Prophets and Messengers of Allah, may the blessings and peace of Allah be on them, were sent by Allah to teach people the meaning of these words, and to show them how to live in accordance with that meaning. They were sent in order that people might know the nature of reality that is the Real that is Allah, and in order that people might know how to live with that knowledge. They were sent with a way of life which would lead those who followed it to self-knowledge and to knowledge of Allah, the same knowledge, for who ever knows their self truly knows their Lord.

It follows, since they all came from and affirmed the same and only One Reality, Allah, that all the respective Prophets' teachings were essentially the same, although sometimes differing slightly in their application in accordance with the particular needs of the particular time and people for whom each Prophet was sent and meant. Moses and Jesus, for example, were sent specifically to the Tribe of Israel, whereas Muhammad, may the blessings and peace of Allah be on him and on all the Prophets, was sent for all mankind and the jinn.

It follows that all the people who have ever lived or are alive or are to live on this earth have only ever had or will have one choice, that is whether to be mumin or kafir. In Reality there is not even that choice, since you can only be what Allah has decreed you will be. Allah is the doer of you and your actions. You are answerable for your actions. On the Last Day you will not question Allah, but Allah will question you. Right now the choice is yours.

The Dajjal is not something separate from kufr. The Dajjal is the final and most extreme expression of kufr before the end of the world, just as the Mahdi will be the final and most eloquent embodiment of Islam before the end of the world. It will be remembered that the Mahdi will be a drop compared to the ocean of the Prophet Muhammad, may the blessings and peace of Allah be on him. It is the final confrontation between the Mahdi and the Dajjal and their respective followers which, according to the *Hadith*, heralds the end of the world. During that final confrontation the Prophet Jesus, peace be on him, will reappear on earth and kill the Dajjal. There will then follow the peaceful rule of the Mahdi as leader of all the Muslims, who will be spread all around the world. When Jesus eventually dies, he will be buried next to the Prophet Muhammad, may the blessings and peace of Allah be on both of them, in Madina. After this period there will come a time when Allah will take the arwah, that is the spirit forms, of all those who trust in Allah from their bodies and this earth, so that there is only one Muslim left on the face of the earth, in China. When he dies, there will be a period when those who are left on the earth will live like animals. At the end of this period, Israfil the angel will blow the first blast of his trumpet, at which every living thing will die. The earth will remain lifeless for a period. At the end of this period Israfil will give a second blast on his trumpet at which the world will disintegrate, as is described in the *Qur'an* and the *Hadith*, until it has become one vast flat plain of silver sand. All those who have ever lived will be brought to life again, and this is easy for the One Who gave you life in the first place. Then, depending on their actions and the intentions behind those actions whilst they were in this world, it will be decided who is for the Fire, and who is for the Garden. The Fire is for the kafirun. The Garden is for the muminun. Dajjal and his followers are for the Fire. The Mahdi and his followers are for the Garden. You are either for the Fire or for the Garden. Right now the choice is yours.

○   ○   ○   ○   ○

The freemasons are the leaders of the takeover by Dajjal as an unseen force. The results of their activities are evidenced by Dajjal as a world wide social and cultural phenomenon. They will be the ones who acclaim and support Dajjal the individual when he appears. Without the freemasons the takeover would not have progressed as far as it has. Since, at the moment of writing this, they control all the kafir institutions and systems in the world today, it would seem that they have never been in an apparently stronger position than now to orchestrate their plans for world domination through the producer consumer process, backed by their banking system, by means of dividing and ruling. The point has even been reached where they are planning mass sterilisation of women in the third world countries so that, in the name of women's 'liberation', they can manipulate and balance the forces of supply and demand in the emerging new world market.

The high degree of control exercised by the freemasons today is witnessed by the fact that they are able to instigate a war, provide the arms for the two sides to be able to fight it, at a price of course, and then take over control, or strengthen control if they already have it, once the fighting is over, any opposition to them having been considerably weakened by the inevitable consequences of war. Look, for example, at what has happened in Bosnia.

This technique of manipulation control by divide and rule is effected by operating on two fronts at the same time. There is what goes on behind the scenes as it were, and there is the official stage production which is put on for the benefit of the general public. The manner in which the hidden activities are conducted is highly ruthless, and the efficiency with which they are carried out is matched only by the lengths to which the freemasons are prepared to go to put on a convincing constitutional, legal and just stage production for the benefit and continued misguidance of the unsuspecting public. The success of the show, that is of the official version of events, is only made possible by the fact that the different kafir sub-systems are able to interlink and co-operate, by virtue of the fact that they are controlled by one and the same ruling elite, the freemasons, who staged the french revolution to begin with, and who have never ceased to increase the magnitude of their stage productions and the control underlying them since that time.

The interaction of the medical and legal kafir systems provides perhaps the most eloquent example of the freemasonic co-operation which is necessary to ensure a good stage production fronting the acquisition of ultimate control. It is not entirely a coincidence that, taking London as an example, the High Court of Justice and the Royal College of Surgeons have their backs facing each other, but are separated only by a stone's throw. Although they apparently face in different directions, they can work in close conjunction with each other when necessary.

To give but three examples of how the legal and medical systems, aided of course by the media system, can work together, we may examine the removal of Lord Northcliffe, a former chief proprietor of *The Times* newspaper, which occurred after the first world war, and the trial of Ezra Pound, the famous poet, and the notorious Nuremberg trials, which took place immediately after the second world war.

◊   ◊   ◊   ◊   ◊

Under cover of the first world war, Palestine – which had been selected as the 'homeland' of the Zionist Jews whose forefathers, the Khazar Jews, were in fact from the Caucasus – was occupied by the British. The famous Balfour Declaration, addressed to Lord Rothschild, was officially delivered on the 2nd of November, 1917, during exactly the same week in which the Russian Revolution was successfully concluded:

> His Majesty's Government view with favour the establishment in Palestine of a National Home for the Jewish People, and will use their best endeavours to facilitate the achievement of this object, it being clearly understood that nothing shall be done which may prejudice the civil and religious rights of existing non-Jewish communities in Palestine, or the rights and political status enjoyed by Jews in any country.

It is interesting to note in passing that Communism, like Zionism, was predominantly a Khazar Jewish affair, as Douglas Reed records in his book, *The Controversy of Zion*:

> The British Government's White Paper of 1919 (Russia, No.1, a Collection of Reports on Bolshevism) quoted the report sent to Mr. Balfour in London in 1918 by the Netherlands Minister at Saint Petersburg, M. Oudendyke: 'Bolshevism is organised and worked by Jews, who have no nationality and whose one object is to destroy for their own ends the existing order of things.' The United States Ambassador, Mr. David R. Francis, reported similarly: 'The Bolshevik leaders here, most of whom are Jews and 90 per cent of whom are returned exiles, care little for Russia or any other country but are internationalists and they are trying to start a worldwide social revolution.' M. Oudendyke's report was deleted from later editions of the British official publication and all such authentic documents of that period are now difficult to obtain. Fortunately for the student, one witness preserved the official record.
>
> This was Mr. Robert Wilton, correspondent of the London Times, who experienced the Bolshevik revolution. The French edition of his book included the official Bolshevik lists of the membership of the ruling revolutionary bodies (they were omitted from the English edition).
>
> These records show that the Central Committee of the Bolshevik party, which wielded the supreme power, contained 3 Russians (including Lenin) and 9 Jews. The next body in importance, the Central Committee of the Executive Commission (or secret police) comprised 42 Jews and 19 Russians, Letts, Georgians and others. The Council of People's Commissars consisted of 17 Jews and five others. The Moscow Che-ka (secret police) was formed of 23 Jews and 13 others. Among the names of 556 high officials of the Bolshevik state officially published in 1918–1919 were 458 Jews and 108 others. Among the central committees of small, supposedly 'Socialist' or other non-Communist parties (during that early period the semblance of 'opposition' was permitted, to beguile the masses, accustomed

under the Czar to opposition parties) were 55 Jews and 6 others. All the names are given in the original documents reproduced by Mr. Wilton.

After the conclusion of the first world war, and while the League of Nations was being set up in order to rubber-stamp the Mandate which would grant the British government 'international' approval to administer Palestine on behalf of the Jews until a sufficient number of Jews had been installed in Palestine to be able to take over control there themselves, Lord Northcliffe, the chief proprietor of, inter alia, *The Times* newspaper, accompanied by a journalist, Mr. J.M.N. Jeffries, visited Palestine and saw exactly what was going on, as Douglas Reed records:

> This was a combination of a different sort from that formed by the editors of The Times and Manchester Guardian, who wrote their leading articles about Palestine in England and in consultation with the Zionist chieftain, Dr. Weizmann. Lord Northcliffe, on the spot, reached the same conclusion as all other impartial investigators, and wrote, 'In my opinion we, without sufficient thought, guaranteed Palestine as a home for the Jews despite the fact that 700,000 Arab Muslims live there and own it ... The Jews seemed to be under the impression that all England was devoted to the one cause of Zionism, enthusiastic for it in fact; and I told them that this was not so and to be careful that they do not tire out our people by secret importation of arms to fight 700,000 Arabs ... There will be trouble in Palestine ... people dare not tell the Jews the truth here. They have had some from me.'

The editor of *The Times*, however, Mr. Wickham Steed – who during the war had already refused to publish the eyewitness accounts of the true nature of the (Khazar Jewish) Russian Revolution which had been written by its chief foreign correspondent for Russia, Mr. Robert Wilton – refused to publish Lord Northcliffe's series of articles on the situation in Palestine; when instructed by Lord Northcliffe to come out to Palestine to see things for himself, he refused to do so; and when he was told, again by Lord Northcliffe, to publish an editorial attacking Mr. Balfour's attitude towards Zionism, he refused yet again. After returning to England, Lord Northcliffe requested the resignation of Mr. Wickham Steed, on the 2nd of March, 1922. The editor refused to do so and informed a director of *The Times* that Lord Northcliffe was 'going mad'. Douglas Reed continues the story:

> On June 8, 1922 Lord Northcliffe, from Boulogne, asked Mr. Wickham Steed to meet him in Paris; they met there on June 11, 1922, and Lord Northcliffe told his visitor that he, Lord Northcliffe, would assume the editorship of The Times. On June 12, 1922 the whole party left for Evian-les-Bains, a doctor being secreted on the train, as far as the Swiss frontier, by Mr. Wickham Steed. Arrived in Switzerland 'a brilliant French nerve specialist' (unnamed) was summoned and in the evening certified Lord Northcliffe insane. On the strength of this Mr. Wickham Steed cabled instructions to The Times to disregard and not to publish anything received from Lord Northcliffe, and on June 13, 1922 he left, never to see Lord Northcliffe again. On June 18, 1922 Lord Northcliffe returned to London and was in fact removed from all control of, and even communication with his undertakings (especially The Times; his telephone was cut). The manager had police posted at the door to prevent him entering the office of The Times if he were able to reach it. All this, according to the Official History of The Times, was on the strength of certification in a foreign country (Switzerland) by an unnamed (French) doctor. On August 14, 1922 Lord Northcliffe died; the cause of death stated was ulcerative endocarditis, and his age was fifty-seven. He was buried, after a service at Westminster Abbey, amid a great array of mourning editors.
>
> Such is the story as I have taken it from the official publication. None of this was known outside a small circle at the time; it only emerged in the Official History after three decades, and if it had been published in 1922 would presumably have called forth many questions. I doubt if any comparable displacement of a powerful and wealthy man can be adduced, at any rate in such mysterious circumstances.

Douglas Reed concludes:

> Lord Northcliffe therefore was out of circulation, and of

the control of his newspapers, during the decisive period preceding the ratification of 'the mandate' by the League of Nations, which clinched the Palestinian transaction and bequeathed the effects of it to our present generation. The opposition of a widely-read chain of journals at that period might have changed the whole course of events. After Lord Northcliffe died the possibility of editorials in The Times 'attacking Balfour's attitude towards Zionism' faded. From that time the submission of the press, in the manner described by the Protocols, grew ever more apparent and in time reached the condition which prevails today, when faithful reporting and impartial comment on this question has long been in suspense.

Lord Northcliffe was removed from control of his newspapers and put under constraint on June 18, 1922; on July 24, 1922 the Council of the League of Nations met in London, secure from any possibility of loud public protest by Lord Northcliffe, to bestow on Britain a 'mandate' to remain in Palestine and by arms to instal the Zionists there (I describe what events have shown to be the fact; the matter was not so depicted to the public, of course).

It is interesting to note in passing that Douglas Reed, who had joined the staff of *The Times* newspaper at the end of the first world war, was sent to Boulogne to act as Lord Northcliffe's secretary during the first week of June 1922. He was thus one of the last people to be with Lord Northcliffe before he was pronounced 'insane'. It is clear that in the opinion of Douglas Reed – who subsequently was to be *The Times* chief foreign correspondent for Central Europe and the Balkans – Lord Northcliffe was his normal self during that week:

> I cannot judge, and can only record what I saw and thought at the time, as a young man who had no more idea of what went on around him than a babe knows the shape of the world. When I returned to London I was questioned about Lord Northcliffe by his brother, Lord Rothermere, and one of his chief associates, Sir George Sutton. The thought of madness must by that time have been in their minds (the 'certification' had ensued) and therefore have underlain their questions, but not even then did any such suspicion

occur to me, although I had been one of the last people to see him before he was certified and removed from control of his newspapers. I did not know of that when I saw them or for long afterwards. In such secrecy was all this done that, although I continued in the service of The Times for sixteen years, I only learned of the 'madness' and 'certification' thirty years later, from the Official History. By that time I was able to see what great consequences had flowed from an affair in which I was an uninitiated onlooker at the age of twenty-seven.

For, under cover of the second world war, the swiftly growing number of Jews in Palestine were armed, and, with the creation of the successor to the League of Nations, the United Nations, the state of Israel was both proclaimed and then swiftly officially and 'internationally' recognised by the members of that institution soon after the war had come to an end.

o   o   o   o   o

Ezra Pound was only too well aware that what passed itself off as education in the western world was nothing less than a conditioning process which guaranteed ignorance of the overall nature and unity of existence, at the expense of being highly informed about specific and isolated pockets of life, the height of that ignorance being the person who thinks he or she knows all there is to know, when in fact the opposite is the case. Ezra Pound was also only too well aware that both the first and the second kafir world wars had been engineered, precipitated and orchestrated by the freemasons, who as a result had made much money out of them, as well as increasing their control both over and in not only the governments of all the countries involved, but also their educational, business, medical, legal and media systems, thereby ensuring and insuring, via their banking, insurance and other finance systems, virtually complete control over much of the kafir producer consumer process which was being established in those countries. Ezra Pound was brave enough to broadcast what he saw was going on over the radio from Italy midway during the second world war. He was foolish or foolhardy enough not to realise the degree of control which the freemasons already exercised over the systems which he hoped to liberate by warning the people of the danger which threatened to engulf them, and by suggesting an alternative way of life and of government and commerce, based on the teachings of Confucius, which at the time he was in the process of translating. It would appear that he was unaware of the only viable alternative way of life to the kafir system that is the Dajjal system: that is, the way of Muhammad, may Allah bless him and grant him peace.

When the American forces reached the part of Italy where Pound was, he was immediately arrested. At that point he imagined that he was going to be taken to America to advise the government as to how to best adopt and implement the Confucian mode which he had been suggesting into the American way of life. The basis of this mode echoed the resolve of the original founding fathers of America, in that interest in any form or guise should not be charged on any kind of debt or loan.

Pound's subsequent treatment soon demonstrated that he was sadly mistaken in his belief, and showed how inimical the controlling freemasonic elite of America were to any suggestions which threatened their chief source of revenue and control, that is the creation of debts and the charging of interest thereon, so that the debtors had no choice but to work continuously in their producer consumer process, in order to raise the money to pay off the old debts, whilst at the same time incurring fresh ones. The takeover had already been virtually completed in America, and accordingly as far as the ruling elite of America was concerned, Ezra Pound was public enemy number one.

Soon after his arrest, Ezra Pound was taken to Pisa, where he was put in solitary confinement in an iron cage which stood in the middle of a military compound, and which provided no shelter from the sun by day, nor from the cold of night, nor from the wind and the dust and the rain. No-one was allowed to hold a conversation with him. Eventually he became so ill that he had to be put inside a tent in order that he be kept alive. After several weeks he was transported to America, still suffering from exposure and ill health.

On arrival in America Ezra Pound was given no time to recover, but was immediately brought before a judge and charged with treason, the very charge which he had been levelling at the freemasons, since in his opinion they were destroying and corrupting the America in which he personally believed – the America which the original founding fathers had envisaged – and were, through their manipulation control techniques, busy establishing the America which in fact exists today.

Ezra Pound was not permitted to have the defence lawyer of his own choosing. Instead he was allocated a lawyer who was himself a freemason, as was the judge who presided over the judicial proceedings, and as were the medical experts who were appointed both by the prosecution and the defence lawyers.

As far as the freemasons were concerned, it was important that Pound should not give evidence, nor indeed come to trial, since this would mean that his knowledge of the takeover would become known to all those who followed the trial, and might become too well publicised, even though the main media systems in America – as in Europe – were, and still are, controlled by the freemasons. Anyone who has attempted to set up their own broadcasting station in a kafir country will know just how tight the control exercised by the freemasons is.

Accordingly Pound's lawyer advised him that the best tactic was to avoid the danger of his being convicted for treason, which is an offence carrying the death penalty, by maintaining that he was unfit to stand trial by reason of insanity. In order for this stratagem to succeed, it was necessary that Pound did not speak a word in court. Pound, who was already an ageing and, because of the treatment which he had just received, a sick man, submitted to the pressure exerted by his lawyer and by his wife, and agreed to adopt this approach.

Pound appeared before the judge and a grand jury on his arraignment, his lawyer made the submission that Pound was unfit to stand trial, and the judge ordered a medical enquiry to be undertaken by medical experts who were to be selected by both the prosecution and the defence lawyers.

It is usual in such cases for the medical experts to disagree sharply, since they are only usually selected by the respective sides in the case because their opinion is going to support and strengthen the arguments put forward by the lawyer who chose them. It would have been expected in this case therefore, that the medical experts chosen by the prosecution would have come to the conclusion that Pound was perfectly sane and fit to stand trial. However, because it had already been agreed behind the scenes what was to happen to Ezra Pound, it came as no surprise that the prosecution medical experts – who like the defence medical expert, all the lawyers concerned and the judge, were freemasons – instead of supporting the contention that Pound was fit to plead and should not be allowed to escape the so-called demands of justice, in fact agreed completely with the defence medical expert in stating, once the necessary but unnecessary rigmarole of due observation, examination and psychiatric tests had been performed, that Pound was indeed 'insane' and therefore unable to stand trial.

This decision was of course portrayed by the freemasonic controlled media as an example of the humane treatment which an insane person, who could not really be held responsible for what he said or did, could expect to receive from a just and understanding legal system. In reality the freemasons were making very sure that what Pound had said or done to expose them did not become common knowledge.

Once the medical experts had come to their inevitable conclusion, and once that conclusion had been given weight by voicing it in the correct judicial setting, Pound's committal to an insane asylum for an indefinite period was a mere formality. The freemasons, as a result of the skilful and polished use and combination of their medical and legal systems, had succeeded in silencing one of their most eloquent and knowledgeable opponents with utmost ease, and all with the appearance of complete what is called legality and due judicial process. The Pound pantomime had been a resounding success: The audience were satisfied and unaware of what had really been going on.

Ezra Pound spent the next fifteen years in an insane asylum. He was allowed visitors, and indeed attracted quite a cult following, but his views were still effectively curtailed. He knew that if he spoke out again, and attempted to organise a more widespread dissemination of his political views by means of his visitors, then he would either be no longer allowed to have visitors, or else he would be brought back to court, adjudged sane, and immediately put on trial for treason. He by now must have realised that he could be found guilty of treason and sentenced to death just as easily as he had already been found insane and unfit to stand trial. Perhaps he saw that there was very little he could do at his advanced age, and acting virtually alone, to change the system. He had tried to kill the many headed monster by cutting off one or two of its heads, and had failed. He was probably unaware of the way to its heart. He chose to remain alive and be a celebrated poet.

Throughout all these goings on, the freemasonic controlled media discredited Pound by all possible means, fully endorsing his so-called insanity, and subtly casting doubt on any of his views concerning economics and politics and the way in which the kafir system, that is the Dajjal system, was, and still is, being controlled. The media presented the public with the picture of a man who was a mad but gifted poet, who in his own almost inspired but certainly idiosyncratic way was competent and even entertaining in his chosen sphere of literary activity – but who was otherwise totally inadequate and unqualified to make any relevant observation whatsoever on the way in which America was being governed and controlled by the freemasons, not only by means of their banking, insurance and other finance systems, but also through all the other large kafir institutions and systems, whether business, educational, media, medical, legal, or governmental.

All efforts were made to ensure that Pound's views were given as restricted a circulation as possible. Since the freemasons controlled the publishing world, which not only provides the educational system with most of its teaching resources, but also makes sure that the bookshops are filled with suitably opiate material for public consumption, nearly all of Pound's writings which attacked the kafir system, that is the Dajjal system, with an accuracy which was a little too uncomfortable to be tolerated, were successfully withdrawn from the market. Only his 'pretty' poems were allowed to have continued general circulation. Even today, many of the editions of Pound's Cantos have certain passages blacked out, wherever sensitive areas or key people, such as the Rothschilds, for example, are – or rather were – indicated or directly mentioned.

Finally, after fifteen years, when Pound was no longer capable of being a threat to the kafir system, that is the Dajjal system, simply because he was old and worn out and preparing for death, he was released from the insane asylum. He returned to Italy, where he subsequently died. If you ask anyone today who Ezra Pound was, they will probably tell you, a famous poet. Hardly anyone knows his real story, simply because it is very well hidden in the kafir information retrieval systems, and not available for all and sundry. The way in which Pound was effectively silenced was only possible because of the efficient interlink which existed, and continues to exist, between the American governmental, legal, medical and media systems, an interlink which was and is made possible by virtue of the control exercised by the freemasons.

    ○   ○   ○   ○   ○

It is clear that the success of the performance of the kafir stage production, which is used to disguise the true nature of the freemasonic ruling elite's ruthless manipulation control techniques, depends on the acceptance by the general population of the kafir definitions of what is 'normal' and what is 'legal'.

The kafir medical experts define what is 'normal' and what is 'abnormal', that is what is to be considered sane or insane. The kafir legal experts define what is 'legal' and what is 'illegal', that is what action is to be considered permissible or not permissible. Since the kafir expert is concerned with reputation and with the opinion of others, it follows that there is always more than one current definition of what is normal and what is legal, because the person who can come up with what the kafir calls an original idea or two thereby ensures a good position in the kafir experts' hierarchy – provided he or she is given suitable publicity and enough of it.

However, although the various kafir definitions of what is normal and what is legal differ widely, they all have one basic characteristic in common, that is that they all uphold the kafir view of existence. This means, in effect, that the apparent differences in opinion amongst the kafir experts are only surface conflicts. In fact they are all agreed when it comes to rejecting the way of the Prophets and affirming the way of the kafir system, that is the Dajjal system. Kufr is one system. The kafirun appear to be one body, but they are divided against each other.

The kafir educational system is used to inculcate and condition the general population with the definitions which have been framed by the kafir experts. The media is used to reinforce and sustain this conditioning. It is for this reason that alternative ways of education which do not support the kafir view of existence tend to be made illegal before they can ever become popular. It is a criminal offence in most kafir states for parents not to send their children through its educational conditioning process. Any 'alternative' educational establishment which is permitted to exist usually has to teach 'the national curriculum' if it is to survive – and is extremely unlikely to receive any form of government funding.

If the local authorities discover families who have slipped through the net, they have wide powers to take their children into what is called care, so that the children can no longer be deprived of their conditioning. Since it often happens that the parents who try to save their children from the educational system do not themselves know what the alternative to it is, the task of the care authorities in satisfying the court that the children should be taken into care because the parents cannot cope is made easier.

Similarly, the most influential media systems, that is radio and television, are monopolised by the kafir system that is the Dajjal system. It is a criminal offence in most kafir states to make an independent radio or television broadcast without a licence. Only those organisations which support the system, whether directly or indirectly, are likely to be granted such a licence.

In this way penetrating criticism of the kafir system that is the Dajjal system on a mass basis is effectively prevented. Instead, limited coverage is given to such 'extremists', since its effect is to persuade the average viewer or listener that the apparent relative stability of the kafir system, that is the Dajjal system, is far more preferable than the brave new world envisaged by the angry and inept minority, whose views are presented in the worst possible light on the media system.

Naturally not all of the imperfections of the system can be hidden from every one, and accordingly the media system usually presents programs in which it appears not only that these failings have been noticed and are being criticised, but also that something is being done to remedy them. The more established the system is in any particular kafir state, the more people are permitted to criticise it – simply because their words will not really change anything. These 'current affairs' programs alternate with dream and fantasy programs which are usually laced with ever more explicit soft pornography, thereby equating 'progress' and 'artistic licence' with the extent to which sexual activity and vulgar language are depicted and used. Having been shocked or lulled by the news you can then be excited by sports time, or entertained by music and drama time, or captivated by competition time, and suddenly another precious day has gone.

The effect of the media system is to make life a cerebral affair. Much of the action goes on in a person's head, via the radio or the television, or the computer, so that 'reality' is indeed virtual. It is a form of hypnosis. Everything happens by means of a technological interface. The result of being plugged into the media system for too long is that in the end you will accept almost anything, without actually doing anything about it, provided that your stomach is full, and your bed is warm, and your home is comfortable.

The individual in a kafir society is bombarded with so much information by the media system, that in the end he or she is usually left feeling completely helpless when confronted with the idea of changing the system, even when he or she has a pretty good idea of how it works. There are many people in today's kafir societies who are not at all happy with the way their lives are being organised, but who feel powerless to change either themselves or their environment. There are also those who, as a result of their educational and media conditioning, accept the world with which they are presented by that conditioning without question.

By controlling the educational and media systems, the kafir ruling elite ensure that their definitions of what is 'normal' and what is 'legal' prevail. The people in a kafir state are presented with these definitions from birth to death. Many of them only see what they are told to see. Very few realise how deeply implanted these definitions are in their consciousness, or seek to find the real meaning of existence, which is covered over by these definitions. The result of a kafir education, that is the view of existence which comes with and as a result of it, is kufr, is what might be called the Dajjal mentality. Ironically but predictably, anyone who disagrees with it is described and dismissed as having been 'brainwashed'.

All these kafir definitions are not based on an understanding of the true nature of existence. Indeed they are used to cover up the truth of things. They do not originate from Prophetic revelation, which derives from the source of existence and the destination to which all existence returns, Allah. Indeed it is only by basing one's life on Prophetic revelation, that is both one's existential life pattern as well as one's understanding of the nature of life itself – and today the only Prophetic revelation which is still intact and available to the seeker of knowledge is the *Qur'an* – that it is possible to cut through the web of kafir conditioning which covers over real knowledge, that is knowledge of the Real, Allah. In order to really understand existence, it is necessary to be 'heartwashed'!

The only way to base one's life on what is in the *Qur'an* is by finding a community of Muslims who most nearly follow the example and life style of the people who were the first to base their lives on what is in the *Qur'an* and the *Sunnah*, that is the first Muslim community of Madina al-Munawarra, which means the illuminated place where the life transaction is, who formed round the Prophet Muhammad fourteen hundred years ago. Allah says in the *Qur'an* that this was the best community which has ever been on the face of the earth, and since all creation is from Allah, He knows what He is talking about. The companions of the Prophet Muhammad received their knowledge of Allah, and of how to live, by keeping company with the Prophet Muhammad, whose every action embodied what is in the *Qur'an*, whose every word contained wisdom, and whose very presence transformed and illuminated those who were near him, may the blessings and peace of Allah always be on him and them.

The transaction of the real muslim community is the same today. The people in such a community receive their learning and knowledge by the baraka, that is by the blessing of their leader, who is a man of Allah and who is guided by Allah. Such a man is called a wali of Allah, that is a friend of Allah. He loves Allah and Allah loves him, and the people who also love Allah and whom Allah loves gather round him. There is no competition between the awliya of Allah. Each has his or her own station with Allah. The greater the wali's fear of Allah, the higher his or her station is with Allah. The greatest of the awliya meet and talk with the Prophet Muhammad in the Unseen, either in dreams or in vision. They accordingly have an access to the living life transaction of Islam which those who lay claim to leadership, merely by virtue of the fact that they have read more books than anyone else, do not have.

Living Islam is not to be found in books. It is transmitted from person to person. However this transmission is only possible because the Muslims have the *Qur'an*, which means 'the Recitation'. The key to understanding what is in the *Qur'an* is to recite it out loud, neither too soft nor too strong, either in a gathering or alone, with your attention on your heart.

The *Qur'an* is the uncreated word of Allah. It is the only book on the face of the earth today which has not been written by a human being, but which was revealed by Allah via the angel Gabriel to the Prophet Muhammad, may Allah bless him and grant him peace – who himself could neither read nor write – and which has not been changed, even by one letter, since it was first revealed. Allah has promised that the *Qur'an* will be preserved intact until the end of the world.

In the light of the *Qur'an* the definitions of the kafir experts are seen to be what they are: often ignorant, often limited, and often inaccurate ideas based on speculation and without certainty. The contents of the *Qur'an* can be used to ascertain the accuracy of any statement, since the *Qur'an* is the definitive collection of statements on the true nature of existence, coming as it does from the Source of all existence, Allah. Some of the more enlightened and sincere scientists from the High Tec North are now discovering that whatever they have accurately 'discovered' is corroborated by what is in the *Qur'an* – revealed more than thirteen and a half centuries ago – and further that there is much in the *Qur'an* which they have not yet discovered, and which they can never hope to discover, since their methods are too gross and clumsy and misconceived, to make such discoveries.

Everything in creation has meaning, but the kafir definitions often obscure and cover over what this meaning really is. Since the kafirun have no certainty but only speculation, their definitions are for ever being re-defined. The kafir experts cover up the inadequacy of their definitions by grandly stating that the reason why these definitions are changing is because they are continually evolving and progressing, not because they are inadequate and misinformed. A leading proponent of the big bang theory was once asked what there was before the big bang took place. He replied that there was an unwritten agreement amongst all scientists not to ask that question – let alone to attempt to answer it. The truth, behind this unwritten agreement, is that they all know that if they admitted their ignorance, then they would lose their professional titles and their salary and their reputation. The best of them know that if they really wanted to discover the true nature of existence then they would have to leave their laboratories, and seek out a man or woman of Allah, that is a person with real knowledge.

One of the key speculative theories of the present so-called civilisation is the Darwinian theory of evolution. The conceptual framework of this theory has been borrowed by most kafir theorists at some time or other to support their ideas. Basically the theory is used to further the kafir doctrine of 'progress and development' in all spheres of activity. Any course of action or any development in technology, for example, which on the face of it appears to be clearly suicidal – the atomic bomb, for example – can always be validated by claiming that it is what has 'evolved' from what came before it, and that therefore it must be better.

The part of Darwin's theory which has received most publicity is the proposition that man is not descended from Adam, but from the apes. We learn from the *Qur'an* that the opposite is the truth. All mankind comes from Adam and Eve, despite what the kafir geneticists may say. There was a people in the past who rejected the Messenger whom Allah had sent to them and who, instead of following the life pattern which he had brought, lived like animals. As a result Allah turned some of them into apes and some of them into pigs. When Allah wishes something to happen, He says, 'Be' – and it is.

Allah says in the *Qur'an* that a people who do not follow the Prophetic life pattern destroy themselves. Even a cursory examination of today's present kafir societies plainly proves this to be the case. These kafir societies are not evolving and getting better. They are getting worse as they disintegrate.

Everything in existence is subject to birth and death, and to growth and decay. When the present kafir system, that is the Dajjal system, disintegrates and finally collapses, the survivors will have no option but to embrace Islam, if they have not already done so.

The Prophet Muhammad, may the blessings and peace of Allah be on him, said that there would not be an age which was not worse than the one before it, until the end of the world. If anything, therefore, the world and what is in it is not evolving but rather devolving. It is approaching its end. The Prophet Muhammad said that you should not be children of this world, but rather children of the next world, because this world is leaving you and the next world is approaching you.

The kafir experts who supply the official definitions of what is normal and what is legal are incapable of giving this kind of advice, simply because they are totally unaware of the true nature of the journey which we all have to make, willingly or unwillingly. They do not know from where they come, and they do not know to where they are going, and their paltry definitions amply reflect their ignorance. Surely we come from Allah, and to Allah we will surely return.

The end to which such definitions are used is not to further man's understanding of the nature of existence, but is rather population manipulation and control in the producer consumer process. These definitions are used, in effect, to programme and condition people into accepting this process as being the meaning of their lives, and the reason for their existence. Allah says in the *Qur'an* that He did not create man and jinn except to worship Him.

As has been seen from the examples of Lord Northcliffe and Ezra Pound, these definitions also provide the means by which the freemasonic ruling elite can eliminate or at least control whoever recognises the kafir system that is the Dajjal system for what it is – and who might disrupt its functioning unless they are stopped – by subjecting them to judicial and medical processes which the majority of the population have been conditioned to accept as legal and normal.

The kafir experts who frame and sustain these definitions are clearly identified by the descriptions contained in the Qur'an as being the mufsidun, meaning 'those who corrupt', that is, the people who say they are putting everything right, when in fact they are only creating disruption, division and dissension.

Thus although the actual word 'Dajjal' does not appear in the Qur'an, the activities of Dajjal, the last and ultimate expression of kufr in the creational process before the end of the world, are clearly indicated and identified. The kafir system as a whole, with all its interlinking sub-systems, all controlled by their so-called experts – and the Prophet Muhammad said that kufr is one system – is Dajjal as a world wide social and cultural phenomenon. The way in which the producer consumer process is operated, and the way in which its supporting subsystems are used to control and manipulate the people enslaved by the producer consumer system, are clear evidence of the takeover which has been and is taking place by Dajjal as an unseen force. The kafir system that is the Dajjal system dominates nearly all of the countries of the world today, and it can only be a matter of time before Dajjal the individual appears.

○   ○   ○   ○   ○

Another example of the manner in which the Dajjal system operates as regards the elimination of opposition by so-called 'constitutional means' is to be found in the manner in which the famous Nuremberg trials were conducted. This particular stage production was perhaps one of the most thoroughly and carefully orchestrated cover-ups in the history of the Dajjal takeover, and cost millions of pounds.

○   ○   ○   ○   ○

Hitler, like Ezra Pound, was well aware of the freemasons' activities, as were his immediate followers. He instigated a widespread propaganda campaign designed to reveal these activities. He even embarked on the second kafir world war. Like Pound he under-estimated the degree of control already exercised by the freemasons. There was even a stage when, partially financed by Zionist financiers on Wall Street, he believed that the American government would be supporting him, so little did he know of the takeover which had been going on in earnest in that country for at least the fifty years prior to the commencement of the second world war.

What Hitler did not realise was that he was just the man that the freemasons were looking for. He had sufficient charisma to attract a large enough following who would be prepared to fight for him, and he was sufficiently greedy for power and sufficiently ruthless in the methods which he was prepared to use to try and attain the power which he desired, for the freemasons to be able to discredit him entirely once the war was over. In effect, Hitler was used by the freemasons to bring about his own destruction, whilst at the same time providing them with the situation from which they could make handsome profits out of the war, and from which they could eventually increase their control on a world wide basis.

The second world war provided nearly every country after the war with sufficient reason to amass vast quantities of armaments, thereby providing the freemasons with countless potential conflict situations to exploit, for it is inevitable that once a country has arms there is going to emerge someone who wants to use them. That someone is given backing by the freemasons, who also help the people opposed to that someone, on the understanding that the winner of the conflict will then return past favours, usually by purchasing more arms, borrowing more money on interest, and giving freemasonic backed corporations favourable contracts, to establish the producer consumer process in the country in question, and to exploit its natural resources. Since the freemasons back both sides in the conflict, without either of the two sides realising it, the outcome of the conflict is immaterial, since the freemasons cannot lose, whichever side 'wins'.

As with Pound, the freemasons had to come up with an effective counter-move at the end of the second world war in order to effectively discredit Hitler's ideas, by portraying him as a man who was so insane that nothing which he had said could possibly be believed to have contained any truth. Having used Hitler to create a profitable conflict situation, the freemasons had to then disassociate themselves not only from any involvement in his rise and downfall and the overall orchestration of the war, but also from the many truths which were undoubtedly voiced by Hitler concerning their activities. Since Hitler was himself a kafir, this task was relatively simple.

Although Hitler was aware of the freemasons' bid for world control, he did not have access to the only viable alternative to the kafir system, that is the Dajjal system – that is, trust in Allah, and a way of life based on the way of life embodied by the Prophet Muhammad, and followed by the community which formed around him at Madina al-Munawarra,

Dajjal – the king who has no clothes   81

that is the illuminated place where the life transaction is, may the blessings and peace of Allah be on him and them.

Indeed Hitler did not even have any of the ideals which Ezra Pound had possessed. Like the freemasons, all that he wanted was power. In effect, Hitler wished to beat the freemasons at their own game, by replacing their pyramidical power structure with his own pyramidical power structure.

In the final analysis, the second kafir world war was merely a power struggle between kafir powers, and not a confrontation between iman and kufr – that is, a struggle between those who accept the wisdom of the Prophetic lifestyle and those who reject it – although of course there were individuals on both sides, who found themselves unwillingly swept up in the conflict, and whose only way of keeping sane was by trusting in Allah. There was even one Muslim colonel from Hyderabad who decided to fight for the English on the basis that if the Germans won the war, they would be so efficient in running the kafir system, that is the Dajjal system, that it would take twice as long for it to reach the state of collapse which it has now reached today. Allah says in the *Qur'an* that although the kafirun appear to be one body, they are divided against each other.

Since Hitler was unaware of the degree of control which the freemasons already exercised over the western world, he was foolish enough to imagine that he could succeed in his power bid for world domination. The freemasons on the other hand, knew that they would win the war even before they encouraged Hitler into 'starting' it. The only 'losers' were the people who were unfortunate enough to be misled into fighting in it. One of the main purposes of the second world war was to increase the extent of the territory now controlled by the Communists who had seized power in Russia under cover of the first world war. This is why war was declared on Germany but not Russia, even though Russia also invaded Poland 'before' the second world war began – and even though Russia ended up occupying all of Poland and half of Germany 'after' the war had ended.

One of the freemasons' main concerns was the cover-up job which it was essential should be performed once the war was over. Their task was twofold. Firstly, it was necessary to discredit Hitler's views on freemasonic meddling and manipulation in world affairs by giving them as little publicity as possible, and by bringing him into utter disrepute.

Secondly, it was necessary to create the impression that the actions which had arisen as a result of those views were other than what they really were. Hitler's views – especially his critique and condemnation of usury – had to be represented as the imaginings of a mad man, and accordingly without any basis of truth or accuracy. His actions, and the actions of those who followed him, had to be portrayed as the horrifying manifestation of the insane prejudices of a racially prejudiced tyrant, rather than the misguided attempts of a man who was trying to free Europe from the stranglehold control of the freemasons, but unfortunately by using the wrong methods.

Many of Hitler's views were either derived from or reinforced by the discovery and publication of *The Protocols of the Learned Elders of Zion*, a small book, originally written in Russian and published by Sergyei Nilus in 1905 – possession of which was punished by death at the time of the Communist takeover in Russia – and which presents a partial yet informative outline of the freemasonic blueprint for world control, the new world order.

The contents of *The Protocols* merely reinforced what Hitler had himself already observed in the way of freemasonic control exercised by what he called the dictatorship of the world stock exchange, the monopoly of raw materials, the control of land if not its ownership and, above all, usury in all its forms.

The freemasons, who at that stage of the takeover had already gained almost complete control of the media in the western world, entered a highly energetic cover-up campaign designed not only to establish the idea that *The Protocols* were a forgery, but also, and more important, to affirm that there was no truth in the contents of *The Protocols* whatsoever. Newspaper articles to this effect appeared in all the leading publications of the western world – including *The Times*, once Lord Northcliffe had been removed – and indeed even still continue to appear occasionally today.

The two most popular stories as to the origins of *The Protocols* were, firstly, that they could be traced back to a satirical dialogue between Machiavelli and Montesquieu in hell, aimed at Napoleon III, and published as part of the German novel *Biarritz*; and, secondly, that they were alleged to have been composed during the last few years of the nineteenth century by members of the Russian secret police in Paris, who had drawn their ideas from a French pamphlet written by a French lawyer called Maurice Joly.

This cover-up campaign culminated in the matter being taken before a Swiss freemasonic controlled court, which – having directed that the provisions of the Swiss Civil Code would not apply to the hearing, and having permitted only one of the forty defence witnesses to give evidence, and having allowed the plaintiffs to appoint two private stenographers, instead of the court stenographer, to keep the 'official' record of the evidence given by their sixteen witnesses – duly gave the desired declaration, on the 14th of May 1935, after the case had lasted nearly two years, in favour of the Swiss Israelitic Alliance and the Israelitic Congregation in Berne, and indeed for the benefit of freemasons in general, that *The Protocols* were a deliberate forgery, probably originating in the Paris Offices of the Russian Political Police, and intended for use by the Tsarist government against Russian liberals. It is not altogether surprising that in view of all the procedural irregularities which had taken place, the Swiss Court of Criminal Appeal quashed this judgement in its entirety, on the 1st of November 1937.

It should perhaps be mentioned in passing that although the Khazar Jews continue to claim that *The Protocols of the Learned Elders of Zion* is 'a horrifying old forgery' – whose circulation on the open market they have gone to such great lengths to prevent – there is, as Henry Ford once pointed out in 1921, a strong resemblance between what *The Protocols* originally envisaged and proposed, and what has since happened and is actually now taking place, ('They have fitted the world situation up to this time. They fit it now.'), whether it be the creation of the United Nations at an international level, (i.e. the World Government of the proposed new world order); or the creation of highly regulated police states at a national level; or the creation of economic impotence through interest-based debts and crippling taxation at a community level; or the creation of confusion and sexual immorality by spreading false political and social theories amongst the Goyim (those who are not Jews) through the media at an individual level; or the introduction of organised sport to replace institutionalised religious worship at every level; to give but a few examples.

A 'forgery' is either an imitation of something original or the creation of something that purports to be an original. A good forgery is often so close to the original that there is virtually no difference between them, or else it is so accurate that it is as 'true' as an original, even if it was not created by whoever is said to have created it. In other words, a 'forgery' is capable of not misrepresenting whatever it purports to imitate or describe.

Even if *The Protocols of the Learned Elders of Zion* is a forgery, which has never been conclusively proved to be the case, it may be that much of what it describes is nevertheless true. Whether it be fact or fiction, it still makes interesting reading. The reader will have to satisfy him or her self as to where the truth lies, by reading *The Protocols*, if that is possible. As in the case of Pound's writings, the freemasons who control the publishing business and its distribution outlets have ensured that virtually all copies of *The Protocols* and any translations thereof have long been withdrawn from the market for public consumption.

Similarly, the writings of Alfred Rosenberg, who was one of Hitler's men and who wrote extensively on *The Protocols*, and who amongst other things traced the sources of the Russian Revolution back to freemasonic activity, were and continue to be withdrawn from the general public's gaze.

As well as withdrawing all written records of Hitler's views which were damaging to the image of the freemasons, literally hundreds of books, backed by other media presentations on radio and on the screen, were written and broadcasted in order to distort what Hitler had actually been saying. Very few people today know what Hitler actually said or believed. His views have been covered over by a barrage of emotional invective, which has prevented the vast majority of people today from actually being in a position to coolly and critically examine what he actually had to say, in order to see what truth if any there was in his words. If you ask people today what motivated Hitler in his actions, most of them will give a predictable involuntary shiver, and dutifully come out with the freemasonic media manufactured picture of a tyrant who was irrationally prejudiced against the Jews, for no reason other than that they were Jews. There is no doubt that Hitler did hate some Jews, but he did have his reasons, and some of them are understandable.

As far as Hitler's actions and the actions of those who followed him are concerned, they were clearly excessive, and this made it all the easier for the freemasons to portray them as being far more excessive than they really were. It is always easier to exaggerate something that has happened, than to invent something which never even happened at all. The freemasons took full advantage of this in their attempts to depict Hitler and his followers as fanatical racist madmen, who wished to utterly destroy all Jews altogether and to establish the Aryan master race.

Using highly emotive techniques of media manipulation, which include the display of the incriminating close up, but not the overall picture, backed up by highly loaded vocabulary, the freemasons were highly successful in portraying Hitler as a disordered paranoid psychopath, who was imagining a conspiracy which did not exist, in order to justify his purely racist and entirely irrational discriminatory prejudice and hatred of the Jews as a whole. Of course there was some truth in their allegations, but they maintained, through the media systems, that this was the whole truth, when in fact large vistas of the truth had been omitted from the picture which had been prepared for the general public.

Thus, for example, Douglas Reed, who was *The Times* newspaper's chief correspondent for central Europe and the Balkans in the 1930s wrote in his book *The Controversy of Zion*:

> In the case of 'the Jewish persecution' in Germany I found that impartial presentation of the facts gradually gave way to so partisan a depictment that the truth was lost. This transformation was effected in three subtle stages. First the persecution of 'political opponents and Jews' was reported; then this was imperceptibly amended to 'Jews and political opponents'; and at the end the press in general spoke only of 'the persecution of Jews'. By this means a false image was projected on to the public mind and the plight of the overwhelming majority of the victims, by this fixing of the spotlight on one group, was lost to sight. The result showed in 1945, when, on the one hand, the persecution of Jews was made the subject of a formal indictment at Nuremberg, and on the other hand half of Europe and all the people in it were abandoned to the selfsame persecution, in which the Jews had shared in their small proportion to populations everywhere.

Douglas Reed continues:

> When the general persecution began I reported it as I saw it. If I learned of a concentration camp containing a thousand captives I reported this; if I learned that the thousand included thirty or fifty Jews I reported that. I saw the first terror, spoke with many of the victims, examined their

injuries, and was warned that I incurred Gestapo hostility thereby. The victims were in the great majority, certainly much over ninety per cent, Germans, and a few were Jews. This reflected the population-ratio, in Germany and later in the countries overrun by Hitler. But the manner of reporting in the world's press in time blocked-out the great suffering mass, leaving only the case of the Jews.

Similarly, when the Soviet troops – who it will be remembered also invaded Poland prior to the beginning of the war – finally overran Poland and eastern Germany towards the end of the war, it was they who took over most of the concentration camps and – just as Hitler had used them to dispose of his political enemies – used them to dispose of Stalin's political enemies, many of whom had been prevented from escaping across the river Elbe by the armies of the Western Allies – an awful scenario of which the general public were never informed, as Douglas Reed again points out:

> The Western masses knew nothing of these happenings in British-American occupied Germany at the time, and might not have objected violently if they had known, for at that period they were still under the influence of wartime propaganda, particularly in the matter of the Nazi concentration camps. They seemed to me completely to have forgotten that the concentration camp was originally a Communist idea, copied by Hitler, and that the further the Red armies were allowed into Europe the more certain its perpetuation became. Their feelings were inflamed by the horrifying news-reel pictures, shown to them on a million screens as the Allied armies entered Germany, of piles of emaciated corpses stacked like firewood in these camps.
>
> I was a member of those audiences and heard the comments around me with misgiving. Wartime propaganda is the most insidious poison known to man, and I believe these picturegoers of 1945, deprived of truthful information for years, had lost all ability, perhaps all desire to judge what they saw. I think most of them thought the human remains they saw were those of Jews, for this was the suggestion hammered into their minds by the press day by day. They constantly read of 'Nazi gas chambers for Jews

... Nazi crematoria for Jews', and few of them in later years troubled to read the stories of inmates and find out who these victims truly were. One instance: a German woman who spent five years in Ravensbruck camp (Frau Margaret Bubers Newmann) says the first victims were the sick or afflicted, or those incapable of work, and the next ones were 'the inferior races', among whom the Poles were placed first, and the Czechs, Balts, Hungarians and others next.

Thus the piles of dead received as little true compassion as the living who were driven back by the Western allies into the concentration-camp area, and today it may be only a matter of historical interest, pertaining to such a book as this, to show that the 'Nazi' concentration camps, at the time when the Anglo-American armies entered Germany, were predominantly under Communist control, that Jews were among the tormentors, and that anti-Communism was a surer qualification for the death-chamber than anti-Hitlerism!

Douglas Reed concludes:

> Communists ran these camps, tortured and murdered the victims. If there was any difference between them and the Gestapo jailers it was only that they were more villainous, because they denounced and killed men who were supposed to be their comrades in battle against a common foe. As the Eastern Jews, in particular, play so large a part in Communism, Jews logically appear among the persons implicated in these deeds. That is not in itself surprising at all, for Jews, like all other men, are good and bad, cruel or humane; but it was kept hidden from the public masses, who received a picture of torture-camps inhabited almost entirely by Jews, tormented by depraved 'Nazi' captors. In fact, the Jews formed a small proportion of the entire camp-population; the tormentors in the last three years of the war were largely Communists, whose motives have been shown; and among these tormentors were Jews.

The media campaign directed against Hitler – designed to persuade the people of the west and of the east that there was no truth whatsoever in Hitler's statements about the activities of the freemasons, and that all the courses of action which he had initiated in order to bring his allegedly madly imagined state of affairs to an end were crimes which ought to be punished – culminated in the notorious Nuremberg trials, one of history's most carefully contrived judicial pantomimes.

Naturally the media coverage portrayed these trials as one of the major landmarks in the history of human rights and impartial due legal process. The view was expressed that the accused were fortunate even to get a trial, let alone a fair one, since any less impartial victors might well have summarily executed them on the spot in angry revenge. This media cover-up picture of the Nuremberg trials continues to be sustained today, as it has been since the trials first took place. It needs but a brief glance at the record of these trials to discover that their outcome had been virtually decided before they began, and that they were designed to inflict as much torment on the accused as possible, before they were finally disposed of by being hanged on the Jewish Day of Judgement, Hoshana Rabba.

The records of the Nuremberg trials, for those who care to go beyond the trite media picture of dastardly criminals being brought to justice by the just, provide a clear example of the extent to which the kafir legal and kafir medical systems can be employed to eliminate opposition.

o   o   o   o   o

Unlike Ezra Pound, whose political opinions had received hardly any publicity or coverage in the media system, the German propaganda machine had aired Hitler's views to such an extent that it was impossible to pretend that they did not exist. Whereas Pound's views had been contained by keeping him silenced, Hitler's views had to be rendered ineffective and made to look ridiculous by distorting them through exaggeration, thereby discrediting them.

This could only be achieved by presenting Hitler and his immediate followers as violent and inhuman psychopaths who, blinded by ignorance and racist hatred, had somehow mesmerised and terrorised the German people not only into attempting to eliminate all the Jews in Europe, but also into fighting a war which they did not really wish to fight in order to achieve that object.

One of the means by which this impression was created was the Nuremberg trials. In the name of international law, which is otherwise known as the law of international expediency, and of justice, their words and actions were accordingly manipulated and arranged, so as to create the desired picture, which was then spread abroad by the freemasonic controlled media system.

○   ○   ○   ○   ○

It was imperative that the accused should be found fit to stand trial, even though they were subsequently to be presented to the world as mentally deranged beings, who could hardly be described as humans. Clearly if any of them could successfully plead that they were unfit for trial, then the impact and force of the picture which was to be presented to the public would thereby be diminished. Accordingly the appropriate medical experts were selected to adjudge the accused as being normal enough to stand trial, and it comes as no surprise to learn that this was the conclusion to which they all came: The only way to avoid standing trial was by committing suicide, a course of action which only a very limited number of the accused chose to adopt.

As in the case of Ezra Pound, the accused were kept in solitary confinement and in unsavoury conditions, albeit not out in the open, in order to soften them up for the impending judicial proceedings. It was during this period of solitary confinement, which lasted several months, that the accused were subjected to the famous Rorschach tests, the results and interpretations of which were subsequently used to great effect in the post-trial propaganda campaign against the followers of Hitler. The Rorschach tests were initially begun by an English psychiatrist, who some years later was to commit suicide on New Year's Eve by swallowing one of the cyanide capsules which had been found on Goering after his own suicide. Allah says in the *Qur'an* that the one who does not follow the way of the Prophets is self-destroyed. This psychiatrist was not considered ideally suited for the leading psychiatrist role in the Nuremberg stage production, and was accordingly replaced by a more expert American expert early on in the show. It was this man who conducted the Rorschach tests on the accused and subsequently wrote volumes on his so-called 'expert' findings.

The basis of the Rorschach tests is to present the 'patient' with a series of large symmetrical ink blots, each differing in shape and colour. The patient gives a verbal reaction to each blot as it is shown, stating what he or she sees in it. The medical 'expert' then interprets the patient's reactions, on the basis that what the patient has seen in the blot is in fact a reflection of the patient's own reality.

It comes as no surprise to learn that the reactions of the accused to the Rorschach tests were interpreted so as to give medically tested credibility to the popular image which was being created, of the Nazis being depicted as dangerous psychopathic sub-human beasts.

The underlying assumption behind these tests – that is, that the Rorschach tests are a valid means of measuring what is 'normal' and 'abnormal' and what is 'sane' and 'insane' – is a fallacious one, not only because, as we have already seen, kafir conceptions of what is 'normal' and what is 'sane' are not connected to the true nature of existence, but in fact cover it up, but also because the methodology used is itself faulty. What the Rorschach method fails to make adequate provision for is the psychological make-up of the medical expert who carries out the tests. Since there is some truth in the assumption that the patient does see his or her own reflection in what is in front of him or her, it follows that this is also true for the medical expert, and that therefore the medical expert's reactions to the responses of the patient to the Rorschach test provide in themselves a further secondary Rorschach-type response, so that any evaluation of the patient's response by the medical expert is in reality an evaluation by the expert of his or her own self.

In other words, the medical expert's interpretation of the Nuremberg accused's responses was in itself a reflection of the experts' own inner reality, just as much as the accused's reaction to the blots was initially a reflection of the accused's own inner reality. The conclusion which the medical experts reached regarding the accused in fact applied to themselves, just as the opinions which the medical experts had reached as regards Ezra Pound's sanity were in fact descriptions of the state of their own sanity.

○   ○   ○   ○   ○

This is one aspect of the underlying unity of existence of which the kafir 'expert' is often unaware – that the patients whom a doctor has tend to reflect his or her reality, just as the people who come before a judge tend to reflect his or her reality. This is partly why different doctors have different kinds of patients, and different judges have different types of cases. As far as the Nuremberg trials are concerned, there was no difference between the accusers and the accused, and no difference between the judges and the judged – and, what is more, and contrary to established legal practice, the accusers and the judges were in reality one and the same.

The idea that the kafir 'expert' is somehow a detached observer of life is one of the hallmarks of the kafir view of existence. He or she thinks that because of his or her special knowledge – or rather superior ability in amassing and juggling with information – he or she is capable of forming a detached and 'objective' view of reality in which he or she is neither directly nor indirectly implicated. The truth is that there is no split in existence. There is only One Reality. No one is separate from the rest of existence even if they imagine that to be the case. The truth is that everyone in creation only sees what is in their own heart. Whatever is in your heart appears before you in creation. Whatever you see in creation is a reflection of your self. All you ever get back from the world is the echo of your own voice.

It follows that the only real doctors are the awliya of Allah, that is the friends of Allah, who have been given the idhn, that is the authority, to cure the hidden illnesses of the heart and the self by Allah, and to lead people from ignorance to knowledge and gnosis of Allah by Allah. The awliya of Allah who teach with idhn are the only doctors in the world who see things as they are, which is to say as they are not, with a direct seeing. The kafir medical expert gives reality to what he imagines to be real but which in fact is illusory. The awliya of Allah give reality to the Real, Allah.

It follows that the awliya who teach with idhn cannot lie. Whoever comes into their presence receives a true reflection of his or her own self, and at the same time benefits from and is transformed by the light of Allah which is their light. Since all this happens by Allah, and since the awliya know this, they are unable to charge money for what they do. This is the sign of the rightly guided man of Allah, that he is rightly guided by Allah, and that he does not ask for money – the complete antithesis of the kafir medical expert.

For the same reasons the awliya of Allah are the people who are best equipped to judge between people, when a judge is needed, because their furqan – that is, their ability to discriminate between what is just and what is unjust – is guided by the *Qur'an* and by the *Hadith* and is by Allah. Since they are the ones who have the most knowledge of Allah, it follows that they have most knowledge of all that comes from Allah, and are therefore in the best position to decide matters. Since their hearts have been purified, they see with a clear seeing. Since they have great fear of Allah, it is not possible for them to be motivated by self interest or personal greed, since they know this would take them to the Fire. Further, since their self has been obliterated in Allah it follows that there is no self to be interested in, or rather they see that the whole of existence is their self, so that personal greed is an impossibility. The awliya of Allah are the complete antithesis of the kafir legal experts, who are not in a position to judge anything because they do not see anything as it really is.

○   ○   ○   ○   ○

The Charter which was drawn up principally by American and English legal experts, and which defined how the Nuremberg trials were to be conducted, was framed in such a manner that it ensured that the desired end result of the trials would be achieved with ease. The official legal definitions of what was to constitute a crime, and the ways in which the commission of that crime was to be capable of being proved, were so wide and so favoured the prosecution lawyers, that even a child could have convicted the accused of the crimes with which they were charged.

It must be emphasised that the accused were not tried in accordance with the rules and laws of any existing legal system, since this would have made the task of convicting them all far more difficult, and much more time-consuming and expensive.

Instead, the freemasonic legal experts created a legal system just for the purpose of the Nuremberg trials, with its own special rules of procedure and evidence, and with its own special definitions of the crimes with which the accused were charged. Had the accused been given any right of appeal to, for example, the English Court of Appeal or the House of Lords, the manner in which the Nuremberg trials were conducted would have been easily proved to be what existing legal systems would have defined as a gross irregularity in the conduct of those trials, and accordingly the accused would all have had to be acquitted and their convictions quashed. It was in order to escape this possibility that a separate self-contained legal system, without any rights of appeal, was created specifically for the purposes of the Nuremberg trials.

There were four major crimes of which most of the accused were charged with committing. The definitions of these crimes were so vague and so all-embracing that a great many acts of war – which are inevitably committed by all concerned on both sides during the course of war, because that is the nature of war – could easily be shown to come within the ambit of these definitions, whenever it was convenient or expedient so to do. The four major crimes were Crimes against Humanity, War Crimes, Crimes against Peace, and Conspiracy to commit these crimes. It should be pointed out that since it was the freemasons who had engineered the war in the first place, it follows that they were just as 'guilty' of these crimes as the accused, if not more so.

The Charter also stated that it was a crime to belong to 'a criminal organisation'. The Charter defined nearly all the organs of government and administration and all the armed forces of Germany, and its official and secret police forces and intelligence agencies, as being criminal organisations. Naturally their counterparts among the Western Allies were not regarded as criminal organisations, despite the fact that they had been operating in basically the same way and using basically the same methods as the Germans throughout the war – for ultimately there is really no difference between one kafir and another, whether they be English, American, Russian or German.

Membership of one of these allegedly criminal organisations was defined as being prima facie evidence of the fact that the person concerned belonged to the Conspiracy to commit the other major crimes defined by the Charter.

Since all the accused, and indeed more than half of the population of Germany, belonged to at least one of the bodies which were defined as being criminal organisations, it followed that they were all automatically implicated in the Conspiracy to commit the other major crimes before the trials had even begun. All that had to be shown, once the trials had started, for the accused to be found guilty of the Conspiracy charge, was membership of one of the what had been defined as criminal organisations.

In effect, the freemasons were accusing the German leaders of the very conspiracy in which they themselves were involved, and which Hitler had unsuccessfully tried to expose and destroy. By boldly turning the tables in this way, the freemasons hoped to provide an effective smoke-screen to cover up and obscure the true nature of their own activities. It would seem that their hopes were fulfilled, for even at the time of writing this, the wind still has not blown the smoke away.

The fact that the Nuremberg Charter defined nearly all of the national institutions in Germany as being criminal for the purpose of the trials, as well as ensuring that the accused would be automatically found guilty of the Conspiracy charge, not only effectively allowed the freemasons to charge whoever they wished to charge, but also indirectly ensured that there would be very few witnesses for the defence indeed. Whilst the judicial machinery for the trials was being prepared, large quantities of leaflets were distributed amongst the German people, requesting members of the what had been defined as criminal organisations to give themselves up, and asking any potential witnesses in the impending proceedings to step forward and identify themselves. Any member of one of the so-called criminal organisations who gave him or her self up could then be charged, if the prosecution thought it necessary, and all without any of the bother and expense of having to go out and find them.

Any potential witness who was foolish enough to identify him or her self was often immediately arrested and charged with belonging to one of the criminal organisations and accordingly with Conspiracy to commit the other major crimes. If however, the person in question agreed to act as a prosecution witness, and not as a defence witness, then it could easily be arranged that in return the charges against him or her would be dropped. If it was not possible to eliminate a potential defence witness in this way, then he or she was often successfully deterred and discouraged from giving evidence by being beaten up. The few defence witnesses who survived this screening process were, like the accused, kept imprisoned in solitary confinement in order to break them down and weaken their morale. No real distinction was ever made between the accused and the few defence witnesses who were able to give evidence at the trial. By the time the trials were under way their value as witnesses, and the weight of their testimony, had been so effectively eroded and undermined by the treatment which they had received, that really their only function was to help create the impression that the accused were receiving a fair trial.

This technique of inducing people to give themselves up voluntarily, and of persuading them to incriminate their colleagues in order to save their own skins, is strongly reminiscent of the techniques used by the Mediaeval and Spanish Inquisitions to achieve exactly the same objects, the only major difference between them being that the Inquisitors were after Jews, Unitarian Christians and Muslims, whilst the Nuremberg prosecutors were after fellow kafirun. It may well be that the Nuremberg prosecutors were aware of and followed the example of the Inquisition, since the Inquisitors were then what the freemasons of today are now.

The Nuremberg prosecutors, who in open disregard of the kafir doctrine of the separation of powers legislative, administrative and judicial, were also both the legislators of the Charter and the judges of the accused, based their case largely on documentary evidence. The advantage of this approach was, and is, that you cannot cross-examine a piece of paper as to the truth of its contents, and a verbal denial alone of the truth of those contents or of a particular interpretation of or construction which has been placed upon those contents, is hardly ever sufficient to rebut the evidence apparently contained in the document in question, especially if the judge is in fact already entirely in agreement with the prosecution case.

The rules relating to documentary evidence which usually apply to judicial proceedings in the kafir courts of the west, and which give at least a limited guarantee of the possibility of being able to establish whether or not what is stated in any particular document is accurate, were for the purposes of the Nuremberg trials waived completely. This meant that the Nuremberg prosecutors could conduct their case in a manner which normally, even by kafir standards of normality, would have been condemned and brought to a halt for being biased, oppressive and contrary to the laws of what the kafir legal systems define as 'natural justice' and 'international law'. Indeed it was even openly argued by the prosecution lawyers that since the accused's actions were breaches of international law, therefore they could not expect to enjoy the protection of international law, let alone to be tried in accordance with it.

Basically the prosecution lawyers were allowed to adduce whatever document they wanted in evidence even if it contained second or third hand hearsay, let alone first hand hearsay, and even if the document was not an original but a copy. This meant that forged documents could also be introduced into the prosecution evidence without being effectively challenged by the defence. Even if a document was challenged as being of suspect origin, naturally there would always be a sworn affidavit available, made by a sufficiently high-ranking legal expert, which stated that all documents were original documents and had been verified as such by whoever had found them.

The Nuremberg prosecutors were given carte blanche by virtue of Articles 18 and 19 of the Charter. Under Article 18 of the Charter the

Tribunal was to confine the trial to an expeditious hearing, and to take strict measures to prevent any action which would cause unreasonable delay, and to rule out irrelevant issues and statements of any kind whatsoever. Article 19 of the Charter stated that the Tribunal was not be bound by technical rules of evidence, and that it should adopt and apply to the greatest possible extent expeditious and non-technical procedure, and that it should admit any evidence which it deemed to have probative value.

Anyone who has the time to read the record of the Nuremberg trials will see how time and again the Tribunal used Article 18 to silence the defence, while allowing the prosecution to adduce whatever so-called evidence they wished by virtue of Article 19. Of course the Charter also provided, by virtue of Article 3, that any attempt to question the validity of the Tribunal's jurisdiction, or its right to try the accused in the first place, should be automatically dismissed without further ado.

The Nuremberg prosecutors were not only able to adduce whatever piece of paper they wanted in evidence, but also often did so without first having served copies of these documents on the defence prior to their being produced. Furthermore, it sometimes happened that when an incriminating document's contents were worded in a language other than German, no translation was provided for the defence lawyers. Whenever this happened, therefore, it meant that the defence lawyers were forced to rely solely on the simultaneous translation service provided by IBM, which translated whatever was being said at the time into English, French, Russian and German, usually about a sentence behind and often inaccurately.

In effect, this meant that the defence lawyers did not know what case they had to meet until the very last moment, which gave them very little time to prepare their case. Furthermore, the defence lawyers were not permitted to converse with the accused in the court room. They could only communicate by written note. This again limited what a defence lawyer could do when an unexpected point was raised by the prosecution, since written communication was so much slower than the whispered word, when it came to trying to ascertain what any particular accused's response was to the point in question.

The Tribunal also permitted the prosecution to adduce in evidence sworn affidavits of alleged prosecution witnesses who were, so it was said, 'unable to attend'. This meant that the defence lawyers were unable to test the truth of the contents of these affidavits by cross-examining the people who were alleged to have made them in the witness box, and to ask them the questions which had purposely not been asked by the prosecutor who had prepared the affidavits. The Tribunal permitted the production of such affidavits under Article 19, blandly stating that it would take into account the fact that such statements did not have as much probative value as they would have had if the person making them had been in the witness box and available for cross-examination, and that accordingly not so much weight would be attached to them.

The truth of the matter is that the nature of the evidence was such that, although to a layman it must have seemed as if it was all being presented in accordance with sound judicial precept and established legal practice, in fact it was not only heavily biased, but also the members of the Tribunal could put whatever interpretation and whatever weight they wished on it. Indeed the conclusions they were to draw had already been reached long before any of the evidence was formally presented for their consideration.

By basing their case on documentary evidence, and by adducing that evidence in the manner in which they were permitted to do so, the prosecution lawyers were able to say what they wanted without fear of being effectively challenged by the defence lawyers, and without having to rely on live witnesses, who might possibly have come out with evidence which was favourable to the accused.

The prosecution lawyers were also helped by the fact that the accused had only been permitted to choose their legal representatives from a list of lawyers which had been prepared by the prosecutors, who no doubt had been sure to ensure that only freemasons, or lawyers who would not put up too much of a fight or ask too many awkward questions, or lawyers who were unfamiliar with the mainly American and English judicial techniques and procedures which were being employed by the prosecutors, were included on that list.

In effect, any lawyer who might possibly be aware of what the freemasons were up to, and who would be prepared to oppose and expose their activities, was excluded from that list of eligible defence lawyers, and accordingly prevented from representing the accused. Furthermore, although the Charter granted the accused the right of conducting their own defence if they so wished, in practice they were in fact deterred and prevented from exercising that right. This meant not only that they were prevented from saying more than was minimally necessary during the course of the proceedings, but also that they were represented by tame lawyers, since any lawyer worth his or her salt would have objected far more strongly about the manner in which, and the basis on which, the proceedings were being conducted than the defence lawyers who were chosen to represent the accused actually did.

The other advantage of basing the prosecution case on documentary evidence was this: At the end of the war the American and English command had set up special documentation centres, and as their forces advanced into Germany, they collected and transported all the official documents which they found to these centres. Literally hundreds of tons of documents were collected. The highly trained personnel at these centres subsequently sifted through the considerable tonnage of these documents and retained all those which helped to support the prosecution case. Those sections of the written word or the filmed event which did not help the prosecution case were either erased or cut and shredded when and wherever possible. Any documents or films which might establish the so-called innocence of the accused, or assist their defence lawyers in their attempts to exonerate the accused, were retained and either destroyed or at least certainly not disclosed to the defence.

As it happened, there were some documents amongst the many thousands which were made available to the Nuremberg prosecutors, which had passed unnoticed through the documentation centre screening process, and which turned out to be favourable to the defence case. As soon as this fact was appreciated, the documents in question suddenly disappeared from the safe in which all the documents which were to be adduced in evidence were kept in safe keeping.

The prosecution lawyers thus had access to and control over all the documents which they wished to adduce in evidence, whilst the defence lawyers had virtually no access to any documents at all, except the useless documents which the prosecutors allowed them to have.

The Nuremberg prosecutors could produce whatever document they wanted, whenever they wanted, without having warned the defence lawyers of their intention so to do – with the exception, that is, of the less important and less incriminating documents – and certainly without having permitted the defence lawyers to have a copy of the document in question before it was actually produced to the court. As it was, it quite often happened that when documents were suddenly produced in this manner, there was no copy available for the defence lawyer who needed it, and if several defence lawyers each needed a copy of a certain document, it often happened that if there were copies available, they were insufficient in number so that they had to be shared.

These tactics ensured that the defence lawyers, ill-equipped as they were, were never in a position to meet the case which was being levelled at the people whom they represented. At best often all that could be mustered was a flat and empty denial of whatever was being alleged, a denial which was easily muffled and silenced by the mountains of paper ammunition which was at the disposal of the prosecution.

○ ○ ○ ○ ○

It is clear that many of the accused in the Nuremberg trials had been responsible either directly or indirectly for the deaths of other people during the war. If they had been charged with murder, or attempted murder, or conspiracy to commit murder, and tried in an ordinary court of law in accordance with existing legal principles and procedures, they probably would have been found guilty on at least one of those counts. However it must be remembered that the purpose of the Nuremberg trials was not merely to find the principal followers of Hitler guilty of capital offences so that they could be legally eliminated. The main purpose of the Nuremberg trials was to create a sufficiently grandiose yet illusory diversion in order to direct the general public's attention away from the activities of the freemasons, and cause them to lay the causes of the second world war fairly, or rather unfairly, and squarely at the door of the German people.

○ ○ ○ ○ ○

The outcome of the Nuremberg trials was a foregone conclusion. What is interesting is the extent to which the freemasons were prepared to go in order firstly, to create the illusion of a fair trial, conducted in accordance with due judicial process, secondly, to arrange the presentation of evidence in such a way that a completely false yet convincing picture of how the war was started and what the Germans did in it was made to emerge, and thirdly, to make sure that this false yet convincing picture was subsequently spread across the face of the earth and accepted by the great majority of those who either saw or heard about it.

The freemasons, like the magicians of Pharaoh, are today's masters of illusion. They mesmerise people with illusions, so as to be able to control and manipulate them, and the Nuremberg trials illusion was perhaps one of their greatest feats of illusion, masking a masterly exercise in manipulation control, thanks to the combined efforts of the medical and legal experts, and ensuring not only that the important followers of Hitler were both utterly discredited and eliminated in the process, but also that the general public of the world were taken in by that illusion.

The publicity which this exercise in mass manipulation received and needed was of course provided by the freemasonic controlled media systems, which were in a position to provide the appropriate pictures and excerpts from speeches and loaded commentaries needed to create the desired impression of an impressive and just judicial assembly who were trying, with all the apparent detachment and impartiality in the world, a motley and inhuman group of psychopathic desperadoes, who really did not even deserve the fair trial which they appeared to be getting, in the first place.

Clearly the part played by the media systems of the kafirun was and continues to be very significant. Creating the desired picture was relatively child's play. The real challenge was to make sure that this picture subsequently found its way by one means or another into the recesses of the majority of the general public's minds. The fact that it did, and has, indicates not only the extreme efficiency of the freemasons, but also the high degree of control which they exercise over a great many people through their media systems. 'Big Brother' may not have been watching you, but he has certainly been programming and conditioning you.

In reality there was little or no difference between the people who tried the accused in the Nuremberg trials and the accused who were tried. In reality the second kafir world war was no more or less than a power struggle between opposing pyramidical kafir power systems. Allah says in the *Qur'an* that the kafirun appear to be one body, but in fact they are divided against each other. The Prophet Muhammad, may the blessings and peace of Allah be on him, said that kufr is one system. Thus in effect, the second kafir world war was one unified event involving one system, that is the kafir system, that is the Dajjal system, involved in destroying itself. Allah says in the *Qur'an* that a people who do not follow the way of the Prophets are self-destroyed, that is, they destroy themselves and each other.

The success of the Nuremberg trials, as far as the freemasons were and are concerned, can be measured by the fact that if you say to anyone in the street today – that is anyone who has been exposed to the usual educational and media conditioning process – the one word 'Hitler', or 'Nazi', or 'Nuremberg', then the magical figure and phrase of 'six million' Jews murdered in the concentration camps will probably spring to his or her lips, or at least flash across his or her mind – even though it was never actually established during the Nuremberg trials, or subsequently, that anything like that number of Jews were killed in this way, and by the methods purported to have been used by those who controlled the concentration camps.

When the figure of six million was being decided on by the freemasons who were most concerned with publicity, Chaim Weizmann, who was one of the public figurehead founders of the Zionist movement, is reputed to have supported the six million mark, by stating that people would not believe a little lie, but they would believe a big one. As Douglas Reed pointed out in his book *The Controversy of Zion*:

> In six years of war the Germans, Japanese and Italians, using every lethal means, killed 824,928 British, British Commonwealth and American fighting-men, merchant sailors and civilians. Assuming that the Germans killed, say, half of these in Europe, they killed (according to this assertion) fifteen times as many Jews there. To do that, they would have needed such quantities of men, weapons, transports, guards and materials as would have enabled them to win the war many times over.

Further, it should be remembered that the phrase, 'concentration camp', is now a very emotionally loaded term, due to the way in which it has been used by the media. Concentration camps were basically prisoner of war camps. Prisoner of war camps were first popularised by the British as they established the British Empire and then tried to keep it, especially during the Boer War in South Africa – but in fact there have always been prisoner of war camps as long as there have been wars in which people have been taken prisoner in large numbers, and they have always been unpleasant places in which to be – especially when run by Communists.

The reality of the second kafir world war is that the actions of nearly all the people concerned in it, on both sides, at some time or other came within the ambit of one or other of the crimes as defined by the sweeping terms of the Nuremberg Charter, which in effect, made it a crime to plan a war and fight it in the way that kafir wars are usually planned and fought.

Kafir wars are fought indiscriminately, whereas jihad, that is a fight in the way of Allah by those who trust in Allah, is fought on the basis that you may only fight in self-defence; and that you may not kill anyone who says the shahada – that is, anyone who affirms that there is no god only Allah and that Muhammad is the Messenger of Allah; and that you must not kill in anger, since that will take you to the Fire; and that you may not pillage and rape if Allah gives you victory; and finally, that if you die in the jihad, then you will die directly witnessing Allah and go straight to the Garden.

The kafir fights in complete ignorance of what lies on the other side of death, and is therefore careless about how and whom he or she kills, and what he or she does. The mumin fights with intense awareness of what lies on the other side of death, fearful in the knowledge that fighting for the wrong reason, or killing the wrong person, can result in him or her ending up in the Fire – and accordingly the mumin is very careful about whom he or she kills in times of war and in what he or she does.

In an age where modern technology has all but perfected the technique of killing people more swiftly and efficiently than ever before, it is possible to become quite blasé about the unjustified taking of human life. Whoever has an intellect – and whatever 'side' they may be on – would be well advised to remember what Allah decreed for the Tribe of Israel:

> We decreed for the Tribe of Israel that whoever kills a human being for other than manslaughter or corruption in the earth, it shall be as if he had killed all mankind; and whoever saves the life of someone, it shall be as if he had saved the life of all mankind. (*Qur'an: Surat'al-Ma'idah* – 5.32)

When viewed from this perspective, it is clear that numbers are not significant. Whether the number is 600,000, or 60,000, or 60, or even just 1, it is equally awful and unlawful to kill anyone 'without just cause' – as defined by God. Allah also says in the *Qur'an*:

And whoever kills a believer of set purpose, then his reward is Hell, for ever there, and the wrath of Allah is on him and He has cursed him and has prepared for him an awful punishment. (*Qur'an: Surat'an-Nisa* – 4.93)

It is interesting to note that the definitions of the major crimes embodied in the Nuremberg Charter did not take the next world into consideration at all. If one views the actions of both sides from the limited perspective of the terms of the Charter then everyone who fought in the war was guilty of those crimes – and especially the freemasons who not only masterminded the war but also drew up the Charter. The victors however were in a position to turn a blind eye to this fact, whilst the vanquished were prevented from voicing it publicly. As Justice Holmes once observed, 'History is what the people who won say it is.'

o o o o o

It is interesting to note that in the relatively minor wars which the freemasons have arranged since the end of the second world war, the actions of notably the American and English forces – which have borne an evident and marked resemblance to those of the German forces in the last war – have not been punished at the hands of military tribunals, but rather praised as being the valiant attempts of those who were prepared to sacrifice their lives for their country or 'democracy' or control over oil-fields, in the name of peace, freedom and justice, in the war against 'the communists', or 'the terrorists', or 'the fanatics', or 'the extremists', or whomever else the freemasonic controlled media has depicted as being 'the enemy'.

Basically the people who control the current media systems can depict whoever they want as being 'the enemy'. This is done by using highly emotive vocabulary to describe 'them' – such as the words 'communists', 'terrorists', 'fanatics', 'extremists' and more recently 'fundamentalists', whose very mention triggers an immediate emotional response in any listener who has been adequately conditioned by the educational and media systems. This emotional response takes the form of an automatic feeling of rejection and condemnation of whoever has been described by these key kafir definitions, so that the person in whom the response arises is totally incapable of seeing who the people so described really are, or of examining what they are really saying.

Furthermore, it is impossible for anyone who relies on the kafir media version of events ever to find out what the truth of the matter really is, since all that he or she has to go on is what he or she is presented with, and this – as we have seen from the examples of Lord Northcliffe and Ezra Pound and the Nuremberg trials – is often very far from the truth. The people who control the media can basically create any illusion they wish, and as long as the validity of their techniques remains unchallenged, get away with it. Indeed it is now possible, using current advanced computer graphics software, to create virtually any image or picture that might be useful. Any person, for example, can be inserted into or removed from a 'photograph' with ease, thereby providing 'evidence' of any false alibi or accusation that might be needed.

In the past, the term 'fanatic' was usually reserved for Muslims; the term 'communist' was usually reserved for any non-Muslims who wished to take over control of any particular government from its current masters; and the term 'terrorist' was usually reserved for the people in either of these two groups who were prepared to act rather than just talk. In recent years, however – in fact ever since European communism was officially discarded in favour of universal 'democracy', and the imaginary iron curtain dismantled – the word 'Communist' has ceased to be a key term. Instead, 'the Muslims' have been substituted by the media as the new threat to democracy, peace and the new world order.

By combining one or more of the other key terms with either the word 'Muslim', or the word 'Islamic', the way of Islam has been increasingly and greatly discredited and misrepresented in the kafir media system, and 'the Muslims' have increasingly been presented to the general public as the new backward public enemy, ever ready to kill indiscriminately and to blindly die for their cause. If any Muslims are attacked and fight back in self-defence, the media defines this as 'terrorism'. If anyone attacks the Muslims this is defined as 'retaliation'. The fact that the vast majority of Muslims in the world today are not even fighting anyone is of course never mentioned. The current media equation is: Terrorism = fanatical paranoid Muslim fundamentalists = Islam = all Muslims.

As we have already seen, the difference between the Muslims and what the kafir calls the capitalists, is the same as the difference between the Muslims and what the kafir calls the communists. The Muslims accept Allah and His Messengers, whilst both the capitalists and the communists reject Allah and his Messengers.

In fact during the last decade of the twentieth century, the world has witnessed the almost overnight transformation of the communists into capitalists. Birds of a feather flock together.

Even when capitalism and communism were presented by the media as being 'at war' with each other – which, at the time of writing this, is still the case with Cuban and Chinese 'communism', although no doubt 'democracy' will soon miraculously prevail in these two cases as well – in reality there was never any real difference between the capitalists and the communists. Capitalism and Communism are the same. Their roots are the same. The capitalists and the communists are kafirun. They appear to be divided against each other, but they are the same body. Kufr is one system.

The capitalists and the communists both base their societies on identical interlinking pyramidical systems structures. They share the same kafir view of existence. They fight for the same things and worship the same idols. Their leaders follow the same behavioural life pattern. They both use kafir ideologies, and although they employ a different vocabulary, that is a different term of reference to describe their actions and what they are doing, they in fact both affirm and sustain the producer consumer process, which can only operate as it does today if the many are enslaved by that process for the benefit of the few.

Although they used to pretend to be at war with each other, and to be separated by their imaginary iron or bamboo curtains, the capitalists and the communists in fact always used to trade with each other and to sustain each other's economies. This is even more the case now, as the new global free market economy, financed by the international banking and stock market systems, continues to expand and be exploited as the true nature of the emerging brave new world order becomes ever more apparent.

And as in the past, so today, the capitalists and the communists both use exactly the same methods and manipulation techniques to condition their people to accept the goals of the consumer producer process, and to be content with its apparent rewards, despite and in spite of the reality of the human situation, which is that only the remembrance of Allah makes the heart peaceful.

As we have already seen, this conditioning is only possible where the educational and media institutions and systems are in the control of the few, the kafir ruling elite, who create the illusion not only that their legal system is what they call just, not only that their medical system is what they call advanced, not only that their educational system provides what they call knowledge, but also that the consumer producer process is what man was created for, and that there is no viable alternative way of life to it.

Indeed it is one of the favourite arguments of the kafir politician to say, whenever the kafir system, that is the Dajjal system, is criticised, that it may not be perfect but at least it is better than anarchy. The word 'anarchy' is another key emotional term in the kafir media system vocabulary. The emotional response which it is desired to evoke in the listener is a vision of absolute chaos, which with any luck will reach apocalyptic proportions if the listener has a good imagination backed up by the typical kafir's fear of creation and poverty, a fear which always exists in an ignorant person who does not know how existence works. This apparent lack of choice, which typifies the 'either you accept society as it is or else there will be anarchy' approach to life, is another example of the persuasive power which the media system exercises over the people whom it helps to condition.

Indeed it is one of the characteristics of the kafir system, that is the Dajjal system, that as long as a person accepts his or her conditioning and the prevailing kafir definitions of the nature of existence, it is impossible to envisage or imagine any other alternative to that system, so strong is the influence of that conditioning. This is one of the reasons why any drug which is capable of lifting a person's consciousness free of that conditioning, and altering that perception of existence, is usually defined as being illegal by most kafir legal systems. The only drugs which are permitted in a kafir state are those which will mildly stimulate or mildly tranquillise.

This does not mean that drugs are necessary in order to alter the consciousness. None of the Messengers of Allah, may the blessings and peace of Allah be on all of them, ever used or advocated the use of drugs as a means to self-knowledge. The way of the Prophet Muhammad wakes you up to the true nature of existence in a way which nothing else can, rendering all drugs obsolete.

It is only those who have seen the kafir system, that is the Dajjal system, for what it is, and who have rejected it, who are able to begin to appreciate the only viable alternative to that system, which is Islam. The only way to really appreciate what the way of Islam is, is to follow that way, for to read about the journey, or to examine the map, is not the same as actually making the journey itself. Life is a journey, but you have to be wide awake to appreciate it. Islam is the science of waking up.

Whoever sets out on this journey progressively tastes the deep sanity which springs from the knowledge of how existence works, and the peace and certainty which this knowledge brings.

Allah says in the *Qur'an*, '**I did not create man and jinn except to worship Me.**' To embody the guidance contained in the *Qur'an*, as exemplified by the Prophet Muhammad and the first Muslim community of Madina al-Munawarra, is to worship Allah in every moment. Many people in the High Tec North who have become dis-enchanted with the kafir system, that is the Dajjal system – no matter how high up in one of its hierarchical sub-systems they may be or may have been – are beginning to find out the truth of these words for themselves. Many people in the Poor South who were beguiled by the surface attractions of the illusory rewards of the producer consumer system, which had been successfully introduced into their countries by the colonisers, are now beginning to rediscover the living life transaction of Islam for themselves.

The resurgence of Islam in these times, which was predicted by the Prophet Muhammad, may Allah bless him and grant him peace – and which is already very much in evidence despite the attempts of the kafir media systems to disguise and discredit it – cannot be compared to the rise of Hitler's movement, and to his attempts to replace one kafir power structure by another kafir power structure. Hitler and his followers were part of the phenomenon of Dajjal as a world wide social and cultural phenomenon and Dajjal as an unseen force. The present resurgence of Islam is the sign that the present dominant kafir culture is about to be replaced and eclipsed by another way of life, which is its complete antithesis and entirely different to it, that is the Prophetic way of life.

It follows that all the kafir governments which at the time of writing this control nearly all of the Muslim countries in the name of Islam, but in accordance with kafir modes of manipulation control, will inevitably be replaced by real Muslims who govern in accordance with what is in the *Qur'an* and the *Sunnah*. These so-called 'islamic' governments are part of the Dajjal system. The people who control them are identified in the *Hadith* as being people whose hearts are devoid of the *Qur'an*, because it cannot descend beyond their throats. Their appearance on the face of the earth is one of the signs of the approach of the end of the world. The Prophet Muhammad said that they would go out of Islam faster than an arrow leaves the bow and passes through its target, and that they would be the worst people on the face of the earth.

The destination of the munafiqun, that is the people who say that they are muslims when in reality they are not, is the deepest part of the Fire.

о о о о о

The present resurgence of Islam is the necessary preliminary phase prior to the appearance of the Mahdi, just as the present ascendance in the influence of the kafir system that is the Dajjal system, throughout the world, is the necessary preliminary phase prior to the appearance of Dajjal the individual.

о о о о о

The examples provided by the treatment of Lord Northcliffe, Ezra Pound and the Nuremberg so-called war criminals – and there are many others – are dramatic ones. They demonstrate the extreme lengths to which the people who control the kafir system that is the Dajjal system are prepared to go in order to ensure the continued survival of that system and their control over it. They are by no means the only examples. You only have to observe what is going on around you, to recognise how the Dajjal system operates and is organised. The machinations of this system in all its various activities in all spheres of life, and the actions of its controlling elite, are everywhere in evidence for whoever looks closely, no matter how hard and cunningly that elite attempts to hide and disguise those activities and actions.

Their actions and activities are always manifest, but it is the meaning of these actions and activities which is so often obscured by the kafir educational and media smoke screen and conditioning techniques. By presenting a fragmented view of existence these systems prevent people from adding the bits and pieces together and from arriving at an overall understanding of what is going on. The people who split existence – or rather who create that illusion, since in Reality existence cannot be split because there is only Allah – are described in the *Qur'an* as the fasiqun, meaning 'those who divide'.

Division characterises the actions and activities of the kafirun, and division is the inevitable result of the way in which the kafir system, that is the Dajjal system, operates. This is why cancer is a physiological illness of this age. This is why schizophrenia and autism are psychological illnesses of this age. This is why nationalism and modern tribal warfare are social illnesses of this age. Whether within the individual, or in the family group, or in kafir society as a whole, we see division, the result of the way of life of the fasiqun, that is the people who operate and uphold the kafir system, that is the Dajjal system, by dividing and ruling.

Clearly there are many people who suffer from the manner in which the Dajjal system operates and who are enslaved by it, but who do not realise what the cause of that suffering is nor realise the nature of the prison they are in. As a result of their conditioning they continue to play an active and often important part in the running of the very system which unbeknown to them is the cause of their pain and the invisible walls of their prison. Drinking alcohol or taking drugs is no cure, rather these 'remedies' are part of the disease. It is the actual existential pattern of behaviour, together with the mental outlook that goes with it, which is the disease, simply because they are not in harmony with the true nature of existence, and accordingly that imbalance manifests in illness whether physiological, psychological, social or political.

Inevitably the most desperate lash out blindly in anger, causing damage and even death. As the saying goes, violence is the last resort of the incompetent, and – since it has become customary for the kafir media to equate such violence with terrorism, and to equate such terrorism with Islam – it must be emphasised that the Prophet Muhammad, may Allah bless him and grant him peace, forbade the killing of women and children and the elderly in times of war, as well as the wanton destruction of property. Killing defenceless people and destroying property at random may be the hallmark of extreme frustration, or the sign of a very hard heart, but it has nothing to do with the teachings of Islam.

If Muslims are attacked and forced to defend themselves, then they are obliged to fight with honour and within the limits of behaviour which were clearly demonstrated by the Prophet Muhammad and his companions, may the blessings and peace of Allah be on him and them.

It is said that sayyedina 'Ali, may Allah be pleased with him, sometimes refrained from killing his opponents on the battlefield because he could see with his inner sight that their children were going to be Muslims. On one occasion, when he was about to deliver the coup de grâce, his opponent spat defiantly in his face and made him angry, whereupon 'Ali let him go. When his opponent asked him why he had done this, he replied that if he had killed him in anger, it would have taken him to the Fire. His opponent was so impressed that he accepted Islam and became a Muslim.

The influence and overall control of the kafir system, that is the Dajjal system, are so widespread and insidiously present in all aspects of people's lives today, that the majority of people are unaware of what confronts them. The Dajjal system is as much a part of their lives as the air around them, which they breathe and depend on without knowing it. The freemasonic control which is exercised over them is so much a part of their every day lives, it is so close up to them, that they do not see it, just as they do not see that their being is from Allah, and that they are entirely dependant on Allah for their every heart beat. The truth of things is a blur in the corner of their eye. They have been born into the Dajjal system, and they have been brought up to accept that this is the way life is. They have been educated in the Dajjal system's ways and they have continually been misled by the media to affirm it, even after their formal education has been completed.

Even when someone is aware that all is not well in the state of kufr, he or she is often not able to say why or what. A person may glimpse an instance of blatant kafir media manipulation, or witness a particular example of the injustice of the kafir legal system at work, or admit deep down that he or she has learnt nothing of real value in the official curriculum at school or university – and yet be unable to form a clear picture of the system as a whole, or to pull free from the influence of the producer consumer process in which he or she is trapped.

Everyone is faced with the basic realities of life. Those simple bare necessities, such as food, shelter and clothing, have to be acquired and the bills have to be paid – which for most people means work and play from day to day – and once a man and a woman meet and start a family, then everyday life can easily become too filled and busy to have time to find out what it is all about.

In reality every atom is in its place and everything which appears to take place in existence is a part of one unified event. In Reality that one unified event does not exist. There is only Allah. Allah is the Inwardly Hidden and the Outwardly Manifest. Allah is the First before time began and the Last after time ceased. Wherever you look there is the face of Allah. Everything is passing away except the face of Allah. Surely we come from Allah and to Allah we surely return.

The difference between the kafir way of life and the muslim way of life is that the kafir way of life prevents you from seeing this, whilst the muslim way of life not only opens this knowledge up to you, but also enables you to live with it at peace and in tranquillity. The kafir thinks that he or she exists, and is troubled, whilst the mumin knows that Allah exists, and is at peace.

The needs and demands of everyday life in a kafir society, whether actual or merely media created – which because of the complex nature of the system are themselves both complex and profuse – make it difficult for most people to stop and reflect, let alone to make the decision as a result of that reflection to abandon the kafir way of life, to de-programme and de-condition, and to find out who they really are and what the true nature of existence really is.

Indeed the influence of the kafir system that is the Dajjal system is often so all pervasive and persuasive that anyone enslaved by it usually believes that the kafir way of life is the only viable way of life there is, is not aware that he or she has been programmed and conditioned, and thinks that his or her kafir view of existence is clear and unclouded. In other words, like goldfish born in captivity, some people do not even realise that they are trapped.

Even if, despite all this, the point of departure is reached, and the decision to really find out what it is all about is made, it is still often difficult to act on this inward intention existentially without coming up against the preventative and deterrent provisions of the kafir legal system, which have been designed to prevent people straying too far from the limits of what the kafir system that is the Dajjal system has defined as 'normal' and 'legal'. Furthermore, there are often strong social pressures from relations and friends who may be relatively content with the system as it is, and who will be correspondingly appalled at your decision to leave it, and therefore be prepared to do all that they can, whether by means of financial inducement, emotional blackmail or even physical force, to dissuade you from acting on your decision.

Anyone who chooses a teacher or follows a leader and joins a group or community of like-minded people will almost inevitably be regarded as having been brainwashed into joining a cult (if they are Christians) or a sect (if they are Muslims). Unfortunately this is in fact often the case, because – as both Jesus and Muhammad foretold, may the blessings and peace of Allah be on both of them – there are many false teachers and leaders at this point in time, even within the Muslim community, which can be very confusing for anyone who is genuinely seeking knowledge. Ultimately everyone is given the teacher they deserve.

Even more unfortunately, the genuine teachers and leaders within the Muslim community – who are rightly guided and who do have the idhn, that is the permission, from Allah and His Messenger, to teach – are often tarred with the same brush by the kafirun and the munafiqun working together – although for the discerning mumin this in itself tends to be a confirmation that a rightly-guided teacher is on the sirat al-mustaqim – for any teacher or leader who is on the sirat al-mustaqim is bound to be opposed and slandered by the kafirun and the munafiqun, as was the case with the Prophet Muhammad himself, and his close companions and followers, may the blessings and peace of Allah be on him and them.

It is inevitable that the sincere muminun – and indeed all the Muslims as a whole – will always be hated and slandered by the kafirun and the munafiqun. The more followers any Muslim teacher or leader attracts – whether rightly-guided or not – the more that teacher or leader and his followers will usually be subjected to a vicious media campaign, in which they will be described as 'paranoid', 'fanatical', 'fundamentalist' and if not expressly then by implication 'terrorist', and finally, if they have ever criticised the barbaric treatment that has been meted out to the Palestinian Arabs during the twentieth and twenty-first centuries, they will be automatically branded not as 'anti-Zionist', but as 'anti-semitic' – and therefore by implication no different from Hitler and the Nazis – even though it is the Palestinian Arabs who are in fact 'semitic', and even though the majority of European and American Zionists are not descended from the Tribe of Israel, but from the Khazars of the Caucasus, and are therefore in fact 'turkic'.

If, in spite of any kafir media campaign, any such teacher or leader remains popular with his followers, and if the degree of his influence continues to be regarded as a threat by the architects of the new world order, then more pressure will be brought to bear. His movements will be curtailed. He may be prevented from leaving the country in which he is resident. He may be placed under house arrest and allowed no visitors. He may be accused of some crime – usually a conspiracy of one kind or another – and brought to trial. He may end up in prison. He may even be killed.

In such a climate it is not surprising that the genuine teachers tend to remain concealed and without much of a following, while those who are genuinely in search of real knowledge find it hard to find anyone whom they feel they can really trust. By the grace of Allah, however, the heart finds the heart.

The sign of a true teacher is that he calls people to worship Allah and to the way of Muhammad, may Allah bless him and grant him peace. The sign of a false teacher is that he calls people to himself. Do not accompany the one whose state does not change you, and whose speech does not guide you to Allah. Whoever seeks a teacher will find one in accordance with his or her own sincerity and strength of resolution.

For those who, despite all the contrary forces – which, in effect, are a test of any seeker's sincerity and strength of resolution – still feel impelled to seek real knowledge and the balanced way of life which must necessarily accompany that search, many subsequently find that they are only prepared to go so far, either because they do not want all that there is to be wanted, or because their inherent social conditioning is just too strongly implanted to overcome, or else because the usually irrational fear of being punished, silenced or eliminated by the system acts as a deterrent, and induces the would-be searcher back into playing the producer consumer game. Only those who fear Allah alone are free from fear of other than Allah, and accordingly are free from fear of the kafir system, that is the Dajjal system, and its varied means of norm enforcement.

The people who only fear Allah alone are those who follow the way of the Prophet Muhammad, may Allah bless him and grant him peace. Clearly those people who have not yet encountered the way of Islam, although they may have a misconceived idea of what it is, as a result of their educational and media programming, and who are at present caught up in the consumer producer process, will have fear of the powers that appear to be in the kafir system, that is the Dajjal system, even though they have already inwardly rejected that system.

Furthermore, the existential panic and anxiety about the possibility of not having adequate provision and shelter – which inevitably arise in the heart of whoever does not know how existence works – reinforce fear of the system, and act as an added incentive to continue to act in accordance with the dictates of the consumer producer process, which promises to relieve that panic and anxiety by coming up with the goods. The deal is that if you play the consumer producer game, then you will acquire the money to buy the goods which you have been conditioned to want. In fact this is a lie, since, as we have already noted, one of the ways of keeping people working in the producer consumer process is to only pay them a sum which will not meet all their needs, so that firstly, they have to continue to work to live, and secondly, they have to continue to work to pay off the debts swelled by interest which they have been encouraged to incur by the various kafir finance systems. The nature of the kafir system that is the Dajjal system is such that only the controlling elite are in a position to fully enjoy the rewards of the labours of all the others. Indeed it has to be this way, since there simply are not enough luxury items in existence for everyone in a kafir society to be able to enjoy them all.

Even the people who receive more than their fair share of the myriad goods which today's consumer producer system manufactures do not find that their existential panic and anxiety have been quelled, and accordingly they often become lost in the endless search for the latest model and the ultimate thing, neither of which really exist. It is like drinking sea-water – the more they drink, the thirstier they become. Only those who are destined to find out stop, and reflect.

The fact that mere consumption is not the answer to anxiety about provision is true for two main reasons. Firstly, this anxiety is the result of ignorance of how existence works, and accordingly will only begin to disappear when that ignorance is replaced by knowledge. Secondly, the restlessness which every man and woman feels deep in their heart is no less than the longing for knowledge of Allah, and accordingly that longing and that restlessness can only be appeased by knowledge of Allah. Real knowledge of Allah only comes with remembrance of Allah, and accordingly it is only in the remembrance of Allah that the heart finds rest. It is only possible to remember Allah if you follow the way of the Messengers who have been sent by Allah during the various ages of mankind, may the blessings and peace of Allah be on all of them. The Messenger who was sent by Allah for the present age is the Prophet Muhammad, and accordingly it is only by following his way that fear of existence and existential panic and anxiety about provision and shelter will disappear. The choice is yours, right now.

Although the choice is clear, it is not always an easy one to make for whoever has been conditioned by the Dajjal system, even if the person in question is in the process of rejecting that conditioning. The conditioning provided by the Dajjal system is insidiously strong. It has an addictive quality about it. It creates in the mind of the individual the impression that the only way to dispel fear and anxiety is by taking the remedies offered by the system, that is to work and to play when you are well, and to do what the doctor tells you when you are ill, and above all not to try and change the status quo either inwardly or outwardly.

In effect, whoever has been conditioned by the Dajjal system is never really permitted to grow up, even though he or she is capable of having children and holding down an office job and driving a car. Whoever has been conditioned by the Dajjal system is kept in awe of that system, in the same way that a young child is not only in awe of the parents but also thinks that they are the best parents in the world and that they know everything. Whoever is not involved in seeking knowledge of Allah is a child, for it is only when you reach a certain age that you begin to wish to know the nature of existence. Some people never emotionally or intellectually reach that age. Some people simply do not have an intellect, which in the *Qur'an* is called aql, nor do they have what in the *Qur'an* is called lubb, meaning 'a core', that is access to the innermost secret of their being.

There is no blame in this. Everyone can only be who they are. Allah has made some people kafir and some people mumin. Allah has made some people ignorant and some people knowledgeable. Allah has made some people blind and some people seeing. They are not the same, but there is no blame. The mercy of Allah covers the whole of creation and pervades it in every respect. The kafir does not see this whilst the mumin does.

Clearly there are those who are utterly blind, and there are those who are utterly seeing, and there are those who are somewhere in between blindness and sight. A distinction must therefore be drawn between the one who is quite content with the Dajjal system such as it is for what it is worth, and the one who cannot bear it and is only interested in following the way of Muhammad in all its rich simplicity, and the one who does not particularly like the Dajjal system but who has not yet encountered the way of Muhammad, may Allah bless him and grant him peace.

Allah says in the *Qur'an* that people either follow the way of the Prophets or they follow the way of their fathers. Clearly there are a great many people in the world today who have not had access to the living and vibrant life transaction of the Prophet Muhammad, as it was lived by him and the first Muslim community of Madina al-Munawarra – and who accordingly have been following the way of their fathers, no matter how ignorant or cultured that way might be, simply because they do not know any better or any other way. These people cannot really be described as being kafir – indeed many of them are from or originate from what have been traditionally regarded as 'the Muslim countries', but have not in fact been brought up as Muslims – since a kafir is one who has actually been presented with a clear exposition of what Islam is and what Allah requires of him or her, and who has then openly rejected what he or she has heard, and subsequently attempted to shut out all mention or manifestation of the way of Islam.

It also often happens that a person, because the self is poisoned with ignorance, at first rejects the way of Islam, because to a sick person what is sweet often tastes bitter and what is bitter often tastes sweet, but then in the ripeness of time he or she accepts the way of Islam. Allah says in the *Qur'an* that it is Allah who expands the heart to accept Islam, and Allah does as He wishes.

It follows that there are a great many people in the kafir states of the world who, although they are at present trapped by the system and caught up in the daily whirl of the consumer producer process, will, when Allah wishes it, and once they have encountered real Muslims and experienced what Islam really is and means, themselves become muslim.

Of course there will also be those who utterly reject the way of Islam. Allah says of these people in the *Qur'an* that their ears and eyes and hearts are veiled, so that they cannot hear what a Muslim says or see what a Muslim does with any true understanding. Whether you talk to them or not, it is the same. They are blind, deaf and dumb, even though they appear to see, and hear, and speak.

Allah guides whom He wishes, and Allah leads astray whom He wishes. Allah sends some to the Garden and He does not care, and Allah sends some to the Fire and He does not care. Allah has power over everything. There is no strength and no power except from Allah.

The present resurgence of Islam is a clear indication from Allah that the polarisation of the people of iman and the people of kufr on a world scale is under way. This polarisation is a necessary preliminary phase before their respective leaders, the Mahdi for the muminun, and Dajjal the individual for the kafirun, can appear – and before the two opposites meet as they inevitably must, since anyone who is kafir cannot help but attack anyone who is muslim, and once the Muslims are attacked, Allah has ordered them to fight back in self-defence and to kill their aggressors, that is anyone who attacks them and then refuses either to say the shahada – that is, to witness that there is no god only Allah and that Muhammad is the Messenger of Allah, may Allah bless him and grant him peace – or to surrender by accepting Muslim governance and paying the jizya tax.

o o o o o

One way of measuring the level of ignorance in a kafir society, and the corresponding fear of existence and anxiety about provision and shelter which arise out of that ignorance, which is the hallmark of the kafir system, that is the Dajjal system, is to examine the extent to which people insure themselves and their goods against possible disaster and misfortune, even when they are not required to do so by kafir law.

The kafir insurance system is totally unnecessary for the people who know how existence works, and who follow the Prophetic life pattern – which is its own insurance.

Since everyone meets the consequences of their actions both in this life and the next, it follows that the one who is unaware of what action is fruitful and what action is unfruitful often brings misfortune upon him or her self, solely because of the way in which he or she behaves. Since the kafir does not know this, he or she seeks to avoid the effects of such misfortune by insuring against it before it happens – rather than by abandoning the course of action which is the real cause of the misfortune.

The way of Muhammad is the science of fruitful action. In the *Qur'an* fruitful action is called halal, whilst unfruitful action is called haram. Although these words are sometimes translated respectively as meaning 'what is permitted' and 'what is forbidden', their real meaning is to be found in the consequences of the actions which they describe. If this perspective is lost, it often happens that the conceptual framework, which the kafir calls 'morality', begins to develop. This moral attitude, which is regarded as the mark of being civilised by whoever has it, in fact tends to make people forget where they are going. It works like this:

To begin with there is the knowledge that what is halal is fruitful in this world and leads to the Garden in the next world, whilst what is haram is unfruitful in this world and leads to the Fire in the next world. This applies even to the food which you eat, because if you eat halal food your actions will tend to be halal, and if you eat haram food your actions will tend to be haram. Drinking wine or eating pork, for example, may not in themselves appear to be serious wrong actions, but the actions which may arise out of these actions, such as violence or adultery, for example, often are. They lead not only to an imbalance in the body but also to an imbalance in actions, an imbalance which causes distress in this world and is experienced as the Fire in the next world. In the same way doing what is halal leads to balanced action which results in harmony in this world and is experienced as the Garden in the next world.

This perspective begins to be lost when it is said that halal means 'permitted' and haram means 'forbidden', because it then often happens that some people begin to forget exactly why an action is permitted or forbidden. The original perspective is further clouded when a value judgement is placed on what is permitted and what is forbidden, that is, when what is described as halal is called 'good', and when what is described as haram is called 'bad', again because it becomes easier to forget why it is 'good' or why it is 'bad'.

If the overall perspective of the next world is lost, then people forget why something is really good or really bad. Instead they begin to form fixed ideas of what is good and what is bad. Then, if they forget that Allah looks at the intention behind the action and not the action itself, they begin to be less critical of their own actions, since they no longer fear the Fire or hope for the Garden, and instead become more critical of other people's actions. They begin to judge the outward actions of others – even though unaware of what the inward intention behind those actions might be – in accordance with their own ideas of what is good and what is bad.

Once people forget about the Fire and the Garden, and indeed cease to know that the next world exists, they then begin to call what appears to be expedient 'good' and what appears not to be expedient 'bad'. In effect, their idea of what is good and what is bad is no longer connected to the true realities of life, but rather is attached to whatever they give reality.

Once this stage has been reached, you have what the kafir calls 'morality', that is, a complex web of do's and don't's which are given spurious validity by emotional value judgements, which often have no relation to the true nature of existence, which like kafir law are always subject to change and re-evaluation, and which accordingly tend to cause whoever has this 'moral' attitude to forget where he or she is going – that is, to Allah, via the Fire or via the Garden.

Anyone who becomes aware of the hypocrisy which inevitably arises out of kafir 'morality' usually then rejects it. Once they have rejected it, they have no frame of reference to use when dealing with situations which require judgement, other than their own personal preferences and prejudices, together with whatever they have already learned from their own experience – that is, they have a limited knowledge of what is halal and what is haram, which they have arrived at by trial and error, and the full significance of which they do not realise, because they do not link this limited knowledge of what is halal and what is haram to what will be happening in the next world.

They then have a choice, which is either to do what they want, seeking pleasure and avoiding pain, or else to set out on a journey to discover the full science of what is halal and what is haram by following the way of Muhammad, may the blessings and peace of Allah be on him. If they make the first choice, they are at the mercy of their own desires and the illusory goals which the kafir system, that is the Dajjal system, promises them. If they make the second choice, then they will arrive at the knowledge of what is halal and what is haram and they will know why something is halal or haram. If they follow the way of Muhammad, avoiding what is haram and doing what is halal, then they will arrive at an inwardly peaceful and outwardly balanced state of being, in which the very idea of kafir insurance will be patently ridiculous. The one who does not follow the way of Muhammad, on the other hand, and who subscribes to the producer consumer process, will inevitably think that insurance is a 'good' idea, and waste as much money as he or she can afford on it.

People are encouraged to insure against every possible misfortune by the kafir insurance companies simply because the more people insure, the greater the profit will be for the company. A kafir insurance company cannot be described as a benevolent institution. It exists to make money out of other people's fears and anxieties. Of course it appears to be worthwhile when one of the events which have been insured against actually takes place and the person who took out the insurance eventually collects the money, but as we have already noted, there are more human ways of dealing with loss and misfortune, which in the real muslim community take the form of voluntary giving out, without your having had to pay a premium as a condition precedent, either by individuals in the community who have been given more than they need by Allah, or else from the bayt al-mal, that is the community's central fund into which all the minimal taxes required by the *Qur'an* and the *Sunnah* are paid, for the purposes of redistribution amongst those in need.

A brief historical study of Muslim communities in the past clearly shows that whenever their people held to what is in the *Qur'an* and the *Sunnah*, and only paid the taxes which Allah had told them to pay, and immediately redistributed those taxes once they had been collected in accordance with what is in the *Qur'an* and the *Sunnah*, then those communities prospered. As soon as the people began to abandon what is in the *Qur'an* and the *Sunnah*, they were given leaders over them who likewise ignored the *Qur'an* and the *Sunnah*. The Prophet Muhammad, may Allah bless him and grant him peace, said that every people have the leaders that they deserve. As soon as these leaders began to gather extra taxes, and to keep the proceeds either for themselves or out of anxiety, instead of redistributing them in accordance with what is in the *Qur'an* and the *Sunnah*, then the communities became divided against each other, ceased to prosper, and were eventually destroyed – just as Allah has promised in the *Qur'an*, that every people who reject Prophetic guidance will be destroyed.

When the companion of the Prophet who was called 'Umar became khalif, may Allah be pleased with him, he requested that he be told immediately the moment he strayed outside what is in the *Qur'an* and the *Sunnah*, so fearful was he of Allah and the Last Day. He was only too aware that the life transaction of Islam is its own insurance. A person once came to him and asked him to do the rain prayer, since there was a bad drought at the time. Sayyedina 'Umar, may Allah be pleased with him, replied that the reason for the drought was the fact that too many of the people in the community had become lax in following what is in the *Qur'an* and the *Sunnah*. In effect, the outward drought was a reflection of the inward drought of lack of trust in Allah. When that trust was renewed, then the rain which is the mercy of Allah, came.

The Prophet Muhammad, may Allah bless him and grant him peace, said that if anyone were to have been a Prophet after him, then it would have been sayyedina 'Umar, may Allah be pleased with him.

The fact that many of the so-called muslim but actually kafir governments – which are, at the time of writing this, still in control of the Muslim lands because they are being supported by the colonisers who helped to install them there in the first place – collect taxes in addition to what is prescribed by Allah in the *Qur'an* and the *Sunnah*, and then refuse to redistribute them, is not only one of the reasons for the lack of prosperity in these countries, but is also a clear sign of the extent of the influence of the world-wide kafir system, that is the Dajjal system.

Indeed it is a well known fact that the oil revenue of the Muslim countries is being used by the people who control it not so much for the benefit of the Muslims, but rather to support the kafir producer consumer system of both the west and the east, of both the High Tec North and the Poor South. This revenue, or at least a large proportion of it, is either invested in large kafir corporations or else it is deposited in kafir financial institutions where it collects compound interest and is used to provide compound interest-bearing loans to the poorer Muslim countries, thereby increasing their national debts still further. Since these corporations and financial institutions are controlled by the freemasonic elite of the kafir system that is the Dajjal system, it follows that they are using the wealth of the Muslims to destroy the Muslims, for one of the principal aims of the freemasons is to destroy the Muslims, in order to fully achieve world-wide control through their business and finance systems, that is by establishing the kafir system, that is the Dajjal system, world wide – the new world order.

The Prophet Muhammad, may Allah bless him and grant him peace, said that every people has its trial, and that the trial of the Muslims would be wealth. He also said that the downfall of the Arabs would be 'black gold' – a term which in the 'modern' world has only relatively recently been coined to describe oil. This much is clear from what has already happened not only to the rulers of Saudi Arabia, who in the name of Islam are busy establishing a police state, based largely on the kafir models of the west, but also to all the Arab states in the Middle East which as a result of the recent Gulf War – instigated principally in order to secure the oil-fields for the benefit of the High-Tec North – have all been considerably destabilised and virtually bankrupted.

The Prophet Muhammad, may Allah bless him and grant him peace, made it clear that the leader of a Muslim community should not be chosen as leader simply because his father was leader before him. It is not the *Sunnah* to have 'royal' families. If this was the *Sunnah*, then clearly the royal family of the Muslims would have been the family of the Prophet Muhammad, may the blessings and peace of Allah be on him and them, and accordingly virtually all of the Muslim rulers for the last fourteen hundred years would have been descended from the Prophet Muhammad, may the blessings and peace of Allah be on him, and on his family, and on his companions, and on all who follow him and them with sincerity in what they are able, until the Last Day.

A brief historical study of Muslim communities in the past shows that as soon as these communities opted for dynastic rule, they inevitably became corrupted and were destroyed. It is absolutely clear that the leader of a Muslim community should be recognised as such on the basis that his fear and knowledge of Allah are great, and that of all the people in the community he has the best understanding of what is in the *Qur'an* and the *Sunnah*, simply because he most embodies what is in the *Qur'an* and the *Sunnah*.

The corruption in the Muslim lands today is not surprising. It is part of the inevitable process of life. Furthermore, to simply blame the kafir system, that is the Dajjal system, for that corruption is not to see the whole picture. Clearly if some of the Muslim leaders in the past had not already been prone to corruption, then the kafir colonisers would have been unable to plant the seeds of the kafir system, that is the Dajjal system, in the Muslim countries in the first place, nor would those seeds have been able to sprout and grow.

The truth of the matter is that everything in life is subject to birth and death and growth and decay. Even the first Muslim community of Madina al-Munawarra was subject to this cycle. The Prophet Muhammad, may the blessings and peace of Allah be on him, foretold that the dynamic living Islam which that community enjoyed would only last in Madina for thirty or seventy years after he had died. He foretold civil war amongst the Muslims, that is, that Muslim would fight Muslim. He foretold that what had begun as a prophecy and a mercy, would become a khalifate and a mercy, would become a tyranny filled with many injustices. He also said that towards the end of time a just and merciful khalifate would once again be established by the Muslims.

And he never mentioned anything about a 'new world order' being established by the kafirun for any length of time!

It is very easy to make Islam an instrument of tyranny, simply by systematising it, and moralising it, and then inflicting that system and that morality, neither of which have anything to do with the life transaction brought by the Prophet Muhammad, on other people who have no desire to be regulated by such a system and such a morality. Many of those who are alive today have seen and experienced this happening.

The Prophet Muhammad also foretold that not all of his community would go astray. He said that towards the end of the world the Muslims would be divided into seventy three different groups, and only one of those groups would have the living life transaction of Islam which he had originally brought. There can be no doubt that this one group, which has access to the living life transaction of Islam in all its rich simplicity, is comprised of the awliya of Allah – that is the friends of Allah, the people whom Allah loves and who love Allah – along with all those who recognise and follow them.

The awliya of Allah are the ones who have preserved the living life transaction of Islam by the grace and guidance of Allah, in every time and age. They are recognised by the fact that people are drawn to them because of their wisdom and serenity, in the same way that people were drawn to the Prophet Muhammad, may Allah bless him and grant him peace, and so real muslim communities form round them, may Allah be pleased with them, just as the first Muslim community formed round the Prophet Muhammad.

The real muslim community is simply the outward manifestation of what is inwardly in the heart of the wali, in the same way that the tyranny of the kafir state is the outward manifestation of the inward darkness of the tyrants who control it. The heart of the wali is inwardly light and peace, and this manifests outwardly in the form of the harmonious and human transactions which always characterise a real muslim community.

The awliya of Allah are not located in one place. As the ruh, that is the spirit form, pervades the entire body, so they are spread throughout the world. The awliya are the ruh of the world. Just as the body rots once the ruh has left it, so the world will come to an end once there are no longer awliya living in it.

The real muslim communities which form around the awliya of Allah are subject to the same cycle of growth and decay as the first Muslim community of Madina al-Munawarra. They begin with one man, the wali. The community forms around him. The kafirun try to destroy the community, but fail because Allah gives victory to those who trust in Him. Then the wali eventually dies. There follows a period of balance during which the community continues to hold to what is in the *Qur'an* and the *Sunnah*, and is led by rightly-guided men, who were the close companions of the wali, and who received their knowledge of Allah by Allah through him. Then these companions die, and the community is led by those who were the companions of the wali's companions. Then they die, and gradually almost without anybody realising it, the community begins to lose the dynamism and living vibrancy which its first members originally possessed.

With the continued passage of time the stage is reached where there is no longer a unified Muslim community. Its members may still follow much of what is in the *Qur'an* and the *Sunnah*, simply because that is what they have been born into, but many do this because it is what their fathers did, and not because they recognise Islam for what it really is. They no longer have what the original community which formed round the wali had. Everything in creation has its high point, and then thereafter there is a falling away. Basically a real muslim community which lives with anything like the same zest for life, and with anything like the same awareness of the true nature of existence, as the first Muslim community of Madina al-Munawarra, only lasts for three generations. Then it is all over. As quickly as one Muslim community dies another is born somewhere else. The knowledge which the awliya possess, and which does not come from books, is transmitted from person to person. Once a wali has transmitted that knowledge to another wali, then that wali takes that knowledge wherever he or she goes. In this way this knowledge has always been kept alive from the time of the Prophet Muhammad up until now, may the blessings and peace of Allah be on him and on all who follow in the dust of his footsteps.

Not every wali has a muslim community forming around him or her. Allah often hides who the awliya are as a protection for them. In those times during the alternating cycle of iman and kufr when kufr is in the ascendancy, the awliya remain hidden. Their job is simply to keep their knowledge and wisdom alive, and to ensure that the chain of transmission remains unbroken. When the time arrives when iman is in the ascendancy, as it is now, then the awliya emerge into the open, and real muslim communities form around them, and there is nothing that the kafirun and the munafiqun can do to stop them, because Allah gives victory to the ones who trust in Allah, and the awliya and those who follow the awliya are the ones who really trust in Allah. They cannot do other than trust in Allah because of the knowledge of Allah which Allah has given them. Allah said on the lips of the Prophet Muhammad, may the blessings and peace of Allah be on him, in a hadith qudsi, that whoever makes war on a wali of Allah, Allah makes war on them.

Naturally there are ignorant people who claim to be walis when they are not. They deal in esoteric information and pseudo-wisdom, but not in real knowledge of Allah. They are usually recognisable because they are concerned with personal reputation – that is, they are more concerned about what other people think about them than what Allah knows about them; and because they usually charge money for the information which they pass on; and because outwardly they do not follow the existential life pattern of the Prophet Muhammad, even in very essential matters such as eating halal food, and doing the prayer, and fasting Ramadan; and because inwardly they do not have the light and wisdom which only a wali of Allah is given by Allah; and because, in the final analysis, they do not have the idhn to teach – that is, they do not have the permission of Allah to teach. One great wali in the past, Shaykh Ahmad ibn 'Ata'i'llah, said that as for the one who speaks with idhn, his words are heard by creation, but as for the one who speaks without idhn, he is no more than a dog barking. Idhn is from Allah and His Messenger, may Allah bless him and grant him peace.

The true awliya are recognisable by a number of signs. Outwardly they embody the way of Muhammad in every respect. Inwardly they have a light which bathes and cleanses the hearts of those who sit with them. They have the best of manners and are human and compassionate. They have great wisdom and knowledge, which they share without charging a fee. They fear only Allah. They love Allah. They have gnosis of Allah, which is not the same as possessing information about Allah. Their selves have been purified. Allah loves them, and when Allah loves them then, as Allah said on the lips of the Prophet Muhammad, in a hadith qudsi, He is the tongue with which they speak, and the hand with which they grasp, and the foot with which they walk. When you see them, it is as if you see instruments moved by divine decree. This is why and how they make things happen and bring knowledge to life.

The awliya are the complete antithesis of the freemasons. The freemasons are the elite of the kafirun. The awliya are the elite of the muminun. The freemasons only want power. The awliya only want Allah. The freemasons exploit and tyrannise the people whom they control and manipulate. The awliya illuminate and liberate the people whom they serve. Both the freemasons and the awliya are necessary to the creational process, which works by the dynamic interplay of opposites. You have to see which of the two opposites you belong to. If you are a kafir then go and join the freemasons, because they receive the best of their world and the worst of the next world. If you are a mumin then go and join the awliya, because they receive the best of this world and the best of the next world. The choice is yours right now.

      o   o   o   o   o

The life transaction of Islam is the best insurance in the world. It guarantees provision in this world, and the Garden in the next world, for the one who embodies it with sincerity. The minimum that you have to do to ensure clothing, food and shelter, is five prayers a day. The minimum that you have to do to ensure the Garden, is to affirm that there is no god only Allah and that Muhammad is the messenger of Allah, in the moment; and to do five prayers in the day; and to fast during the month of Ramadan in the year, and to pay the zakat tax once every year; and finally, if it is possible, to do the hajj, that is the pilgrimage to Makka, at least once in your life time.

These five essential actions, the five pillars of Islam as they are called, are not only all you need to do to reach the Garden, but are also the basis of a balanced life on this earth which inevitably leads to knowledge of Allah. They alone can transform the heart of whoever does them, and make it peaceful. Of course the more that you embody of the way of Muhammad, may Allah bless him and grant him peace, the more you gain from it, since there is great wisdom in everything which the Prophet did, and this wisdom is only available for the people who do likewise.

Ultimately, Allah is in the expectation of His slave. You will receive from Allah what you expect from Allah. Every one gets what they want. It is related that there was a man who on the Last Day was told that he was for the Fire. He replied, 'Which is greater, my wrong actions or Allah's forgiveness?' Because he had this expectation of Allah, he went to the Garden.

The truth of the matter is that Allah could not show His mercy and forgiveness if no one had wrong actions. To the one who seeks knowledge of Allah, right action and wrong action are the same, because he or she learns from both. If the one who trusts in Allah is wise then he or she does not get stung in the same place or in the same way twice. For the one who desires to see the face of Allah – and that vision is possible both in this world and in the Garden within the Garden in the next world – Allah is his or her only concern. The object in life for such a person is not simply to avoid the Fire and reach the Garden, but solely to see the face of Allah. The only way to reach the stage when and where Allah will give you this vision, if He wishes it, is by following the way of Muhammad.

The danger for the one who neither desires Allah, nor longs for the Garden, nor dreads the Fire, is that he or she will worship Islam instead of worshipping Allah – that is, he or she will mistake the means for the end.

Whoever makes this mistake kills the living life transaction of Islam stone dead, and makes a religion out of it, that is a constricting web of do's and don't's which has nothing to do with the way of Muhammad. This is what the Jews and the Christians have done to the teachings of their respective Prophets, Moses and Jesus, on whom be peace, and unfortunately some of the Muslims have also made a religion out of the teaching of the Prophet Muhammad, may the blessings and peace of Allah be on him, in fulfilment of his prophecy that some of the Muslims would follow the example of their predecessors, meaning the Jews and the Christians, just like a lizard making for its hole.

If you wish to follow the way of Muhammad, then learn from those who have travelled it and who embody it, and not from those who have made a religion out of Islam. The ones who best know the way of Muhammad are the awliya, because they best embody it. The one who desires knowledge should only take it from the one whose actions are the same as his or her words.

So in reality there are two choices. Firstly, you may choose between iman and kufr. If you choose iman, then secondly, you may choose between either the living life transaction of Islam – which thrives around the awliya and which inevitably leads to knowledge of Allah and to the Garden, or the dead religion of Islam – which is followed by the people of book knowledge and fixed 'morality' and which is like a prison. The choice is yours right now.

It is clear that a mumin's insurance, that is the living life transaction of Islam and trust in Allah, is accompanied by a vibrant awareness of the Unseen and of what comes after death. Kafir insurance is the opposite of this. To the kafir, death is not simply a doorway which leads from one world to another world, and which accordingly is not in itself something to be feared. To the kafir, death is the ultimate misfortune which is accordingly to be insured against. This is because the kafir does not know what death is, or what lies on the other side of death – and even if he or she is told, the teller will not be believed.

Life insurance also appears to be necessary to the kafir because of his or her anxiety about provision and shelter in old age. In many ways this anxiety is a well-grounded one in a fragmented society, because the young tend to abandon the old, and leave them to fend for themselves, often alone. This is the complete antithesis of the real muslim community where life insurance policies are completely unnecessary, because everyone looks after each other, from birth to death.

Another inevitable result of the fragmentation of kafir society, and especially a society which makes people want so many things because they have been conditioned to want them in order to keep the consumer producer process in business, is that there is a lot of what the kafirun call crime. It is almost inevitable that people who do not fear Allah and the Last Day, and who cannot get what they have been conditioned to want from the consumer producer process by legal means, will turn to crime. As we have already seen this criminal activity is not discouraged, or rather its true causes are not eliminated, because it provides many of the people who work for the legal system with a reason for living and a steady income.

Crime also provides an added incentive to make people insure their property. As we have already seen, the insurers do not lose out, because they have fixed the insurance system so that they receive more in premiums than what they pay out in claims, and then these profits are further swelled by investing them and earning interest. Thus we see that the kafir insurance system appears to be necessary, because it performs a costly service in a fragmented society where people do not trust each other. The average kafir is obliged to trust in the average insurance company – which is not itself entirely trustworthy, because however 'efficient' it may be, in the final analysis its directors have the annual profits in mind more than the welfare of their customers. Anyone who has read the terms of insurance policies and studied the law which governs the interpretation of these terms, will know that the policies are designed to cover as little possible misfortune as they can in practice, whilst appearing and purporting to do the opposite in theory.

The kafir insurance system is another of the important sub-systems in the kafir system, that is the Dajjal system. Whereas the kafir legal and medical systems make their money out of the actual misfortunes of people – and misfortunes which have often been created by the way in which the system works at that – the kafir insurance system goes one step further and makes its money out of the fear people have for misfortunes which only might happen.

The illusory need to insure – which derives both from groundless anxiety, and from the legal obligation to insure – and which arises out of the inevitable detrimental results of a society which is fragmenting, are both the children of ignorance as to how existence works, and of lack of trust either in Allah or in other people – and in truth these two trusts are the same trust. This state of affairs is in direct contrast to the reality of the mumin whose only insurance is trust in Allah, a trust which is manifested by his or her following the guidance which Allah has sent, and which is contained in the *Qur'an* and the way of Muhammad.

The Prophet Muhammad, may the blessings and peace of Allah be on him, said that if you really trusted in Allah, then you would live like the birds who go out in the morning with nothing, and who return to their nests in the evening with nothing, and who in the meantime have been fed. He also said that whoever does five prayers a day is guaranteed food, clothing and shelter by Allah. The Prophet himself could not go to sleep at night if there was money in his simple room. Accordingly he was what the kafirun call bankrupt at the end of each of his days as a Prophet – and yet there has never been anyone richer than he, nor will there ever be.

The reality of provision is that Allah is the Provider, and He remembers those who remember Him as is promised in the *Qur'an*. The reality of provision is that in the fifth month of pregnancy the ruh, that is the spirit form, is breathed into the foetus, and at that time it is written what his or her provision will be in the world, whether he or she will be happy or sad, when he or she will die, and whether he or she is for the Fire or the Garden. The whole matter has already been decided, even before you were born. Once you are born then whatever is coming to you comes at its appointed time, and whatever is not coming to you will never come. That is why Allah says in the *Qur'an* that what is written for you cannot be avoided, and what is not written for you cannot be reached. That is why Allah says in the *Qur'an* do not exult in what you are given, and do not grieve for what you are not given.

One of the companions of the Prophet Muhammad asked him, 'Are we on a matter which is completed, or are we on a matter which is not completed?' The Prophet replied, may the blessings and peace of Allah be on him, 'We are on a matter which is already completed. The pen has stopped writing, and the ink is dry.'

The kafir tries to make a nonsense of this by conjuring up visions of an idiot sitting and doing nothing and waiting for his or her provision to fall out of the sky, or of another idiot who blindly walks across the road without first looking to see if there is a car coming. This shallow kafir concept – which is usually described as 'fatalism' or 'belief in predestination', has nothing to do with the true nature of existence. Your going out and getting things, and your taking precautions to avoid mishaps, your every breath, your every heartbeat, are all part of what has been written for you.

You cannot do other than what is in your heart, your every move is already decided, but whenever you are faced with a choice you have to make the decision. Right now the choice is yours, but once it has been made, and looking back on it, perhaps you will see that you could not have made any other decision. Allah is the doer of you and your actions, and you are answerable for your actions on the Last Day, and depending on what actions you choose in this life, you will be for the Fire or for the Garden in the life after this.

○   ○   ○   ○   ○

It has been related that 'Umar ibn al-Khattab, may Allah be pleased with him, was asked about this ayah:

> **When your Lord took their progeny from the Banu Adam from their backs and made them testify against themselves, 'Am I not your Lord?' They said, 'Yes, we bear witness', lest you should say on the Day of Rising, 'We were heedless of that.'** (*Qur'an: Surat'al-'Araf* – 7.172)

'Umar ibn al-Khattab said, 'I heard the Messenger of Allah, may Allah bless him and grant him peace, being asked about it. The Messenger of Allah, may Allah bless him and grant him peace, said, "Allah, the Blessed, the Exalted, created Adam. Then He stroked his back with His right hand, and progeny issued from it. He said, 'I created these for the Garden and they will act with the behaviour of the people of the Garden.' Then He stroked his back again and brought forth progeny from him. He said, 'I created these for the Fire and they will act with the behaviour of the people of the Fire.'" A man said, "Messenger of Allah! Then of what value are deeds?" The Messenger of Allah, may Allah bless him and grant him peace, answered, "When Allah creates a slave for the Garden, He makes him use the behaviour of the people of the Garden, so that he dies on one of the actions of the people of the Garden, and by it He brings him into the Garden. When He creates a slave for the Fire, He makes him use the behaviour of the people of the Fire, so that he dies on one of the actions of the people of the Fire, and by it He brings him into the Fire.'"

Yahya related to me from Malik that he heard that the Messenger of Allah, may Allah bless him and grant him peace, said, 'I have left two matters with you. As long as you hold to them, you will not go the wrong way. They are the Book of Allah and the Sunnah of His Prophet.'

Yahya related to me from Malik from Ziyad ibn Sa'd from 'Amr ibn Muslim that Tawus al-Yamani said, 'I found some of the companions of the Messenger of Allah, may Allah bless him and grant him peace, saying, "Everything is by decree."' Tawus added, 'I heard 'Abdullah ibn 'Umar say that the Messenger of Allah, may Allah bless him and grant him peace, said, "Everything is by decree – even incapacity and ability," (or "ability and incapacity").' (*Al-Muwatta'* of Imam Malik: 46.1.2-4)

Allah says in the *Qur'an*:

> **And Allah has created you and what you do.**
> (*Qur'an: Surat'as-Saffat* – 37.96)

○   ○   ○   ○   ○

It is sheer ignorance of this state of affairs which induces the kafir not only to rely on his or her own actions rather than on Allah, from Whom all actions come, but also to insure against what is defined by kafir insurance terminology as 'risk'. In reality there is no such thing as risk, just as there is no such thing as luck. Allah's mercy is greater than His wrath, and the way of Islam is the means to taste His mercy and avoid His wrath.

The reality of the kafir insurance business system, and indeed of all the kafir finance systems, is that they are carefully designed to involve as many people as possible more fully in the producer consumer process, and to make as much money as possible out of that involvement. The insurance system plays a vital role in the functioning of the commodity markets which deal in raw materials from the mineral, vegetable and animal kingdoms, in bulk and in the future. These markets buy and sell crops which have not yet been planted, fruit which has not yet begun to ripen, metals which have not yet been mined, and livestock which has not yet been born. By dealing in the future like this, the profit margin is increased, whilst possible losses occasioned by unforeseen events are insured against, the premiums for the insurance being paid out of the large profits which have been made by paying the producers of the commodity in question a lower price in advance than the price which the buyer would have had to pay if the goods had actually existed at the time of buying.

This is yet another example of how the kafir system, that is the Dajjal system, creates a quite unnecessary pattern of activity in order to make money from it. The winners are those who operate the markets and the insurers. The losers are the people at the bottom of the company pyramid – who in fact are usually the ones who do all the hard work.

Behind this pattern of activity of buying and selling in the future – a pattern of activity which is not permitted for Muslims – is not only sheer greed, but also a deep underlying anxiety about provision. The Muslim who does not have this anxiety, only buys and sells what already actually exists, in accordance with the way of Muhammad, which clearly states firstly, that dealing in the future like this is haram – that is, it is forbidden because it is unfruitful – and secondly, that a trader should not make more than thirty per cent profit on all essential goods and commodities – so that people are not exploited. It is because the Muslim only deals in the present, and not in the future, and because he or she trusts in Allah, and the other Muslims with whom he or she deals, that insurance in the Muslim business world is totally unnecessary.

If kafir insurance was not a way of making money out of people, then the insurance companies would not exist. The amounts which they are prepared to pay out, and the circumstances in which they are prepared to make payment, are all carefully calculated so that overall payments out are a great deal less than the total amount of premiums received and invested – although of course whenever there is a really large-scale 'disaster', which was unlikely to happen but which is covered by an insurance policy, then all these calculations about future probabilities prove to be of no avail, and expert juggling and restructuring is rapidly needed to ensure that the insurance company in question stays afloat.

It is because of the large profits which they usually make that the insurance companies can afford to use the civil legal process to their own advantage, either by employing legal experts to achieve the court decision which conveniently limits their liabilities in claims over which there is a dispute, or by offering sums which are less than the amount which they should really be paying out – because they know that the person or company insured cannot afford to take them to court, and will therefore have to reach a settlement on the insurance company's terms by accepting whatever is being offered. When the situation is such that both parties in a dispute over an insurance claim can afford to go to court, then of course this means continuity of work for the people involved in the civil legal process. This is yet another example of how the interlink between the sub-systems of the kafir system that is the Dajjal system ensures that they keep each other busy, by providing work for each other.

Once a person or company has taken out an insurance policy, or, for that matter, has entered into a hire purchase or mortgage agreement, or borrowed money from the bank, then this means that that person or company is more fully committed to keep working in the producer consumer process, in order to keep up the payment of the premiums, or the hire purchase, mortgage or overdraft repayments. The more you insure, and the greater the financial commitments which you incur, the harder you have to work to pay them off, and accordingly the more you are trapped and enslaved by the producer consumer process.

The media systems are used with devastating effect not only to encourage people to consume generally, but also, more specifically, to fall into debt by living beyond their means. Once they have fallen into this trap it is then relatively simple to create money out of nothing, by charging them interest on the money which they owe. In effect, you are provided with some of the goodies which the kafir system that is the Dajjal system promises you, now, but at the price of having to pay much more for them than you would have had to pay if you could have bought them outright in the first place.

The main purpose of the 'have it now, pay later' techniques is to create debts, because then the interest on the debts can also be collected. Furthermore, this kind of transaction encourages the buyer to insure the goods, especially if we are talking about something expensive rather than something cheap, because there is nothing more frustrating than having to continue to pay for something which has been written off or stolen, especially if you are being charged interest into the bargain! The chances are that in fact the thing, whatever it is, will not be written off. This will mean that you have not only had to pay interest on the original debt, but also will have incurred the additional expense of the insurance as well.

By inflating the cost of goods in a kafir society by these methods, the freemasonic controlling elite ensure that the people they control continue to be enslaved by the consumer producer system, whilst making a profit out of them.

Living in debt beyond their means encourages or drives many people to gamble, since only a miracle win is going to wipe out their growing debts. Of course the vast majority of gamblers tend to end up further in debt as a result – because all forms of gambling only exist in order to make money out of gamblers, and not to help them. As a result, many people end up trying to find enough money not to pay off their debts, but simply to be able to service them, by making the required monthly payments. Once they have reached a 'no win – no escape' situation, many people are then encouraged to insure against the possibility of their not being able to keep up their repayments on their debts as a result of ill-health or redundancy. Thus virtually all debts today are further increased by the additional premiums which are paid out on payment 'protection' plans.

The combined activities of the various kafir finance institutions make the accumulation of vast pools of wealth a reality. Even a million one pound monthly premium payments by a million small-time policy-holders, gives the insurance company twelve million pounds to play with. In the present complex kafir states of the High Tec North, where virtually every kind of activity involves one form of insurance or another, of course the actual figures are not mere millions, but run into hundreds and thousands of millions and billions. And of course much of what has been said about the kafir insurance companies applies equally to the kafir hire purchase finance companies, and to the kafir building societies, and especially to the kafir banks.

○   ○   ○   ○   ○

Of all the kafir finance institutions, the kafir banks accumulate the most wealth, because they not only charge interest on debts, but also they encourage people to save money, if they have it to save, and to deposit whatever they save in the banks. Although the banks pay interest on money in deposit accounts, they of course invest that money and receive far more from it than the amounts which they have to pay out on it. Furthermore, they also have most of the money which is lying in the current accounts to play with, and on this money they have to pay no interest at all. Thus whatever return they receive by investing current account money is all profit. The banks have found in practice that on average out of every thirteen pounds lying in the bank, there is only ever an actual collective demand by the clients of the bank for one of those pounds in cash. This leaves the bank with twelve pounds out of every thirteen to play with.

The overall sum which the banks have to play with is phenomenal, because virtually all of the other kafir finance institutions, and virtually all of the business corporations and concerns, and indeed most of the people in the street, deposit their money with the banks. The banks are the means by which vast pools of wealth are accumulated – and, for example, out of every thirteen billion pounds deposited with them, they are free to invest twelve billion pounds in order not only to maximise their own profits, but also, more significantly, to finance and facilitate whatever social engineering there happens to be on the political agenda. The new world order could not exist without the banks.

The banks are controlled by freemasons. The giant corporations of the kafir producer consumer system, that is the Dajjal system, are controlled by the freemasons. The governments of the kafir states are controlled by the freemasons. It follows that the freemasons are in a position to use the vast pools of wealth which have been accumulated by the banks to finance those projects which will provide business for their large corporations, and furthermore, this activity will be sanctioned by official government approval and permitted by the kafir legal system.

These large projects, which affect the lives of all those who work in them, are decided upon without asking all those who have been affected whether or not that is what they want. The project is set in motion, and the people who work in it work because they need the money, not because they necessarily believe in the project. Naturally the freemasonic controlling elite decide on those projects which are profitable to them. In effect, any project is profitable to them, firstly, because the people who do the work are paid less than the money which is received by the company which employs them, and secondly, because the money which they do earn has to pass through the banks, who then use whatever is not being spent by the client to finance yet another project.

The kafir system, that is the Dajjal system, is a self-perpetuating system. Once it has people working in and for it, their activity generates more activity, and all this activity generates money. The large corporations and companies do not really exist. They merely provide an effective facade to disguise the activities of the freemasons who control them, and an illusory structure within which the people who work for them are trapped. Using the large kafir corporations and companies as a front, the freemasons channel the vast amounts of money to which they have access to finance the social projects which ensure continued profits and therefore power for themselves, and which also ensure the continued subservience of the people who are caught up in working in those social projects.

It is clear from this perspective that the kafir taxation system is in fact just one more kafir finance system, which ensures that people do not have too much money to play with, and are accordingly obliged to keep on working in the kafir producer consumer process. Once the taxes have been collected – and their overall bulk and effect is disguised by giving them different names, and by taxing not only earned income but also any transaction where capital is gained or transferred and where consumer items or services are purchased or utilised – the money which has been accumulated in this way can then be used to finance the social projects of the freemasonic ruling elite's choice. Thus, for example, the freemasonic controlled government will give the juicy contract to the freemasonic controlled building corporation to build all the buildings needed to house all the activities of the bureaucratic infra-structure which is used by the government to gather the taxes which are needed to control the country which it rules.

The argument, which states that since the government has been elected by the people, therefore it follows that the government policies are the policies which the people want and support, is nonsense. Firstly, the government which is publicly elected is not the real government. It is just a figurehead government, which distracts the attention of the people away from the real ruling elite who are the freemasons. Secondly, the reality of the 'democratic' election process today is that the figurehead government is always elected by a minority of the actual total number of people living in the kafir state in question, even though it has been elected by a majority of those who bothered to vote.

The reason why so many people do not bother to vote is because they at least have an inkling of the fact that they have no real choice in the matter. They are presented with a limited choice of apparently acceptable candidates, usually not more than two, both of whom make promises which they usually never keep, and neither of whom necessarily represent the views of those who usually end up voting for them, simply because there is no one else to vote for. People are encouraged to vote, through the media system, on the basis that since it is their country, they should have a say in who rules it, but in fact they can only choose someone who has his name on the ballot slip – and the only people who ever get their names on the ballot slip in the first place and get elected are people who either secretly or unwittingly support the activities of the freemasonic ruling elite, and who in turn are supported by that elite, since it is impossible to conduct a successful election campaign without the use and support of the media, all of which costs a great deal of money.

Whoever the people vote for, or even if they do not vote – which means that they do not wish to be governed by any of the candidates standing for election – the so-called government still gets elected, and the real ruling force behind the facade of the election pantomime, that is the freemasonic ruling elite, remains in power. Of course some kafir states do not even bother with elections. Instead the figurehead ruler claims to have the interests of the people at heart, and may even call the country 'a people's republic' to prove it, although of course this meaningless phrase changes nothing.

The people who really rule the kafir states of today are the people who control the kafir finance and business institutions, that is the freemasons. The freemasons decide what the social projects are to be. The freemasonic controlled business institutions carry out those social projects, enslaving the working population within those social projects in the process. The freemasonic controlled finance institutions finance these projects.

The key kafir finance institution is the banking system since it handles the life blood of the consumer producer process, that is money. The importance of the banking system lies in the fact that it not only facilitates financial transactions on a national level, but also enables transactions between different countries using different currencies to take place. As a result of these international transactions, money itself becomes a commodity. As well as making money by charging a commission every time one currency is changed into another currency, money can also be made simply by buying and selling different currencies at strategic intervals. These transactions are very magical since often no money actually changes hands, and yet by buying and selling on the same day, a profit can be made and recorded in the bank computer's memory.

This activity is very similar to what happens on the stock exchange, which is ostensibly the place where companies and corporations raise money to finance their operations, by promising to pay the share holder a dividend, that is interest, on the money which he or she is effectively lending to the company.

This method of raising money is attractive to the corporation or company, because it may work out cheaper than borrowing it from the bank. This method of lending money is attractive to the shareholder, because if the company or corporation makes large profits, then the annual return on the loan will probably be greater than the interest which would have accrued if the money loaned had been deposited with the bank.

What in fact happens is that the different shares, like the different currencies, become commodities in themselves. You can buy and sell them. You can buy and sell them for different reasons. You can buy and sell them to gain or relinquish control of the company or corporation whose shares they are. This works by virtue of the reasoning that if you are providing most of the finance for the company or corporation then you should have the final say in how it is run. Naturally the freemasons have a controlling interest in all the important corporations, because only they have access to the funds which are necessary to acquire such an interest. This system of control by owning the bulk of the shares of any large business concern means that the freemasons can takeover virtually whoever they want, simply because they can provide whatever price is needed to achieve this object. Once they have a controlling share, they can then staff that company or corporation with their own people. This is one way in which the Dajjal takeover sometimes manifests.

The usual reason for buying and selling shares is simply to make money by investing it wisely, or to raise money quickly if you need it. Another reason for buying and selling shares is to make a quick profit without actually having had to part with any money at any stage in the transaction. Like the gambling which goes on in the currency exchange, it all happens on paper, or on the computer screen via the internet. One of the favourite techniques is to buy shares, even though you do not have the money to pay for them, hoping to sell them again at a higher price, before the time for your having to pay for them falls due. Alternatively you can sell shares which you do not possess, in the hope that you can buy them from someone else at a lower price than what you will be paid for them, and before the time arrives when you are meant to be 'handing them over' to the person to whom you originally sold them before you had them. In using either of these techniques it is possible to make a large profit from nothing other than skilful juggling along the telephone lines. Of course if, like the freemasons, you already have the capital at your disposal in the first place, then you can buy and sell shares at leisure, hoping that the market forces will eventually enable you to sell for more than you bought, or to buy for less than what you will eventually sell.

It is on the commodity, stock and money exchanges that the power struggles for control of the kafir producer consumer system, that is the Dajjal system, are conducted. It is from these power struggles that money is made. Thus even at the very tip of the producer consumer pyramid, the principle of divide and rule is applied. The main division is between those who control and those who are controlled. In financial terms this is the difference between those who lend money, and those who borrow money.

Any large corporation in its infancy has to borrow money in order to grow. One of the ways in which this is done is to borrow money from one source, then to go to another source and borrow more money using the sum you have already borrowed as security for the second loan. Having in effect, doubled your money on the strength of nothing, you then go to another source and borrow more money again using the money you have accumulated thus far as security. This process can usually be repeated up to eight times in succession by a corporation which is sufficiently large enough to command a good credit-rating. Having amassed sufficient funds by this method, the corporation then has to embark on a business venture which will reap sufficient profits to pay back all the loans and the interest thereon. In order to do this its controllers must be ruthless, and all the successful ones are.

There comes a time when a successful corporation has generated enough activity, and accrued sufficient capital not to have to borrow any more. At this stage it can begin to take over other smaller corporations and companies, either by agreement or by sharp dealing on the stock exchange. There comes a point where a really large corporation has amassed enough capital in enough different countries to be able to have its own internal banking system, which works independently from, but not in competition with, the main international banking system. In effect, the multi-national corporation 'bank' is in a position to pursue all the profitable activities enjoyed by kafir banking as a whole – such as loaning money on interest and financing profitable projects for a price – whilst the corporation is released from the liabilities which it would incur if it still relied on the main kafir banking system – such as, for example, having to pay bank charges every time large sums of money are transferred from one country to another, or being subject to exchange control regulations, or having to pay interest on loans raised for new projects.

By having their own 'banks', the multi-national corporations ensure their freedom to act. Since they and the main kafir banking system are not in competition with each other, because all the chief controllers concerned are freemasons, the money which the large multi-national corporations expend, sooner or later finds its way into the main banking system, which can then make it grow by lending twelve thirteenths of it at interest, or by investing that proportion profitably on the stock exchange.

The main kafir banking system does not stop creating money out of nothing at this stage. Firstly, the money which has been created by charging interest can then be loaned out again and thus accrue further interest. This process can continue ad infinitum. Secondly, the man who borrows a thousand pounds for example, will probably put some of it in the bank. Although to him it is a minus amount, in the sense that it is not really his to spend because he will eventually have to pay it back, to the bank it is a plus amount in the sense that twelve thirteenths of what has been deposited can be loaned out again, or otherwise invested. This process can also continue ad infinitum.

As far as 'small man in the street' transactions are concerned, the aforementioned banking practices do not appear to be significant, although of course when all the small transactions in the world are added together, it is clear that the banking system makes a considerable profit even out of these. Where these practices do become significant is in the large multi-national transactions. Loans of several million dollars or pounds accrue much interest in a short time. This means that the subservience of the debtor to the loaning bank is correspondingly greater. It also means that the pool of wealth, which the loaning bank accumulates by multiplying it through charging interest on what is loaned, increases at such a rate that in the end it does not really matter whether or not a particular loan is repaid. No-one in the bank is going to starve if the loan is not repaid. What is important, however, is that the bank is in a position to dictate to the borrower the conditions on which the obligation to repay the interest or the loan or both will be waived, and it is in an even stronger position to lay down further conditions under which further sums will be loaned, such as, for example, in what projects the new loans must be invested. In effect, by creating the debt, the bank gains control over whoever has borrowed the money.

The ultimate expression of the 'control through debt' and 'motivation through fear' syndromes is to be seen in the activities of the International Monetary Fund and of the World Bank. Basically the I.M.F. lends money to the so-called 'developed' countries of the High Tec North, whilst the World Bank lends money to the countries of the 'third' world, that is the so-called 'less-developed' countries of the Poor South. These two financial institutions have so much money, on paper at any rate – or rather, in computer – that it has no meaning as money per se. What it really means is control over every government in the world – because there is not a government in the world today which is not in debt – and once a government is in debt it can then be told how to spend the money which is subsequently lent to it; and it can be told that if it does 'this' then there will be more funds available; and it can be told that if it does 'that' then there will be no more funds available.

This is the principal way in which the freemasonic controlling elite of the kafir system, that is the Dajjal system, attempt to control the world. The freemasonic controlled banking system loans money to governments, and continues to loan to them even after they have become heavily indebted, and can never hope to repay all the money back, on the condition that they do as they are told. This is the reality of what is called neo-colonialism. Although it is said that the countries in question have been given their so-called independence, in fact this has only been granted once the country in question has become totally involved in the kafir consumer producer process, and totally reliant on the kafir banking system to finance that process.

Most of the larger national debts in the non-Muslim countries were created and developed during the eighteenth and nineteenth centuries, while most of the national debts in the Muslim countries were created during the twentieth century, largely thanks to the efforts of Jamal'ud-Din Al-Afghani, Muhammad Abdou and Rashid Reda, who, having been granted the dubious privilege of becoming members of Lord Cromer's freemasonic lodge – Lord Cromer was a member of the notorious Barings banking family – eventually managed to 'persuade' the Muslim rulers of the day, more by means of bribery than the original teachings of Islam, that certain types of usury were 'not haram', and that it was not only 'halal' but indeed preferable to use paper money – thereby facilitating the introduction of the utterly haram banking system into the Muslim lands in the name of progress, development and modernisation.

o   o   o   o   o

Since all national debts have been structured in such a way that they will never be repaid – even England's national debt, which was initiated with a £1.2 million loan to King William of Orange, was deliberately structured on the basis of irredeemable annuities – and since by the operation of compound interest combined with the additional borrowing that always occurs in times of war, all national debts can only and have only grown ever larger – at the time of writing this, for example, England's national debt is now approaching the £300 billion mark – one of the inevitable results has been that taxation of the general population in virtually every kafir state in the world has also continued to grow steadily through the years – which is why nowadays many people who do vote tend to vote for whoever promises to tax them the least.

This in fact is the economic basis of 'modern democracy': a state whose government is elected to service the national debt by taxing the general electorate. This is the reality of the 'control through debt' and 'motivation through fear' syndromes. This is the basis of the new world order. Inexorable economic control disguised by liberal political debate.

○   ○   ○   ○   ○

Thus, to summarise, the people who really rule the kafir states of today are not the politicians who appear on television, but rather the people who control the major finance and business institutions, that is the freemasons. Effective control is exercised especially by using the kafir banking system to create debts by charging interest, which grow so large that they can never be repaid. In order to speed up the process of creating debts, the freemasons, as we have already seen, create conflict situations out of which profits are made by selling the goods – especially armaments and food – needed by the sides who have been drawn into conflict, at a high price, and out of which debts are created by providing those goods on credit at interest.

The conflict situations created by the freemasons vary, from manipulating market forces – especially in the commodity markets and on the stock and money exchanges – to engineering war on a large scale. Thus, for example, in order to curb the wealth of the Muslim oil-producing countries during the boom of the 1970s – and especially after the price of oil was quadrupled by OPEC in 1973 in response to the High Tec North's support of Israeli military aggression against the Arabs in the Yom Kippur War – the cost of crude oil from the Middle East was soon reduced, not only by re-negotiating the price per barrel, but also by devaluing the currencies of all the oil-producing countries – by revaluing the exchange rates within the international banking system, as well as by manipulating supply and demand and therefore value on the international money markets.

During the 1980s, Iraq was armed, at its own expense, in order to wage war on and weaken Iran. Once this had been achieved – increasing both Iraq's and Iran's dependence on the international banking system in the process – Iraq was then encouraged to invade Kuwait, while at the same time Saudi Arabia and the Gulf states were warned that if American troops – accompanied by token forces from other countries to create the impression of its being an 'international' affair – were not permitted to come to their rescue, at their expense, then they would be the next to be invaded by Iraq. The troops came, the Gulf War ensued, all the latest technological weapons (including the chemical ones and their vaccines) were tested, Kuwait was destroyed and had to be rebuilt, at its own expense, much of Iraq was destroyed and its population decimated, and Saudi Arabia and all the Gulf states spent billions on financing the war and buying obsolete armaments in order to ensure that the same thing did not happen all over again.

During the early 1990s therefore, vast profits were made by the armaments industry, and vast profits were made by the international banking system as funds poured out of the Middle East into the High Tec North at one rate of exchange and then eventually back again, once it was all over, at another rate of exchange. As a result the oil-wealth of the Middle East had been reduced to virtually nothing, and as if to emphasise the hold which the international banking system now enjoys over Saudi Arabia and the Gulf states, the BCCI Arab bank was closed down almost overnight, wiping out much of the Muslims' 'wealth' throughout the world in the process.

Once again, everything had gone more or less according to plan and the architects of the new world order had triumphed. This was the same kind of carefully orchestrated activity of which both Ezra Pound and Adolf Hitler were fully aware, and tried to prevent, but without any success.

○   ○   ○   ○   ○

Perhaps one of the main reasons why Pound and Hitler failed to expose and destroy the activities of the freemasons was because they were not fully aware of the true nature of existence. The true nature of existence is that nothing exists, only Allah. It follows that anything other than Allah only appears to exist if you give it reality.

The way of Muhammad, may the blessings and peace of Allah be on him, means that reality is given to Allah. The way of kufr means that reality is given to other than Allah.

If enough of the people who are at present enslaved by the kafir system, that is the Dajjal system, and who are accordingly imprisoned

Dajjal – the king who has no clothes

by the kafir view of existence, decide to follow the way of Muhammad, and accordingly cease to give reality to what they have been conditioned to give reality to by the educational and media systems, then the producer consumer process will collapse and cease to exist – especially once the Muslims abandon the banks and their worthless paper and plastic money.

Thus the way to fight the kafir system, that is the Dajjal system, is not to fight it, but to leave it. Ignore it. The way to leave the system is to follow the way of Muhammad, may Allah bless him and grant him peace. The system is already in an advanced state of collapse. Accordingly it is becoming easier and easier to leave it, and to follow the way of Muhammad – and when the system does collapse, it will be the Muslims who will best be able to cope with what happens next. The choice is yours, right now.

✿ ✿ ✿ ✿ ✿

One of the main reasons why the kafir system, that is the Dajjal system, is in an advanced stage of self-destruction and collapse is that the money, which is the life-blood of the consumer producer process, and which is the medium by which control through debt is exercised through the banking system, is only really worth the paper on which it is printed. As the life-blood of the producer consumer system it is totally anaemic.

Money only succeeds in its role as the medium by which control through debt is exercised through the banking system because enough people think it is worth something. Money, however, only has the value which people ascribe to it, but it has no inherent value of its own. Money is only numbers printed on bits of paper or stored in mega-computer data-bases.

Anyone who uses this kind of money is part of a gigantic confidence trick. Once the trick is exposed it is impossible to place any confidence in either paper, or plastic, or micro-chip money.

The endless discussions on the illusory topic of inflation, and the futile attempts to resolve the illusory problem of inflation are only either decoys, smoke screens or red herrings, to disguise the fact that the real issue is not the question of money losing value, simply because it has no real value to lose in the first place.

The reason why money has absolutely no value today, other than the illusory value which the great majority of people are conditioned to give it, is on account of the way in which it has been and is handled by the international banking system and the international money markets. In order to appreciate this fact, it is necessary to look at what money used to be, before the present banking system was first introduced.

        o   o   o   o   o

Money used to be made principally of gold or silver. Since it was made from these precious metals it had inherent value. Even if it was melted down, its value did not change – unlike paper money which at *Fahrenheit 451* ignites and turns to ashes. Coins minted in different countries of the world could nevertheless be used as a means of exchange in any other country in the world, once the quality and purity of the gold or silver used to mint the coin was established, simply by weighing it. As a result, the value of money remained more or less constant, while the prices of the goods for which it was exchanged fluctuated as the market forces of supply and demand varied.

Furthermore, up until the time of the Reformation of the European Trinitarian Church, which occurred during the sixteenth century, usurious transactions were forbidden for and avoided by all believing Jews, Christians and Muslims. During the Reformation, however, the Jews argued that they were entitled to charge non-Jews interest, the Christians argued that instead of 'no interest' they would permit 'low interest', and at a much later stage some of the Muslims argued that if interest was given a different name, like 'service charge', then it was no longer interest. As soon as interest began to be charged, the value of money was affected, since it had now become a commodity in itself, not merely a means of exchange, and accordingly its value was now marginally subject to the market forces of supply and demand.

The first banks were formed to look after other people's money by keeping it in a safe place, although of course even at this stage money still had a palpable and valuable form. The practice arose whereby when someone deposited gold or silver in the bank, the banker would give the depositor a written receipt, whereby he promised to repay 'the bearer on demand' the gold or silver when that receipt was presented to him. The practice then arose that these receipts became transferable. Thus the depositor of the gold was able to buy goods to the value of the gold in the bank, by giving his receipt to the seller of the goods. The seller of the goods could then take that receipt to the bank, and collect the gold, even though it was not he who had originally deposited the gold there.

Since gold and silver are relatively heavy, and since paper is relatively light, the bankers then hit upon the idea of printing paper money. Anyone who deposited gold and silver with them was given this paper money. That paper money could then be used in any number of consecutive transactions, the understanding being that anyone at any time who had these notes come into his or her possession could, if he or she wanted, take them to the bank and exchange them for the gold or silver which they represented.

At this relatively simple stage, during the mid-nineteenth century, every paper note was backed by its equivalent amount of gold or silver. You could exchange one for the other at any time. It was also at this stage, if not before, that the bankers discovered that for every thirteen pounds of gold or silver deposited with them only one of these thirteen pounds was actually physically required by the customer to spend at any one time, which left the bankers free to loan on interest, or otherwise profitably invest, the other twelve pounds.

This meant, in effect, that for every thirteen paper pound notes, only one needed to be backed by gold, and this is what happened. It was no longer the case that every paper note referred back to its equivalent in gold or silver. Instead, for every pound's worth of gold or silver which the banks had in their vaults, thirteen paper pound notes were printed.

At this stage, however, you could still go into the bank, produce a paper pound, ask for a pound's worth of gold, and get it. Provided that not everyone tried to exchange their paper money for gold or silver at the same time, the banks were 'safe', even though in fact not all the paper money was backed by gold any more. At this stage, in real terms, paper money was only really 'worth' one thirteenth of what it used to be worth.

Gradually people became so used to using paper money that no-one even thought of going to the bank and asking for gold or silver in exchange. Everyone believed that the paper money was 'worth' what it said it was worth on its two sides, that is its 'face' value. At the same time the volume of the banks' business was increasing, as the origins of what is today's consumer producer process began to get under way and become established. This meant that the banking system was creating more and more money, not by printing more bank notes, but by charging interest.

Debts owed to the banks – especially vast national debts – grew on paper in the ledgers, as the interest ticked up, but the money created in this way had no direct connection with the money which was already in existence, and which was backed by gold in the proportion of thirteen paper to one gold or silver. In effect, money was being created out of nothing, and this 'out of nothing' money was not even being manifested in the form of pound notes, but was merely being given a tenuous reality by being recorded in a ledger, or as today, in a computer.

This put the banks in a more precarious position. If, for example, everyone decided to draw their paper money out of the bank at the same time, the banks simply would not be able to produce it, simply because the volume of money, which was recorded as existing in the ledgers or in the computers, was so much greater than the number of printed money notes in actual circulation. Thus at this stage there were two credibility tricks which the banks had to play on the growing number of customers, who were needed by the banks for both profit and manipulation purposes.

The first trick was to fool everyone into thinking that all the paper money was still 'backed' by gold, even though people no longer tried to change paper notes for their gold equivalent. The second trick was to fool everyone into thinking that all the money, which existed according to the computer and ledger records, actually existed in the form of paper notes. Neither of these illusions created by the freemasonic magician bankers was real, but as long as the great majority of the population thought they were real, then the whole magical but totally illusory system continued to work, and indeed continues to work today.

As a result of the massive debts created during the first world war – according to 'official' estimates there was a 475 per cent increase in the world's national debts as a whole between 1914 and 1920 – the vast gulf that now existed between the volume of money that had been created through interest, and the volume of paper money that had actually been printed, was so great that it was no longer feasible to maintain the thirteen paper to one gold ratio. During the next decade, therefore, the international banking system abandoned the gold standard altogether, and from this point onwards it was no longer possible to take a paper note into a bank and demand its equivalent in gold or silver. From this point onwards, the 'value' of paper currencies could be altered by the international banking system and the international money markets almost at will. From this point onwards the 'value' of money was increasingly determined by supply and demand on the international money markets and by 'government policy' as regards exports, imports and the balance of payments.

As a result of the even more massive debts created during the second world war, and after two hundred years of compound interest at work, the world's national debts were now so ridiculously large that supra-national banking institutions such as the I.M.F. and the World Bank had to be created in order to regulate a situation where millions and billions and trillions were being made and lost in accordance with predetermined – and eventually fully computerised – mathematical formulas. 'Inflation' had come of age.

Clearly one of the greatest dangers to the freemasonic banking system was and is that too many people would ask for too much paper money at the same time. Although endless amounts of more paper money could easily be printed, with a very large numeral being printed on each individual piece of paper to represent its face value if necessary, there was always the danger that the general public would see through the illusion and realise that however large the number which had been printed on the note, it still was not really worth a penny.

It was only by having a carefully regulated flow of paper money – not too plentiful, and not too scarce – that the illusion of normality and 'business as usual' could be sustained and maintained. After all, very few people whose wealth was tied up in the banking system could bear the thought of the fragile web being blown away, of the whole system collapsing, of their discovering that their tens, or their hundreds, or their thousands, or even their millions or billions or trillions, were all equally worthless.

In order to regulate this supply and demand difficulty, and to keep the now fluctuating value of money within what appeared to be 'reasonable' limits, people like John Maynard Keynes came up with new theories of economics which were in keeping with the new paper-based interest-inflated currencies of the world, and which were designed to replace the Victorian theories of laissez faire, which could only, and had only, worked in a situation where real money, gold and silver with inherent value, was being used.

Basically Keynes drew people's attention to the fact that the demand for paper money in the hand could be regulated, by making spending and saving either more or less attractive, by raising or lowering the bank rate, that is the rate at which interest would be charged on loans and paid out on savings deposits. Put very simply, the higher the rate, the more it costs to borrow and the more interest you will receive on your savings deposits. Accordingly high interest rates encourage people to borrow less, spend less and save more. Conversely low interest rates encourage people to borrow more and therefore spend more, and to save less because if money is not going to 'grow', very quickly, you might as well spend it.

In effect, Keynes's theories of economics appeared to achieve two things. Firstly, when applied to the producer consumer process, they were used to regulate the pace and extent of business activity, by making it more or less profitable and therefore possible. Secondly, they were used to regulate the demand for paper money, by regulating the pace and extent of borrowing and saving – and therefore of spending.

Today there has been a further development in the international banking system's strategy to ensure that not too many people ask for money which does not even exist in paper form, but only in computer memory, at the same time. Basically they are attempting to make it unnecessary to have money at all. This has been done by encouraging not only cheque transactions, but also the increasing use of plastic card transactions.

The way that the plastic card transaction works is that when you produce your plastic card, which contains information as to your identity, together with the bank's guarantee that it will honour your financial commitments incurred by using that card, then a record of that information is made and sent to the bank together with the relevant details of the transaction, and the bank debits your account and credits the account of the person from whom, for example, you have bought the goods.

In this kind of transaction no money passes hands. All that happens is that figures are moved from one field to another in the banking network computer database memory. As more and more of these transactions occur and become commonplace, paper money increasingly ceases to have relevance. If this way of transacting is carried out to its ultimate and logical extent, then eventually there will be hardly any demand for paper money at all, because virtually all transactions will be carried out via the plastic card, and the monetary result recorded in the bank's computer – a plus here, and a minus there – and of course with a little nibble here and a little nibble there for the bank, which not only charges the buyer interest on whatever has been 'borrowed' in order to complete the transaction, but which also charges the seller a percentage of the total amount of any given transaction.

This trend – assisted by the widespread use of direct debit and direct credit facilities – has been reflected in England, for example, by the fact that since 1986 people have no longer had the right to be paid in the 'coin of the realm' – which up until the mid-nineteenth century used to be predominantly gold and silver, rather than paper, until, as we have already seen, the gold and silver were withdrawn from circulation, and paper introduced instead. Now that an employer is no longer obliged to pay employees in the 'paper of the realm', this means that employees can be paid either by cheque or by a direct credit to the employee's bank account, instead of in 'cash'. In other words, virtually everyone in England now 'needs' to have a bank account in order to have access to their pay. In other words, virtually everyone in the country now relies on the banking system.

The general aim is to eventually have the plastic card system operating throughout the world, because that will mean that virtually everyone is dependant on the banking system, and that will mean that everyone is that more easy to control. If, for example, all your 'wealth' is stored in your bank's computer database, then it can be 'frozen' at the touch of a button, or deductions can be made at source in compliance with, for example, a court order. In other words, if you value your 'money', then you will have to behave.

Conversely, on the other side of the 'coin' so to speak, this is why today's bank robber no longer needs a balaclava, a gun and getaway car, but rather a computer, a modem and the software and ability needed to hack into and out of the banking network computer system.

If this trend within the banking system continues along its way, then by the twenty-first century most people's credit cards will be their identity cards. Everyone's personal details will be on the computer, their income and expenditure subject to assessment and analysis, their credit-rating monitored, even their movements recorded via the bank computer's record of the times and places where their plastic cards have been used – and of course everyone will be encouraged to spend more than they actually have, to be constantly in debt, just like whatever government they may 'choose' to elect – which, whatever the state of the balance of payments, will always have a growing national debt to service, as long as the system lasts.

And as the different computer databases increase their interlink capacity – the banking database, the TV licence database, the house-owner database, the car-owner database, the electricity, gas and water supplies databases, the telephone database, the various social benefits databases, the electoral role database, the various police records and national security databases, to name but a few – then perhaps the scenario envisaged in George Orwell's *Nineteen Eighty-Four* will not seem quite as far-fetched as when the book was first published in 1949 – or even as when the year 1984 itself came and went, with the new world order still, at that point, to be publicly announced.

o o o o o

We see, therefore, that the influence of the kafir system, that is the Dajjal system, through its international banking system, has almost reached the stage where paper money is not only worthless, but also it does not matter that it is worthless, because everyone now depends on the banks for their services in conducting their financial transactions. The banks themselves have become the medium of exchange – and now virtually every transaction can be done with a piece of plastic, or over the telephone, or on the internet. Paper money has almost become redundant. And as the internet becomes more established, financial transactions are becoming even more tenuous and even less 'physical' than ever before.

If you use the internet to make a purchase, then you do not even have to hand your credit card over to another person to be swiped, or sign the receipt; you do not even have to talk to a person over the telephone to give them your credit card number, expiry date and security code; all it needs is a few taps on your computer keyboard, a few clicks on your mouse, and goods can be advertised or purchased, bills paid or sent, stocks and shares bought or sold, and fortunes made or lost.

o o o o o

And if the power supply which makes it all possible for this fragile web to function is suddenly cut, then what? Allah is the power which powers the power supply. There is no strength and no power except from Allah.

It is on usury that the new world order is based – and since it is based on usury it is bound to collapse, because usury is forbidden, and because

Allah and His Messenger have declared war on usury:

> O you who believe, fear Allah and give up what remains to you of usury, if you are indeed believers. If you do not, then take notice of war from Allah and His Messenger.
>
> (*Qur'an: Surat'al-Baqara* – 2.278-279)

Who has ever been at war with Allah and His Messenger, may the blessings and peace of Allah be on him, and won? And even if there were no war on usury, all things must pass.

○   ○   ○   ○   ○

People in a kafir society are not only manoeuvred into needing the banking system, but, as we have already seen, they are also encouraged to spend more than they have, and accordingly to become indebted to the various financial institutions, especially the banks. This ensures continued dependence on the freemasonic controlled kafir banking system, whether by the man in the street at his local branch, or by the government of a country at its 'central' bank or at the World Bank or the I.M.F. It is at this stage that the actual extent of the indebtedness is seen to be irrelevant. After all it only exists in the computer.

What is significant is the actual extent of the dependence on the banking system, for the greater the dependence on it, the greater the manipulation control it exercises, and accordingly the greater is the influence of the kafir system, that is the Dajjal system, over the world. The degree and significance of that control and that influence can be measured by the fact that if you merely closed down all the banks for a little while – or rather if you just turned off the banking computer network – then the whole consumer producer process as we know it today would collapse, and then it would be time for the next world order.

○   ○   ○   ○   ○

The aim of the freemasons is to perfect the kafir system, that is the Dajjal system, by involving everyone in the producer consumer process, as far as their work and consumption of goods is concerned, whilst ensuring the smooth running and overall balance of activity in that process, by having everyone and every business concern dependent on their banking system.

In effect, they wish to arrive at the stage where the people of the world are completely caught up in one synchronised and unified field of activity, that is economic activity. If this aim were to be achieved, there would of course be only one currency, which would not even take the form of paper money, but which would be identified solely in terms of computer credits and debits. Ideally everyone would have their basic needs taken care of, but of course some would have them taken care of better than others, and the freemasonic ruling elite would have them taken care of best of all, as has always been the case. This would mean that everyone would be relatively comfortable in the freemasonic idea of paradise now on earth made fact – but they would be completely unprepared for what comes after death.

Fortunately we know from the *Qur'an* and the *Hadith* that this illusory dream will never be realised. The new world order is doomed to fail. There will inevitably be a collapse in the kafir system, that is the Dajjal system, before the freemasons' ideal can ever be made to happen. The social decay which accompanies the way in which the system operates means that the people who are most exploited by the system will cease to play the consumer producer game long before this dream of a unified global economic pyramid can be realised.

The point in time is bound to be reached when enough people realise that the money in their pockets and the money recorded in the computer memory – whether the figures are 'plus' or 'minus' – is absolutely worthless. This will mean that they will cease to become dependent on the kafir banking system, and this will happen long before everyone has been issued with their plastic economic identity cards.

Most important of all is the fact that the present resurgence of Islam means that more and more people are severing connections with the kafir system, that is the Dajjal system, and are accordingly ceasing to be trapped by the system. The more people cease to give reality to the system, the more it ceases to exist. As the number of real Muslims grows, and as they begin to reunite, so the controllers of the Dajjal system will try to wipe them out. These attempts will find their most extreme expression when Dajjal the individual has appeared, and leads his army against the Muslims who have gathered around the Mahdi.

This final and ultimate conflict between the two opposites, kufr and iman, which is referred to in other writings as Armageddon, or Har Meggidon, will result in the death of Dajjal the individual and his followers, and indeed of the whole Dajjal system, thanks to the reappearance and intervention of the Prophet Jesus, on whom be peace.

The period of unified and peaceful Muslim rule, in accordance with what is in the *Qur'an* and the *Sunnah*, under the Mahdi, the rightly guided leader of the Muslims, will then commence. This will be the next world order.

❂   ❂   ❂   ❂   ❂

The mumin understanding of the nature of money is utterly opposite that of the kafir system of economics. This is because it is based on an understanding of the true nature of existence. The mumin knows that only Allah exists, although this knowing differs from person to person. Some know it intellectually and others know it through direct witnessing. It follows that the mumin knows that since money does not really exist, it is worth nothing, right from the start. To the mumin money is just a medium of exchange, but not a commodity in itself. There is thus absolutely no point in hanging on to it whatsoever, and since the mumin has no anxiety about provision and shelter, his commerce is, as we have already seen, based on giving out in the knowledge that whatever he or she gives out will be returned by Allah ten times over.

There is no need for the Muslims to amass capital in the way that the kafir banks do, because their capital is the generosity of Allah, which is limitless. There is no need for the Muslims to borrow and lend on interest, because Allah's return on any gift made in the Name of Allah is far higher than any interest that anyone could hope to charge – that is, the equivalent of one thousand per cent. There is no need to manipulate people by getting them into debt, because since the body politic of the muslim community is unified there is no body of people within it who seek to control and manipulate and exploit the others.

The only elite in the muslim community are the awliya, whose stations are greater than the others because they fear and love Allah more than the others; it is because of their great knowledge of Allah and therefore of how existence works that they know that the more they serve the others, and the more they give out in the Name of Allah, the more Allah will look after them and give them what they want – which in their case is not other than what they need.

Muslim commerce is based on trust and on giving out. It is dynamic and free flowing. There is no need for Keynesian control techniques. Kafir economics is based on exploitation of others and retention. It is static and stagnant. It stinks. As 'Umar Ibrahim Vadillo points out in his book, *Islam Against Economics*:

Islamic Law defines the parameters within which trade and business will be just. Economics defines the parameters within which an economy will be more efficient. Islamic Law and economics are totally different approaches to existence that create two different ways of life. Islam rejects usury, while economics is based on usury. Economics has managed to justify what is Islamically a crime. This is possible because economics has a methodology and an object of study which covers up the inherent injustice of usury. In other words, economics can neither properly analyse nor identify the nature of usury.

And as 'Umar Ibrahim Vadillo concludes in his book, *The Workers have been Told a Lie about their own Situation*:

> The only way out of the usurious system is Islam. Because only Islam is government without state and commerce without usury. The age of judaism and christianity is over. Only by understanding that 'there is no god but Allah', can the people stop worshipping useless perishing things, like the state, money and their job, and be free. Only by accepting 'Muhammad is the Messenger of Allah' can there be justice in the transaction. Islam or Economics, Islam or the Banking System, this is the decision everybody will have to make.

It is clear, from this analysis, that there is no such thing as a halal 'islamic' bank. As 'Umar Ibrahim Vadillo observes in his book, *The End of Economics*:

> The so-called 'Islamic bank' is a usurious institution contrary to Islam. The fallacy of the 'Islamic bank' is an absurd attempt to resolve, as was done in the case of Christianity, the unswerving opposition of Islam to usury for fourteen centuries. Since its origin the 'Islamic bank' has been patronised and promoted by usurers. Their only intention was to incorporate the thousand million Muslims of the world – who in general would scornfully avoid using any banking or usurious institution – into the international financial and monetary system. The artificial creation by the colonial powers of the so-called 'Islamic states', itself a contradiction in terms, whose character is markedly anti-Islamic, was the

historical result of the end of territorial colonisation and the beginning of financial neo-colonisation. The universal establishment of the western constitutional model (the model of the french revolution) brings with it the establishment of artificial and unnatural boundaries, the creation of a repressive ministerial bureaucracy, the exacting of taxes, the imposition of an artificial yet legal money, and the legalisation of usury itself (the banking system), all measures which are profoundly contrary to Islam. The Islamic bank is nothing other than a typically degenerate product of the so-called 'Islamic states'.

And as 'Umar Ibrahim Vadillo concludes in his book, *Fatwa on Paper Money*:

> The founders of the so-called Salafiyya movement or modernist movement were the first to declare publicly from a recognised position, like the University of al-Azhar, that the use of banking was halal. The implications of this declaration can be seen in our day with the implantation in the Muslim lands of the 'Islamic Bank'. The 'Islamic Bank' is a completely usurious institution used as a means to lure the Muslims who still reject the banks to enter in the banking system. The 'Islamic Bank' is a Trojan horse in Dar al-Islam.

    ✪   ✪   ✪   ✪   ✪

Given the dynamic nature of muslim commerce, it comes as no surprise to learn that the value of money, in the time of the first muslim community of Madina al-Munawarra, was based not on how much gold or silver it could buy – because their money was gold and silver – but on how much gold or silver was needed to buy a given volume of grain.

Since grain was readily available, unless there was a severe drought, and could be grown by anyone, it followed that it could not be used – by either withholding it or flooding the market with it – to make the value of money fluctuate, in the way that the artificially limited gold and silver markets of today are manipulated in order to raise and lower the apparent value of today's worthless money, almost at will. This meant that the basic value of money – in other words, its purchasing power – remained stable in Madina al-Munawarra, and accordingly there was no such thing as what the kafirun call 'inflation'. Furthermore, since the taxes required by the *Qur'an* are so low, it followed that there was no stimulus to make people raise their prices in order to beat the effects of the taxes, as happens in today's 'modern' so-called advanced kafir state. Accordingly prices remained stable, and so again there was no inflation caused by rising prices.

Furthermore, since it is not permissible to make more than thirty per cent profit on essential goods, the Muslims in that first community did not raise prices too high out of sheer greed, if they feared Allah and the Last Day – which they did. Since the value of money was stable, and since prices were stable, it followed that incomes were stable, so there was no inflation caused by excessive 'wage demands', as happens today in the so-called 'modern' kafir state.

Finally, since Allah expressly forbids the charging of interest, saying more than once in the *Qur'an* that it is haram, and will take you to the Fire if you indulge in it, it follows that there was no opening for the kind of business institution which today lives off other people's indebtedness to it, by charging interest.

Allah says in the *Qur'an* that the first community of Madina al-Munawarra was the best community that has ever lived on the face of the earth. It follows that in order to know how to live, it is necessary to see how they lived. Having seen this, it is possible to apply their way of doing things to the way we do things today. The kafir argument that their way of life is now 'out of date', and does not and cannot apply to the twenty-first century, is palpably weak. The scenery and the props may change, but the human situation remains the same, and the way of the first community is the best way of dealing with it – and it will remain so until the end of time. Following the way of the first community of Madina al-Munawarra does not mean religiously imitating their way of life in every detail. It does not mean having to abandon today's technology, where that technology can be usefully used, and used with the discrimination between what is halal and what is haram.

The way of the first community was based on what is in the *Qur'an* and on the example of the Prophet Muhammad, may Allah bless him and grant him peace, who was described by his wife 'A'isha as being 'the *Qur'an* walking'. Records of that example still exist today, both in the *Qur'an* and the *Hadith* collections, and in human beings, notably the awliya, who have had the existential way of living of the Prophet and the knowledge which goes with it transmitted to them, person to person, from the time of the Prophet Muhammad and the first community up until the present day, without a break in that chain of transmission.

The nature of the *Qur'an* is such that the guidance in it can be applied to any situation. Where there is no specific mention of what to do in the situation in which you find yourself, it is still possible to see what to do by doing ijtihad. Ijtihad is the process whereby you see what to do in the light of what you know of what is in the *Qur'an* and the *Hadith* and the way of Muhammad. To begin with it is a conscious thinking process, but as the heart becomes more finely tuned and illuminated, ijtihad becomes a reflex action. You know what to do and what not to do in the moment, and without having to think about it. If you are not sure about something all you have to do is open the *Qur'an*, and you will see the ayah that is the sign which contains the answer. Thus it is not only Muslim commerce which is dynamic, but the whole way of life in whatever sphere. The nature of phenomenal existence is such that there is a constant and dynamic interplay of many opposites, which is always in motion and never exactly repeats itself, even though patterns and cycles are clearly recognisable. You are part of that interplay. You are not separate from it.

The way of Muhammad, may the blessings and peace of Allah be on him and on all who follow him, is the way of knowing what to do in that interplay, so that you never fight it, but go with it. By living in this way you arrive at knowledge of Allah from Whom this interplay of opposites originates and returns – not only in the very beginning, and at the very end, but also in every moment. By living in this way you arrive at knowledge of yourself, and you find that the whole of existence is your self, and whoever knows their self truly knows their Lord, Allah. When you live in this way and with this knowledge then you are a human being, who acts with humanity and with humility. You are pleased with Allah and Allah is pleased with you, and in this state you enter the Garden.

✿ ✿ ✿ ✿ ✿

The result of the way in which all the kafir sub-systems and institutions in the kafir system, that is the Dajjal system, work and operate, is to de-personalise and de-humanise the human transaction. Where in the past people used to give to each other, now they charge each other for services rendered. Where once common sense, generosity, wisdom, flexibility, and above all humanity, used to characterise human transactions, now the rules of the various systems which together form the Dajjal system are often applied with automatic and unfeeling inflexibility, even when the outcome is patently ridiculous. The complementary descriptions which are used to affirm and promote the system do not in the least accord with what is actually going on as conditions in general steadily continue to deteriorate. The more citizens' charters and other official guarantees there are, the less people are treated like human beings. Patients in hospitals are now called 'customers' and people in general are now called 'consumers'. The words, the conditioning, the programming, the explanations, the reasons – all of these are no more than a web of illusion which has been spun by the controlling elite of the kafir system that is the Dajjal system, the freemasons, so that they can entangle and enslave the many, as they struggle to free themselves.

The kafir system, that is the Dajjal system, uses people until they are of no further use to that system – and then they are discarded. People are given numbers and treated like robots, because machines are much easier to control than human beings. Machines submit to whatever you do with them without complaint, provided they are kept in running order. There is no need to behave like a human being towards a machine, because machines cannot respond like humans. You just use them until they have come to the end of their working life, and then you get rid of them and carry on with their replacements – until, that is, the time comes for you to be replaced as well.

It is only possible to treat people like robots, because half the people in the kafir system, that is the Dajjal system, already are robots. The so-called people who are completely happy with the kafir system, that is the Dajjal system, are the people who have been taken over, are the living proof of the manifestation of Dajjal as a world wide social and cultural phenomenon and Dajjal as an unseen force, will be the people who recognise, support and follow Dajjal the individual when he appears, will be for the Fire. The people who abhor the kafir system that is the Dajjal system are the human beings who have not been taken over, who if they are not already Muslims will be Muslims, insh'Allah, who will recognise, support and follow the Mahdi when he appears, who are for the Garden.

You belong to either one group or the other group, and there is no third group. You cannot extricate yourself from the creational process of which you are a part, and which is based on the dynamic interplay of opposites. There is no escape. Turning your back on 'the problem' will not make it disappear. Hiding your head in the sand will not change who you are, but will merely make it extremely difficult to see where you are ultimately going. There is no hyper-space button to press and magically transfer you to another location or a different context. You can change your name, or your address, or your possessions, or your job, or your partner, but you cannot change your true identity.

There is one other definable group who in fact belong with the kafirun. This group are the munafiqun, that is the people who say they are muslim but who in reality are kafir, because they do not trust in Allah, and they do not follow the way of Muhammad, even though they know that it exists. The munafiqun can often be recognised by their constant criticism and bad opinion of the muminun. The Prophet Muhammad, may Allah bless him and grant him peace, said that the munafiqun have four main characteristics, even if they do the prayer and fast Ramadan: when they speak, they tell lies; when they argue they are abusive; when they make a promise, they act treacherously; and when they are trusted, they betray that trust.

The munafiqun are a part of the Dajjal system, and when the army of the Mahdi confronts the army of Dajjal the individual, the munafiqun will be with the followers of the Dajjal. In the next world the munafiqun will be in the deepest part of the Fire, because they did not act on what they knew in this world, that is they did not follow the way of Muhammad, even though it was there for them to follow, and they knew it.

The people who are attempting to follow the example of the Prophets who came before the Prophet Muhammad, such as, for example, those who brought the original Vedas, Buddha, Moses and Jesus, are in a difficult position. The sincere among them wish to worship Allah, but it is impossible for them to worship Allah in the way that Allah has indicated that He is to be worshipped, because the holy books which they now have are not the original books which their Prophets were given, blessings and peace be on them, and because the existential life pattern of those Prophets has been lost for ever.

It follows that the people who still attempt to follow the way of these Prophets in the present age, will never have true knowledge of Allah, because this knowledge only comes to the one who embodies what has been revealed to the Prophet whom he or she follows. If the existential life pattern of embodying that teaching has been lost, and if the teaching itself has been lost by having been changed by corrupt people in the past, then it is not possible to follow the original life pattern of the Prophet concerned or his original teaching, and therefore knowledge of the Real, Allah, is not possible, by holding to the remnants of these earlier teachings.

Allah says in the *Qur'an* that everything in creation worships Allah, only some people do not realise this. Every atom in existence is sustained by the power of Allah and is proof of Allah and worships Allah. All the kingdoms in the phenomenal world and in the Unseen praise Allah, but only man is capable of having gnosis of Allah. The one who has this knowledge of Allah worships and praises Allah with a greater understanding than any other created being or thing. The atoms in the body of a kafir bear witness to the limitless perfection and splendour of Allah, but with his or her words and actions the kafir denies the very existence of Allah. The atoms in the body of one who trusts in Allah bear witness to the limitless perfection and splendour of Allah, and so do his or her words and actions, and what is more the one who trusts in Allah knows this, and has knowledge of Allah.

Whoever tries to follow the way of one of the Prophets who came before the Prophet Muhammad, may Allah bless him and grant him peace, is somewhere in between these two opposites. The atoms in his or her body bear witness to the limitless perfection and splendour of Allah, but because he or she is not following a guidance which is still intact, it follows that only some but not all of his or her actions affirms this Reality and his or her understanding of what he or she is doing, and accordingly his or her understanding and knowledge of Allah, is therefore incomplete and inevitably partially distorted.

Only by knowing Allah can you truly worship Allah. The worship of Allah by the one who has gnosis of Allah is deeper than the worship of Allah by the one who only has an intellectual understanding of Allah, is deeper than the worship of Allah by the one who only has limited information about Allah, is deeper than the worship of Allah by the one who has distorted information about Allah, is deeper than the worship of Allah by the one who only worships Allah by virtue of the existence which Allah has given to him or her, but who consciously thinks that Allah does not exist.

The greater the knowledge that a person has of Allah, the more he or she realises that he or she knows nothing. Allah says again and again in the *Qur'an* that Allah knows and you do not know. One of the signs of ignorance is thinking you know when in fact you do not know. This is especially true of the kafirun, but it also applies to those who are content to try and follow the distorted remnants of earlier Prophetic teachings, which are now defunct and not really for this time.

Those who have not yet had access to the living life transaction of Islam cannot be blamed for not following it. Allah says of the people who follow Prophets other than Muhammad in this time, that those who worship Allah with sincerity have nothing to fear from Allah on the Last Day. Allah also says in the *Qur'an* that once a person knows about Islam, no other way of life is acceptable to Allah. Surely the life transaction with Allah is the life transaction of Islam.

The life transaction with Allah always has been the life transaction of islam. All the Prophets embodied the life transaction of islam – one of whose meanings is 'accepting the way things are', including 'submitting the self in worshipping Allah' – but the only life transaction of islam which is still intact today, and which is for today until the end of the world, is the life transaction of Islam which was brought by the Prophet Muhammad, may the blessings and peace of Allah be on him, and on his family, and on his companions, and on all who sincerely follow him – and right now the choice is yours.

o   o   o   o   o

The only viable alternative to the kafir system, that is the Dajjal system, is the way of Islam. All other apparent alternatives never succeed in being established. Either these movements are rapidly eliminated and annihilated by the system, or else they are reshaped and absorbed into the system, or else they are in reality already part and parcel of the system, and any apparent conflict between the two is merely on the surface.

The reason why Islam is the only viable alternative to the kafir system that is the Dajjal system is that the way of Islam is diametrically opposed to the way of Kufr. They are opposites, and one of the secrets of life is that everything lies in its opposite. In the dynamic interplay of opposites, which is the creational process, the interplay between kufr and iman is such, that once you have one, you will inevitably have the other. Anyone who is awake sees that this is true not only of themselves, but also of other individuals, of other families, of other communities, of other towns and cities, of other countries – and indeed of the whole world. Since, at the time of writing this, the kafir system that is the Dajjal system is the dominant force in the world today, it is inevitable that the life transaction of Islam must replace it tomorrow. Everything lies in its opposite, and there is no changing the way of Allah.

The only way of appreciating what the way of Islam is, is to become a Muslim if you are not one already, and to follow that way. No one can bring you to Islam and no one can take you away from it. Allah says in the *Qur'an* that there is no compulsion in the life transaction. It is Allah Who makes the straight way plain from the crooked one – and the straight way is the way of Islam, and it is as narrow as the edge between the two sides of the sharpest sword. This is why the wise who take this way rely on Allah for success.

It is Allah Who expands the heart to Islam. You cannot make people become muslim, even the ones you love. It is Allah Who gives the ability to discern the differences between kufr and iman, and between what is displeasing to Allah and what is pleasing to Allah, and between what is haram and what is halal, and between what words and actions lead to the Fire and what words and actions lead to the Garden.

Above all, it is Allah Who gives knowledge of Allah, to whomever He pleases, as He pleases. You will not acquire knowledge of Allah by looking for it, but only if you look for it will you acquire it. So do not rely on your actions, but rely on Allah.

In reality everything is from Allah, including everyone and whatever they do. The whole cosmos comes from and returns to Allah, and it does not contain Allah, but Allah contains it, and no form or idea in the seen or unseen worlds can be associated with Allah. Allah is not like anything. If you have an idea of Allah, Allah is not like that idea. You are the idea of Allah. The whole of creation is Allah's idea. To understand this you have to put your head on the ground before Allah. Until you have stood, and bowed, and prostrated, and sat in the presence of Allah in the same way that the Prophet Muhammad stood, and bowed, and prostrated, and sat in the presence of Allah, you cannot begin to appreciate what the way of Islam is, nor can you begin to have real knowledge, that is knowledge of the Real, Allah.

The reason why the Jews and the Christians cannot have real knowledge, that is knowledge of the Real, Allah, is that they do not do the same prayer as the prayer that their respective Prophets, Moses and Jesus, once did. The way that Moses and Jesus prayed, peace be on them, and the words that they actually used, have been lost for ever. The prayer of the Muslims, on the other hand, and the words they use, are the same as the prayer of the Prophet Muhammad, and the words that he actually used. When you recite the *Qur'an* you recite the words which the angel Gabriel recited to the Prophet Muhammad, may the blessings and peace of Allah be on him, and which the Prophet Muhammad recited to his followers, may Allah be pleased with all of them.

In reality everything is from Allah. The entire cosmos, both in the seen and in the unseen worlds – in the mulk, and in the malakut, and in the jabarut – is the manifestation of the Names and Attributes of Allah, which display the Beauty and the Majesty of Allah. All that people think good, and all that they think bad, is from Allah, by the decree of Allah. To have knowledge of Allah it is necessary to abandon all value judgements, and all 'moral' judgements. It is necessary to stop thinking, so that you can let the heart take over. Existence does not cease when you stop thinking – rather you see it in a different light. Relax the mind and learn to swim. Clean the heart with remembrance of Allah, in order that you may find what is in it. Allah. Allah said on the lips of the Prophet Muhammad, may the blessings and peace of Allah be on him, in a hadith qudsi, 'The whole universe cannot contain Me, but the heart of the mumin contains Me.' In Reality there is only Allah. Allah said on the lips of the Prophet, in a hadith qudsi, 'La ilaha il'Allah means Me and only Me.' Wherever you look, there is the face of Allah. Everything is passing away except the face of Allah. There is no reality, only the Reality. There is only Allah. Allah.

Allah guides whomever He wishes and Allah leads astray whomever He wishes. Allah gives life and Allah takes away life. Allah increases and decreases provision. Allah said, on the lips of the Prophet Muhammad, may the blessings and peace of Allah be on him, in a hadith qudsi, 'I send people to the Garden and I do not care, and I send people to the Fire and I do not care.' Allah is the doer of you and your actions, and you are responsible for your actions. On the Last Day you will not be asked what others were doing, you will be asked what you were doing, and you will not question Allah, but Allah will question you, and depending on what you did in this world, and the intentions behind what you did, and your expectation of Allah, and the mercy and wrath of Allah, you will either be for the Fire, or you will be for the Garden.

Allah has power over everything. There is no strength to do right action or wrong action, except from Allah. There is no strength and no power, except from Allah. You are helpless – but right now the choice is yours.

          o   o   o   o   o

The only way of following the way of Islam is to keep company with those who do their best to follow the example of the first community of Muslims who gathered round the Prophet Muhammad at Madina al-Munawarra, the illuminated place where the life transaction is, may the blessings and peace of Allah be on him and them. Such a company will only be found round a person whom Allah loves, and who loves and fears Allah, that is a wali of Allah, a friend and lover of Allah.

The wali of Allah is the one who, after the Prophet Muhammad, comes nearest to embodying and understanding what is in the *Qur'an* and the *Sunnah*. The wali of Allah is like a drop compared to the ocean of the Prophet Muhammad, may the blessings and peace of Allah be on him. The wali of Allah is the best of guides because Allah guides the ones whom He loves, and no one is loved more by Allah than the awliya. The awliya are the ones to whom the living life transaction of Islam, and the knowledge which goes with it, have been transmitted in an unbroken chain of transmission, from the Prophet Muhammad, person to person, to the awliya of today.

It is the awliya of today who are the ones who best know and follow the way of Islam. The greatest of them meet and talk with the Prophet Muhammad, may Allah bless him and grant him peace, in true dream and in direct vision, receiving confirmation and guidance whenever it is needed. Help comes to them from the Prophet Muhammad in every moment. The excellence of their knowledge of the means – Muhammad – is only matched by the excellence of their knowledge of the end – Allah. The awliya of Allah have gnosis of Allah, the highest knowledge there is, and it is this knowledge which gives them certainty as to the true nature of existence.

There are three stages of certainty. The mithal, that is the likeness, of these three stages is that firstly you are told of the fire in the forest – and without seeing it you believe the one who told you; then you see the fire in the forest for yourself – and you hear its crackling and smell its smoke and feel its heat, so that now there is no room to doubt its existence; and then finally you are the fire in the forest – utterly transformed and annihilated by and in it.

In this final stage of certainty is the station of the greatest of the awliya, and the meaning of this station is that Allah loves them, and when Allah loves them, then He is the tongue with which they speak, and the hand with which they grasp, and the foot with which they walk. It is because of this that their pleasure is Allah's pleasure, and their guidance is Allah's guidance, and they are the best of guides, and they cannot be associated with Allah who is the Guide.

It is from amongst the awliya that the Mahdi – who will be one of the Prophet Muhammad's descendants, may the blessings and peace of Allah be on him and on all his family – will appear. The Mahdi will be the most rightly guided of guides, and all the real Muslims will recognise that.

○　　○　　○　　○　　○

A distinction must be made between the living life transaction of Islam, which has been transmitted to and preserved by the awliya, and the dead religion of Islam which has been created and perpetuated by the people who obtain their knowledge solely from books. The awliya use books, but they do not rely on them. Their knowledge comes from fear of Allah and by the grace of Allah. If your knowledge does not come from the fear of Allah then you have been deceived. One of the great awliya in the past, Abu Yazid al-Bistami, said to a man who relied solely on books, 'You get your knowledge from the dead, but we get our knowledge from the Living who never dies.' Another of the great awliya in the past, Abu'l-'Abbas al-Mursi, said, 'If the Prophet Muhammad left my sight for a moment, I would no longer consider myself a Muslim.'

At best the ones who rely solely on books for their knowledge of Islam only ever reach the first stage of certainty. They will go to the Garden, insha'Allah, but they are not the best of guides. The danger in following them is that you may end up worshipping Islam instead of Allah, mistaking, in effect, the means for the end.

The way of Islam is so that you can have knowledge of Allah, and worship Allah, and the best knowledge of Allah is gnosis of Allah, and the one who has gnosis of Allah worships Allah with a deeper understanding of Allah than the one who only possesses information – however much – concerning Allah.

At worst the ones who rely solely on books for their knowledge of Islam will side-track you away from Islam, because they do not always act on what they know. Only take your knowledge from those who act on what they know. Is, for example, the leader of their community an Amir – which is the *Sunnah* of the Prophet Muhammad, may Allah bless him and grant him peace; or is the community run by a democratically elected committee – which is the sunnah of the Jews and the Christians?

If there is a dispute between two members of the community, do they go to the Amir for a decision in accordance with the *Qur'an* and the *Sunnah* – a decision which they both agree to accept and abide by beforehand; or do they resort to the kafir legal system for judgement and enforcement?

Is the beginning and end of Ramadan announced to the community by the Amir – after he has satisfied himself that the new moon has been sighted by at least two reliable witnesses; or is all this decided by a committee who have in fact already secretly decided in advance when Ramadan will begin and end, after referring to an astronomical almanac which only records the times when it has been scientifically predicted that the new moons will most probably be born – but not when they will be capable of being sighted, and most certainly not when they will actually be sighted?

Is the collection and distribution of the zakat supervised by the Amir; or does a committee leave it up to each person's individual conscience and choice, leaving it up to everyone to assess their own zakat and then pay it into a collecting box in the mosque or to a charity of their choice – and simply ignoring those who either refuse or forget to fulfil this obligation?

Is the Imam who leads the community in prayer also the Amir or else someone appointed by the Amir; or is the Imam appointed and controlled by a committee who pay his salary? Are there separate facilities for both men and women in the community's mosque; or do they mix freely there – which is the sunnah of the Christians; or is it a place for 'men only' – which is the sunnah of the Jews?

In other words, does the community have Islam in their actions as well as on their tongues? Usually those who have Islam in their actions have remembrance of Allah on their tongues – and in their hearts. The signs which indicate those who are following the way of Muhammad, may Allah bless him and grant him peace, and the signs which indicate those who are following the example of their predecessors – meaning the Jews and the Christians, just like a lizard making for its hole – are very clear indeed, for anyone to see.

Only take your knowledge from the one whose actions and words are the same. In an ignorant age a person's words are mistaken for their actions. Such people do not act from certainty but out of expediency. They fear other than Allah and they do not fear Allah. They are confused and they confuse whoever listens to or follows them. The Prophet Muhammad said that there would be some people who would have the Qur'an on their tongues, but not in their hearts nor in their actions. He said that they would be the worst people on the face of the earth. These are the munafiqun, the hypocrites, destined for the deepest part of the Fire. One of their signs is that they have no fear in their hearts that there may be hypocrisy in their hearts. They can also sometimes be recognised in that they often consider themselves 'experts' on Islam – in the same way that the kafir expert considers him or her self an 'expert' in a particular field – which often results in their praising themselves and slandering the muminun.

Although they use so-called 'islamic' vocabulary, the institutions which the munafiqun either initiate or support are modelled on the institutions of the kafir system, that is the Dajjal system. In effect, they are part and parcel of the system. Today they are to be found particularly in the Muslim lands whose governments are based on kafir models and controlled by the kafir system, that is the Dajjal system. The munafiqun are often used by corrupt governments to gain the people's acquiescence in and acceptance of such governments, by assuring them that these governments are 'islamic'.

Just in the same way that people in kafir states are persuaded to accept the kafir system, that is the Dajjal system, because they are led to believe what the so-called kafir experts tell them, so people in the Muslim lands are persuaded to accept the infiltration of the system into their countries, because they are led to believe the so-called 'islamic' experts who tell them that the ways of the kafirun which their governments have adopted are 'islamic'.

Allah does not always reveal who the munafiqun are, but no doubt as to their identity is left whenever there is a direct confrontation between kufr and iman, since at that point the munafiqun always side with the people of kufr and oppose the Muslims. This is a sure sign of their ignorance and of their lack of trust in Allah, since the reason why they side with the kafirun is that they think that the kafirun are going to come out on top!

The cerebral brand of Islam which they advocate is nothing to do with the living life transaction of Islam, as embodied by the Prophet Muhammad and the first Muslim community of Madina al-Munawarra – simply because they say one thing and do another. The religion of

Islam which they have manufactured is really no more or less than a form of kufr in disguise, just in the same way that the modern religions of Judaism and Christianity are no more or less than different forms of kufr in disguise.

One of the most distinguishing features of these three pseudo-religions is that they are all orchestrated by a hierarchical ruling elite of priests some, but not all, of whom are in fact freemasons into the bargain. They do not oppose the kafir system that is the Dajjal system, but rather they support it, often providing so-called religious ceremonies or even written 'legal' opinions to provide an aura of respectability and credibility to some of the kafir rites and public occasions. In effect, they are a part of the stage show which is put on for the benefit of the general public, in order to disguise the true nature of the activities of the freemasonic ruling elite.

Naturally there are members of each of these three official priesthoods who are sincere in their actions and worship of Allah, but if these people took the trouble to examine the respective teachings of their Prophets even a little more closely, they would find that none of these Prophets, nor indeed any Prophet, ever initiated a priesthood who said 'you need us' to reach Allah.

o o o o o

The real transaction with Allah is between you and Allah direct, and without any intermediary. Your whole life is between you and Allah. Those who have access to the living life transaction of Islam know this.

o o o o o

The teaching of the Prophet Muhammad, may the blessings and peace of Allah be on him, is the only Prophetic teaching which is intact today, because the awliya to whom this teaching has been transmitted are all Muslims. You will not find gnostics of Allah, which is what the great awliya are, amongst the Hindus, or the Buddhists, or the Magians, or the Jews, or the Christians, because gnosis of Allah is only possible for the one who has access to, and follows, a Prophetic teaching which is still intact. All the Prophetic teachings which were once followed in their entirety long before the coming of the Prophet Muhammad have either been lost or altered, and either successfully de-potentised by the kafir system, that is the Dajjal system, or incorporated into it – and this is also partially true of the people who have turned the original teachings of Islam into a dead re-defined religion.

Dajjal – the king who has no clothes

The few Jews who can still claim to be direct descendants of the original Tribe of Israel which was led by Moses, and the Jews who are not really Jews – that is either those who are descendants of the Khazars, or those who are descendants of Oriental or Sephardhic Jews who interbred with other races – do not follow the existential life pattern which was embodied by Moses, peace be on him. The Christians – whether Unitarian or Trinitarian – do not follow the existential life pattern which was embodied by Jesus, peace be on him. The books on which the Jews, and the Jews who are not Jews, and the Christians, rely are unreliable, having been altered and censored by corrupt rabbis and priests in the past, who made changes in order to compromise with kafir rulers, and in order to make a little money on the side.

Furthermore, in both cases it is not even the original revelation which has been changed: In the case of the Jews, there was a point in time in their history – at least six centuries after the death of Moses, peace be on him – when all complete copies of the *Torah* were destroyed by the forces of Nebuchadnezzar when they sacked Jerusalem in 586 BC. The Jews tried to restore it, by gathering together all the surviving remnants and the rabbis who had committed different parts of it to memory, to see if it was possible to reconstitute the original *Torah*. It was not. Still they put an edition together which contained as much as they could find or remember. This was the compilation which was supervised by Ezra during the exile of some of the Jews in Babylon in the 5th century BC, and which he brought to Jerusalem in 458 BC – but it is generally accepted that this compilation was in turn destroyed during the sack of Jerusalem by Antiochus Epeplianus in 161 BC.

It is interesting to note in passing that prior to the exile in Babylon, only the book of Deuteronomy – which had been written in 621 BC and read to the people in the Temple at Jerusalem – had existed in written form. Prior to this – that is, throughout the previous six centuries – the knowledge of the Jews and of their history had been kept alive by means of an oral tradition. Douglas Reed writes in his book, *The Controversy of Zion*:

> Significantly, Deuteronomy which appears as the fifth book of today's Bible, with an air of growing naturally out of the previous ones, was the first book to be completed as a whole. Though Genesis and Exodus provide the historical background and mount for it, they were later produced by

the Levites, and Leviticus and Numbers, the other books of the Torah, were compiled even later.

Even if the original *Torah* was successfully memorised accurately by heart by successive generations of Levites during a period of several centuries without any mistakes or alterations being made, which is unlikely, the fact of the matter is that most of the contents of these five books – and indeed of all the other books in the Old Testament – are in the form of various accounts of what happened before, during and after the lifetime of the Moses, peace be on him, and therefore cannot possibly represent what was actually revealed to him on Mount Sinai. The form that these books take is more in the nature of a 'history' of the Tribe of Israel than of anything else.

During the four centuries between 450 and 50 BC, and especially after the destruction of Ezra's compilation by Antiochus in his invasion of Jerusalem in 161 BC, the book which was called the *Torah* – together with the additional books which purported to record the history of the Tribe of Israel after the time of Moses, and which were often written and compiled from remnants of various sources centuries after the events which they purported to describe had taken place – continued to be written and rewritten and revised and subsequently further altered in the process by corrupt rabbis who wished to bend the law which had been derived from the original living life transaction of islam brought by Moses, peace be on him.

As Dr. Maurice Bucaille points out in his book, *The Bible, the Qur'an and Science*, by the time the Hebrew Scriptures came to be translated into Greek by, it is said, seventy-two Jewish scholars at Alexandria, between 275 and 150 BC, they no longer truly represented the original teachings of Moses – nor had they done so for some considerable time:

> Around the Third century BC, there were at least three forms of the Hebrew text: the text which was to become the Masoretic text, the text which was used, in part at least, for the Greek translation, and the Samaritan Pentateuch. In the First century BC, there was a tendency towards the establishment of a single text, but it was not until a century after Christ that the Biblical text was definitely established.
>
> If we had had the three forms of the text, comparison would have been possible, and we could have reached an

opinion concerning what the original might have been. Unfortunately, we do not have the slightest idea. Apart from the Dead Sea Scrolls (Cave of Qumran), dating from a pre-Christian era near the time of Jesus, a papyrus of the Ten Commandments of the Second century AD presenting variations from the classical text, and a few fragments from the Fifth century AD (Geniza of Cairo), the oldest Hebrew text of the Bible dates from the Ninth century AD.

Dr. Bucaille continues:

> The Old Testament is a collection of works of greatly differing length and many different genres. They were written in several languages over a period of more than nine hundred years, based on oral traditions. Many of these works were corrected and completed in accordance with events or special requirements, often at periods that were very distant from one another.

Dr. Bucaille concludes:

> A Revelation is mingled in all these writings, but all we possess today is what men have seen fit to leave us. These men manipulated the texts to please themselves, according to the circumstances they were in and the necessities they had to meet.

In *The Controversy of Zion* Douglas Reed quotes Josef Kastein (alias Julius Katzenstein) from his book *History and Destiny of the Jews* as stating that the Greek translation was undertaken 'with a definite object in view, that of making it comprehensible to the Greeks; this led to the distortion and twisting of words, changes of meaning, and the frequent substitution of general terms and ideas for those that were purely local and national.' Having pointed out that perhaps the real reason for undertaking the translation must have been that the largest single body of Jews at that time was in Alexandria, where Greek had become their everyday language, and that 'many of them could no longer understand Hebrew and a Greek version of their Law was needed as a basis for the rabbinical interpretations of it,' Douglas Reed observes:

> In view of the changes which were made, at the translation, (see Dr. Kastein's words, above), none but Judaist scholars

could tell today how closely the Old Testament in the Hebrew-Aramaic original compares with the version which has come down, from the first translation into Greek, as one of the two sections of Christendom's Bible. Clearly substantial changes were made, and quite apart from that there is the 'oral Torah', and the Talmudic continuation of the Torah, so that the Gentile world has never known the whole truth of the Judaic Law.

The *Talmud*, which is alleged to record the oral traditions of Moses, did not actually appear in written form until some seventeen centuries after the death of Moses, and at least nine centuries after the *Torah* itself had ceased to exist in its original form: The *Mishnah*, the written form of the alleged oral traditions of Moses was not collated in its present form until the beginning of the third century AD. The two commentaries on the *Mishnah*, the *Jerusalem Gemara* and the *Babylonian Gemara*, were not completed until the fifth and seventh centuries AD respectively, while the commentaries written on these commentaries, the very extensive *Midrash* literature, were written between 400 and 1200 AD.

It was because these various commentaries were so long and detailed that attempts were then made to codify them. The most well-known codes are *The Code of Maimonides* compiled in the 12th century AD, *The Code of Jacob ben Asher* (called *The Turim*) completed in the 14th century AD, and The *Code of Joseph Caro* (called *The Shulchan Aruch*) compiled in the 16th century AD.

The one book which certainly does not exist today is the *Torah of Moses*, peace be on him, the original revelation that he received from God, in the original language in which it was revealed – so that the accuracy and authenticity of any translation or interpretation of that original text could always be ascertained and assessed simply by referring back to that original text whenever the occasion might arise.

○   ○   ○   ○   ○

In the case of the Christians, it would seem that the *Injil*, that is the Gospel, which was revealed to Jesus was never actually committed to either parchment or papyrus. Certainly there is no book called the *Gospel of Jesus* and written in Aramaic, which was his tongue, in existence today. If there is, then the Christians are keeping very quiet about it. Instead their New Testament contains four official gospels according to people who never even met Jesus, which contradict each other many times over, lumped together with the teachings of Paul who also never even met Jesus, which openly contradict the original living life transaction of islam brought by Jesus, peace be on him. It is this book which was compiled and subsequently altered by corrupt priests in the past who wished to amend and embellish the original teachings of Jesus almost beyond recognition, and to make their new religion more amenable both to kafir rulers and to their congregations.

Perhaps the two most flagrant alterations were firstly, the insertion of the one and only reference to the Paulinian doctrine of the Trinity (I John 5: 7), and secondly, the insertion of the one and only reference to the Paulinian doctrine of Incarnation (I Timothy 3: 16) – both of which were conclusively proved by, inter alia, Sir Isaac Newton to be forgeries, and neither of which were ever referred to during the fierce theological debates which took place during the first three centuries after Jesus had disappeared, for the very simple reason that neither of these two verses existed at that time!

According to the English translation of the Italian version of the Gospel of Barnabas – which, like the other officially accepted Gospels, is incapable of being fully authenticated in the absence of an original text – the *Injil* was not committed to 'paper', but was revealed to Jesus by the angel Gabriel in a vision, taking the form of a well of knowledge in his heart, from which he could draw as he wished, and which was the means by which he breathed new life back into the original law of Moses which, it should always be remembered, he had come to revive and re-establish among the twelve tribes of the Tribe of Israel – and not to change 'by one jot or one tittle'.

This made things difficult for the priesthood of the Jews who prior to the arrival of Jesus had been able to claim that they were the true guardians of the original teachings of Moses, and who had made this claim the basis of their leadership and their livelihood. Jesus showed up their hypocrisy and endangered the source of their authority and wealth and this was why they opposed him so vehemently. With the arrival of Jesus, all the misrepresentations and changes to the original teachings of Moses which had gradually been introduced by the Jewish priesthood during the nine centuries which had elapsed since the reign of the Prophet Solomon had ended, peace be upon him, were suddenly in grave danger of being exposed, and their hierarchy of being destroyed. This is why they rejected Jesus, peace be on him, and this is why they plotted with the Romans to have him killed – although they did not succeed:

> And they did not kill him and they did not crucify him, but it appeared so to them. And surely those who disagree about it are certainly in doubt about it – they have no knowledge about it except that they follow speculation. And they did not kill him for certain – but Allah took him up to Himself. And Allah was ever Mighty, Wise.
>
> (*Qur'an: Surat'an-Nisa* – 4. 157-158)

Unfortunately, after the miraculous disappearance of Jesus, and as a result of the subsequent conflict which occurred between the original followers of Jesus (the Nazarenes – who are sometimes described as 'the Judeo-Christians' in order to distinguish them from those followers of Jesus who did not belong to the Tribe of Israel), and the followers of Paul (who after four centuries of debate eventually formulated, inter alia, the doctrines of Incarnation, Trinity, Original Sin, and the Atonement and Forgiveness of Sins), many of the early written eye-witness accounts of the life and sayings of Jesus, of which it is said there were about three hundred, were destroyed – including, inter alia, the *Gospel of the Hebrews*, the original *Gospel of Barnabas* and the *Gospel of Thomas* – especially after the Council of Nicea in 325 AD, at which it was officially decided that Jesus was the 'son' of God, and during which the four official Gospels were selected by the Paulinian Christians.

As Dr. Maurice Bucaille makes clear in his book *The Bible, the Qur'an and Science*, these four Gospels were not eyewitness accounts and only came to be written down at a relatively late date:

> The texts that we have today, after many adaptations from the sources, began to appear around 70 AD, the time when the two rival communities were engaged in a fierce struggle, with the Judeo-Christians still retaining the upper hand. With the Jewish war and the fall of Jerusalem in 70 AD, the situation was to be reversed. This is how Cardinal Daniélou explains the decline:
>
> 'After the Jews had been discredited in the Empire, the Christians tended to detach themselves from them. The Hellenistic peoples of Christian persuasion then gained the upper hand: Paul won a posthumous victory; Christianity separated itself politically and sociologically from

Judaism: it became the third people. All the same, until the Jewish revolt in 140 AD, Judeo-Christianity continued to predominate culturally.'

From 70 AD to a period situated sometime before 110 AD the Gospels of Mark, Matthew, Luke and John were produced. They do not constitute the first written Christian documents: the letters of Paul date from well before them. According to O. Culmann, Paul probably wrote his letter to the Thessalonians in 50 AD. He had probably disappeared several years prior to the completion of Mark's Gospel.

Dr. Bucaille continues:

As far as the Gospels are concerned however, it is almost certain that if this atmosphere of struggle between communities had not existed, we would not have had the writings we possess today. They appeared at a time of fierce struggle between the two communities. These 'combat writings', as Father Kannengiesser calls them, emerged from the multitude of writings on Jesus. These occurred at the time when Paul's style of Christianity won through definitively, and created its own collection of official texts. These texts constituted the 'Canon' which condemned and excluded as unorthodox any other documents that were not suited to the line adopted by the Church.

As regards the four officially accepted Gospels, there are no versions in the original Hebrew or Aramaic, and, as Dr. Bucaille confirms, the earliest Greek versions date from after the Council of Nicea:

Documents prior to this, i.e. papyri from the Third century AD and one possibly dating from the Second, only transmit fragments to us. The two oldest parchment manuscripts are Greek, Fourth century AD. They are the Codex Vaticanus, preserved in the Vatican Library and whose place of discovery is unknown, and the Codex Sinaiticus, which was discovered on Mount Sinai and is now preserved in the British Museum, London. The second contains two apocryphal works.

According to the Ecumenical Translation, two hundred and fifty other known parchments exist throughout the world, the last of these being from the Eleventh century AD. 'Not all the copies of the New Testament that have come down to us are identical' however. 'On the contrary, it is possible to distinguish differences of varying degrees of importance between them, but however important they may be, there is always a large number of them. Some of these only concern differences of grammatical detail, vocabulary or word order. Elsewhere however, differences between manuscripts can be seen which affect the meaning of whole passages.'

Thus not only is it possible – indeed it is highly likely – that significant changes were made to the original texts which pre-dated the Council of Nicea and which have all been destroyed, but also even the texts which date from after the Council of Nicea do not fully agree with each other, cannot therefore be entirely accurate, and in fact have themselves been altered:

> The authenticity of a text, and of even the most venerable manuscript, is always open to debate. The Codex Vaticanus is a good example of this. The facsimile reproduction edited by the Vatican City, 1965, contains an accompanying note from its editors informing us that, 'several centuries after it was copied (believed to have been in circa the Tenth or Eleventh century), a scribe inked over all the letters except those he thought were a mistake.' There are passages in the text where the original letters in light brown still show through, contrasting visibly with the rest of the text which is in dark brown. There is no indication that it was a faithful restoration. The note states moreover that, 'the different hands that corrected and annotated the manuscript over the centuries have not yet been definitively discerned; a certain number of corrections were undoubtedly made when the text was inked over.' In all the religious manuals the text is presented as a Fourth century copy. One has to go to sources at the Vatican to discover that various hands may have altered the text centuries later.

The one book which certainly does not exist today is the *Gospel of Jesus*, peace be on him, the original revelation that he received from God, in the original language in which it was revealed – so that the accuracy and authenticity of any translation or interpretation of that original text could always be ascertained and assessed simply by referring back to that original text whenever the occasion might arise.

✣   ✣   ✣   ✣   ✣

This is not to say that there is no truth left in the books on which the Jews, and the Jews who are not Jews, and the Christians rely. There is truth in them, and some of their contents most probably correspond with the original books which were revealed to their respective Prophets, may the blessings and peace of Allah be on both of them. They do not, however, contain the whole truth, and furthermore, as well as having been censored, deliberate lies have been inserted. It is for this reason that they are not entirely reliable. Finally, even if the original *Torah* and the original Ingil still existed, they have been abrogated by the *Qur'an*.

The original *Torah* as revealed to Moses no longer exists. The original *Ingil*, or Gospel, as revealed to Jesus no longer exists. The people to whom the existential life pattern of these Prophets was transmitted, person to person, without a break in the chain of transmission, are all long dead. The chains of transmission from Moses and from Jesus have been broken and lost for ever. Even if you are filled with the greatest sincerity, you cannot follow the existential pattern of worship and behaviour which was once embodied by Moses and Jesus – and by the bringers of the original Vedas and by Buddha for that matter – and the communities which formed around them, because that behavioural pattern has been lost for ever, and other falsified patterns have been put in its place, in their names and in the Name of God. There is no going back. Only the existential pattern of worship and behaviour which was once embodied by Muhammad, may Allah bless him and grant him peace, the way of Muhammad, has survived up to the present day.

✣   ✣   ✣   ✣   ✣

The *Qur'an* is the only Prophetic guidance on the face of the earth today which has not been changed by even one letter either by alteration, addition or subtraction. It is recorded as it was revealed. It was both memorised by heart and recorded in writing as it was in the process of being revealed. Those who were delegated to record the *Qur'an* in writing were instructed by the Prophet Muhammad – who was himself illiterate and could neither read nor write – not to record anything else, in order to ensure that there could be no confusion between the contents of the Qur'an on one hand, and what he himself said during the normal course of events on the other. The revelation of the Qur'an was completed before the Prophet Muhammad died, may Allah bless him and grant him peace. The written version was gathered together, authenticated and verified by those who knew it by heart within twenty years of the Prophet Muhammad's death, may he have peace and light in his grave – and the number of Muslims who have continued to know the entire Qur'an by heart ever since that time, right up until the present day, has always been quite extraordinary.

Allah has promised that the Qur'an will remain intact until the end of the world. There is no doubt in it. It is utterly reliable. Even the most ingenious kafir so-called scholars and orientalists have been unable to discredit it. Allah says in the Qur'an that if you do not believe that the Qur'an is from Allah, then try and write something like it. No-one has ever been able to meet this challenge – and they never will. Allah says in the Qur'an that even if the whole of mankind and all the jinn banded together, they still could not produce the like of the Qur'an between them.

The Prophet Muhammad, may Allah bless him and grant him peace, said:

> 'Allah sent down this Qur'an to command and prevent, and as a Sunnah to be followed and a parable. It contains your history, information about what came before you, news about what will come after you and correct judgement between you. Repetition does not wear it out and its wonders do not end. It is the Truth. It is not a jest. Whoever recites it speaks the truth. Whoever judges by it is just. Whoever argues by it wins. Whoever divides by it is equitable. Whoever acts by it is rewarded. Whoever clings to it is guided to a straight path. Allah will misguide whoever seeks guidance from other than it. Allah will destroy whoever judges by other than it. It is the Wise Remembrance, the Clear Light, the Straight Path, the Firm Rope of Allah and the Useful Healing. It is a protection for the one who clings to it and a rescue for the one who follows it. It is not crooked and so puts things straight. It does not deviate so as to be blamed. Its wonders do not cease. It does not wear out with much repetition.' (It was related by At-Tirmidhi).

Furthermore, not only the *Qur'an* but also the existential life pattern of the Prophet Muhammad and the community which formed around him, may the blessings and peace of Allah be on him and them, has been preserved and transmitted, from living person to living person, in an unbroken chain of transmission, right up until today. The Prophet Muhammad said that this transmission would continue until just before the end of time, when there will be no more Muslims left on the face of the earth.

If you believe in Allah and wish to worship Allah in the manner which Allah has indicated that He should be worshipped through his Prophets, then you must find out what is in the *Qur'an* and in the *Hadith*, and follow the way of Muhammad, that is the living life transaction of Islam. Right now the choice is yours.

○   ○   ○   ○   ○

Each of the one hundred and twenty four thousand Prophets who have been sent by Allah, may the blessings and peace of Allah be on all of them, were sent for specific people, and at a specific time in the history of mankind. Some were sent for only a few people, some were sent for a particular tribe, some were sent for a particular nation, and only one was sent for the whole world. Noah, for example, only had nineteen followers at the time of the great flood, even though he lived for nine hundred and fifty years. Both Moses and Jesus were sent only for the Tribe of Israel, so only Allah knows what the Jews who are not Jews, and the Christians who are not descended from the Tribe of Israel, are up to today. Only the Prophet Muhammad, may Allah bless him and grant him peace, was sent with a guidance, a good news and a warning, for all people and the jinn from the time the *Qur'an* was revealed to him up until the end of the world.

The times for all the Prophets who came before the time of the Prophet Muhammad are now long over. The people for whom all the Prophets who came before the Prophet Muhammad were sent are now long dead. The time for following the way of the Prophet Muhammad is now. The people for whom the Prophet Muhammad was sent have either died during the last fourteen hundred years, or they are alive today, or they will live at some stage between now and the end of the world.

The only way to follow the Prophetic life pattern today is to follow the way of the Prophet Muhammad, may the blessings and peace of Allah be on him, and on his family, and on his companions, and all who follow him, because his way is the only Prophetic life pattern which has survived intact up until today, and which will continue to survive up until the time immediately preceding the end of the world, when Allah will take the arwah, that is the spirit forms, of all the Muslims who are alive at that time from this world, leaving only the people who will live like animals until the end of the world.

The Prophet Muhammad, may the blessings and peace of Allah be on him, is the first and the last of the Prophets. He was in existence when Adam was still between water and clay. He is the last of the Prophets, the seal of the Prophets, confirming by the *Qur'an* all the messages of the Prophets before him, and thereby abrogating and completing those messages. The *Qur'an* contains all that the teachings of the earlier Prophets contained, and more.

The *Qur'an* is the final edition of the A to Z of existence, and its author, publisher and distributor is Allah, the Originator of all that appears to exist, and the One to whom all that appears to exist returns. Since the Prophet Muhammad was the embodiment of the *Qur'an*, that is the *Qur'an* walking, he was the only complete and perfect man that existence has ever known, may the blessings and peace of Allah be on him – and he cannot be associated with Allah, because Allah is One, alone without any partner.

Allah was a hidden treasure, and He wished to make Himself known, so He created the Universe. When there was only Allah, before time and space began, Allah took a portion of His light and said, 'Be Muhammad!' From this light of Muhammad all the source forms of everything that was ever to manifest either in the Unseen, or in the phenomenal world which is apprehended by the senses, were created. The first source form to be created was the source form of the man and Prophet, Muhammad, may the blessings and peace of Allah be on him for ever.

Since that time all the source forms created from the light of Muhammad by Allah have manifested, and continue to manifest, and will continue to manifest until the end of the world, in the Unseen and in the phenomenal worlds. Everything is made from the light of Muhammad. The light of Muhammad is from the light of Allah. Only Allah exists. Everything in the time and space continuum is an illusion, is not what it appears to be. Do not curse the time and space continuum, for it is Allah. Everywhere you look, there is the face of Allah. Everything is passing away except the face of Allah. Allah is as He was before the creation of the Universe, and He continues to be. There is only Allah.

Say: He is Allah the One, Allah the Everlasting – nothing is born from Him and He was not born from anything and there is nothing like Him.
(Qur'an: Surat'al-Ikhlas – 112.1-4)

The reality of the Prophets, may the blessings and peace of Allah be on them all, is that the next Prophet only came when the teaching of the Prophet before him had been lost. All the teachings of all the Prophets, except for the teaching of the Prophet Muhammad, have been lost. The Prophet Muhammad is the last of the Prophets before the end of the world. If you wish to follow the way of the Prophets you have no choice but to follow the way of Muhammad. Right now the choice is yours and it is a very simple one to make, but a difficult one to put into practice.

The Prophet Muhammad said that a time would come when to hold to the living life transaction of Islam would be like handling hot coals. That time has come. The people who control the kafir system, that is the Dajjal system, are making it difficult to hold to the living life transaction of Islam. This is a test from Allah. The more Allah loves someone, the more Allah tests them. No one was tested as much as the Prophet Muhammad, may the blessings and peace of Allah be on him, because no one has been loved as much by Allah as the Prophet Muhammad.

The reality of the Prophets is that they were all from Allah, and they all brought the same message, because there is only One Allah to know and affirm, and because the nature of existence, which derives from Allah, has always been essentially the same. This means that there is no competition between the Prophets because they all affirmed One and the same Reality, Allah. In the same way there is no competition between the awliya, because there is only Allah, and they know it with direct seeing. The knowledge, the knower and the known are One. The Muslims are the only ones who recognise this. This is why only the Muslims accept all the Prophets, and make no distinction between them, all one hundred and twenty-four thousand of them.

There is no way to worship Allah, as Allah has indicated He should be worshipped, except by following the way of Muhammad, may the blessings and peace of Allah be on him. Only by following the way of

Muhammad will you be able to affirm the true nature of existence, and understand it, and know your self – and truly whoever knows their self knows their Lord. The whole Universe cannot contain Allah, but the heart of the one who trusts in Allah contains Allah, and the way to your heart is the way of Muhammad, may the blessings and peace of Allah be on him.

○   ○   ○   ○   ○

Either you are for the kafir system, that is the Dajjal system, or you are against it. If you are against it, then you are for the way of Islam. If you are not against the way of Islam – and you must find out what it really is, because it certainly is not what the educational and media systems depict it to be – then you are for the way of Islam. No one can take you to Islam, and no one can take you away from Islam.

○   ○   ○   ○   ○

Allah is in the expectation of His slave, and we are all slaves of Allah, and deep down we all know that, because when Allah had created the source forms from the light of Muhammad, He said to all the arwah, that is the spirit forms, of all the people who would ever come into and go out of existence, 'Am I not your Lord?' – **'Alastu birabbikum?'** and they all answered, 'Yes, we bear witness.' – **'Bala shahidna.'** This question and this answer resonate in the heart of every human being. Deep down in the heart, whoever is mumin remembers this – whilst whoever is kafir covers it up and pretends that it did not happen.

The only way to realise the full extent of your being a slave of Allah – and this means that you will not be a slave of anything or anyone or any idea which or who appears to be other than Allah – is to follow the way of Muhammad, who was the perfect slave of Allah. He, may Allah bless him and grant him peace, was so pure that he cast no shadow when he walked in the sunlight. When he laughed, light bounced off the walls. His sweat smelled of musk. He was immersed in remembrance of Allah in every moment. He was always in complete abasement before Allah. He was a complete and perfect man, and therefore his way is the best of ways. There is no better example of how to be a human being than him.

Ask yourself now the questions which you will be asked later, after your death. Who do you worship? Who do you follow? What is your source of knowledge? What is your way of life? Right now the choice is yours.

○   ○   ○   ○   ○

It is not known for certain exactly when Dajjal the individual is going to appear. It is not known for certain exactly when the Mahdi, the rightly guided leader of the Muslims, who walks in the footsteps of the Prophet Muhammad, may the blessings and peace of Allah be on him, is going to appear.

It has been stated by some of the awliya of the present age that both the Dajjal and the Mahdi are alive and on this earth – which would appear to indicate that the time when they finally meet cannot be all that far away, which in turn would appear to indicate that the second coming of Jesus, peace be on him, is also imminent – but only Allah knows for certain when that time will be. They may appear in your life time, they may not.

What we do know is that in the end there are only two basic ways of living while you are here on this earth. Either you follow the way of Kufr, or you follow the way of Islam.

○   ○   ○   ○   ○

From Abu Hurayra, may Allah be pleased with him:

> The Prophet, may Allah bless him and grant him peace, said: 'The Prophets are like brothers; they have different mothers but their life transaction is one. I am the closest of all the people to Jesus son of Mary, because there is no other Prophet between him and myself. He will come again, and when you see him, you will recognize him. He is of medium height and his colouring is reddish-white. He will be wearing two garments, and his hair will look wet. He will break the cross, kill the pigs, abolish the jizya and call the people to Islam. During his time, Allah will end every religion and sect other than Islam, and will destroy the Dajjal. Then peace and security will prevail on earth, so that lions will graze with camels, tigers with cattle, and wolves with sheep; children will be able to play with snakes without coming to any harm. Jesus will remain for forty years, then die, and the Muslims will pray for him.' (It was related by Ibn Hanbal)

From An-Nuwas ibn Sam'an, may Allah be pleased with him:

> One morning the Prophet, may Allah bless him and grant him peace, spoke about the Dajjal. Sometimes he described him as insignificant, and sometimes he described him as

so dangerous that we thought he was in the clump of date-palms nearby. When we went to him later on, he noticed that fear in our faces, and asked, 'What is the matter with you?' We said, 'O Messenger of Allah, this morning you spoke of the Dajjal; sometimes you described him as insignificant, and sometimes you described him as being so dangerous that we thought he was in the clump of date-palms nearby.'

The Prophet, may Allah bless him and grant him peace, said, 'I fear for you in other matters besides the Dajjal. If he appears whilst I am among you, I will contend with him on your behalf. But if he appears while I am not among you, then each man must contend with him on his own behalf, and Allah will take care of every Muslim on my behalf. The Dajjal will be a young man, with short, curly hair, and one eye floating. I would liken him to Abdal-'Uzza ibn Qatan. Whoever amongst you lives to see him should recite the opening ayat of Surat'al-Kahf. He will appear on the way between Syria and Iraq, and will create disaster left and right. O servants of Allah, adhere to the Path of Truth.'

We said, 'O Messenger of Allah, for the day which is like a year, will one day's prayers be sufficient?' He said, 'No, you must make an estimate of the time, and then observe the prayers.'

We asked, 'O Messenger of Allah, how quickly will he walk upon the earth?' He said, 'Like a cloud driven by the wind. He will come to the people and call them (to a false religion), and they will believe in him and respond to him. He will issue a command to the sky, and it will rain; and to the earth, and it will produce crops. After grazing on these crops, their animals will return with their udders full of milk and their flanks stretched. Then he will come to another people and will call them (to a false religion), but they will reject his call. He will depart from them; they will suffer famine and will possess nothing in the form of wealth. Then he will pass through the wasteland and will say, "Bring forth your treasures", and the treasures will come forth, like swarms of bees. Then he will call a man brimming with youth; he will strike him with a sword and cut him in two, then place the two pieces at the distance between an archer and his target. Then he will call him, and the young man will come running and laughing.

'At that point, Allah will send the Messiah, son of Mary, and he will descend to the white minaret in the east of Damascus, wearing two garments dyed with saffron, placing his hands on the wings of two angels. When he lowers his head, beads of perspiration will fall from it, and when he raises his head, beads like pearls will scatter from it. Every kafir who smells his fragrance will die, and his breath will reach as far as he can see. He will search for the Dajjal until he finds him at the gate of Ludd (the biblical Lydda, now known as Lod), where he will kill him.

'Then a people whom Allah has protected will come to Jesus son of Mary, and he will wipe their faces (i.e. wipe the traces of hardship from their faces) and tell them of their status in Paradise. At that time Allah will reveal to Jesus: "I have brought forth some of My servants whom no-one will be able to fight. Take My servants safely to at-Tur."

'Then Allah will send Gog and Magog, and they will swarm down from every slope. The first of them will pass by the Lake of Tiberias, and will drink some of its water; the last of them will pass by it and say, "There used to be water here". Jesus, the Prophet of Allah, and his Companions will be besieged until a bull's head will be dearer to them than one hundred dinars are to you nowadays.

'Then Jesus and his Companions will pray to Allah, and He will send insects who will bite the people of Gog and Magog on their necks, so that in the morning they will all perish as one. Then Jesus and his Companions will come down and will not find any nook or cranny on earth which is free from their putrid stench. Jesus and his Companions will again pray to Allah, Who will send birds like the necks of camels; they will seize the bodies of Gog and Magog and throw them wherever Allah wills. Then Allah will send rain which no house or tent will be able to keep out, and the earth will be cleansed, until it will look like a mirror. Then the earth will be told to bring forth its fruit and restore its blessing. On that day, a group of people will be able to eat from a single pomegranate and seek shelter under its skin (i.e. the fruit will be so large). A milch-camel will give so much milk that a whole party will be able to drink from it; a cow will give so much milk that a whole tribe will be able to drink from it; and a milch-sheep will give so much milk that a whole family will be able to drink from it. At that time, Allah will send a pleasant wind which will soothe them even under their armpits, and will take the soul of every Muslim. Only the most wicked people will be left, and they will fornicate like asses; then the Last Hour will come upon them.' (It was related by Muslim)

From Ibn Mas'ud, may Allah be pleased with him:

The Prophet, may Allah bless him and grant him peace, said: 'On the night of the Isra (the Night Journey), I met my father Abraham, Moses and Jesus, and they discussed the Hour. The matter was referred first to Abraham, then to Moses, and both said, "I have no knowledge of it." Then it was referred to Jesus, who said, "No-one knows about its timing except Allah; what my Lord told me was that the Dajjal will appear, and when he sees me he will begin to melt like lead. Allah will destroy him when he sees me. The Muslims will fight against the kafirun, and even the trees and rocks will say, 'O Muslim, there is a kafir hiding behind me – come and kill him!' Allah will destroy the kafirun, and the people will return to their own lands. Then Gog and Magog will appear from all directions, eating and drinking everything they find. The people will complain to me, so I will pray to Allah and He will destroy them, so that the earth will be filled with their stench. Allah will send rain which will wash their bodies into the sea. My Lord has told me that when that happens, the Hour will be very close, like a pregnant woman whose time is due, but her family do not know exactly when she will deliver."' (It was related by Ahmad ibn Hanbal)

❖ ❖ ❖ ❖ ❖

To conclude, Dajjal the individual will be the final embodiment of all that denotes the way of kufr. The Mahdi will be the final human embodiment of all that it is possible to follow in the way of Islam – for only the Prophet Muhammad was in a position to be all of the Qu'ran walking, may the blessings and peace of Allah be on him. When these two opposites meet, everyone will have a choice – and when Jesus has come again, and the final conflict has been resolved, then the choice will be even clearer.

All this, however, lies in the future, and in the meantime everyone has a choice, the same choice, between iman and kufr.

It is not possible to defer making your choice between the two alternatives until a later date, since once you know that you have a choice, it must be made. Right now the choice is yours.

The *Qur'an* is crystal clear as to what will happen when the opposites meet: Allah gives victory to the ones who trust in Allah, over the ones who reject Allah. The *Qur'an* is crystal clear as to what will happen to you after your death. If you trusted in Allah and followed the way of His Prophet Muhammad, then you will be for the Garden. If you rejected Allah and refused to follow the way of His Prophet Muhammad, then you will be for the Fire. For ever. Right now the choice is yours.

Once you know about the way of Muhammad, the living life transaction of Islam, no other life transaction is acceptable to Allah. Surely the life transaction with Allah is Islam. Right now the choice is yours.

o o o o o

From 'Umar, may Allah be pleased with him:

> One day while we were sitting with the Messenger of Allah, may the blessings and peace of Allah be on him, there appeared before us a man whose clothes were exceedingly white and whose hair was exceedingly black; no signs of journeying were to be seen on him and none of us knew him. He walked up and sat down by the Prophet, may the blessings and peace of Allah be upon him. Resting his knees against his and placing the palms of his hands on his thighs, he said, 'Oh Muhammad, tell me about Islam.'
>
> The Messenger of Allah, may the blessings and peace of Allah be on him, said, 'Islam is to witness that there is no god only Allah and that Muhammad is the Messenger of Allah; to do the prayer; to pay the zakat; to fast in Ramadan; and to go on pilgrimage to the House if you are able to do so.'

He said, 'You have spoken truly.' And we were amazed at him asking him and saying that he had spoken truly. He said, 'Then tell me about Iman.'

He said, 'It is to believe in Allah, His Angels, His Books, His Messengers, and the Last Day, and to believe in the Decree, the good of it and the evil of it.'

He said, 'You have spoken truly.' He said, 'Then tell me about Ihsan.'

He said, 'It is to worship Allah as though you see Him, and though you do not see Him, yet truly He sees you.'

He said, 'Then tell me about the Hour.'

He said, 'The one questioned about it knows no more than the questioner.'

He said, 'Then tell me about its signs.'

He said, 'That the slave girl will give birth to her mistress; and that you will see the barefooted, naked, destitute herdsmen competing in constructing tall buildings.'

Then he went, and I stayed for a time. Then he said, 'Oh, 'Umar, do you know who the questioner was?'

I said, 'Allah and His Messenger know best.'

He said, 'It was Gabriel, who came to teach you your deen.' (It was related by Muslim)

From Abu 'Abdullah Jabir the son of 'Abdullah al-Ansari, may Allah be pleased with them both:

A man asked the Messenger of Allah, may the blessings and peace of Allah be on him, 'Do you think that if I do the obligatory prayers, fast in Ramadan, treat as permitted that which is permitted and treat as forbidden that which is forbidden, and do nothing more than that, I shall enter the Garden?'

He said, 'Yes.' (It was related by Muslim)

Yahya related to me from Malik that he heard that the Messenger of Allah, may Allah bless him and grant him peace, said, 'I have left two matters with you. As long as you hold to them, you will not go the wrong way. They are the Book of Allah and the Sunnah of His Prophet.' (It was related by Malik bin Anas)

✿   ✿   ✿   ✿   ✿

You are on a journey. Your passage through this world is only a brief part of that journey, like a person who enters a room through one door, crosses it, and goes out through another door; or like a rider who comes to a tree, rests under it for a moment or two, and then continues on his or her journey.

Allah says in the *Qur'an* that people will be asked how long their lifetime was in this world, and they will reply that it was only a short time, maybe a day or half a day.

The Prophet Muhammad, may the blessings and peace of Allah be on him, said that you should be children of the next world, not of this world, because this world is leaving you and the next world is approaching you. He also said, 'Love whom you will, they will surely die. Do what you will, you will be judged accordingly.'

Right now the choice is yours.

Follow your heart. Do what you can. You will be drawn to what you love. You will be repulsed by what you hate. You will do what you have to do. Do not deny your heart. Nobody can make you what you're never meant to be. Nothing but this moment knows the moments that will be. And as what remains of your life time unfolds, moment by moment, hour by hour, day by day, and as all the changes come and go, one after another, each so unexpected in the future, each so immediate in the present, each so unreal in the past, then do not forget, but remember, and when you forget, remember:

> You are on a journey. Truly everything comes from Allah and returns to Allah, willingly or unwillingly, via the Garden or via the Fire, including you. Right now the choice is yours. Wake up. Time is passing. You are on a journey. The journey is to Allah.

Allah

The Ka'aba, Makka

When everyone is standing before Allah
On the Last Day
Allah will say
'Who is the King now?'

Say: 'This is my way – I call to Allah with clear understanding, I and whoever follows me, and glory be to Allah, and I am not one of the idol worshippers.'

(*Qur'an: Surah Yusuf* – 12.108)

Who could say anything better than someone who summons to Allah and acts rightly and says, 'I am one of the Muslims'?

(*Qur'an: Surah Fussilat* – 41.32)

There is no god only Allah
Muhammad is the messenger of Allah

The Prophet Muhammad said, may the blessings and peace of Allah be on him, that knowledge is the lost property of the mumin, who may pick it up wherever he or she finds it.

Nothing is what it seems.

This book is for all those who are not satisfied with the official version, and who want the real thing.

There is no real thing, only the Real, Allah.

Allah

Glossary of Arabic Terms

adab : inner courtesy coming out as graciousness in right action.

adhan : the call to prayer.

ahlu'l-dhimma : non-muslims living in Muslim territory and under the protection of Muslim rule by virtue of the fact that they have agreed to pay the jizya tax.

akhira : what is on the other side of death; the world after this world in the realm of the Unseen.

Alastu bi Rabbikum? : 'Am I not your Lord?' The question which Allah asked all the arwah when they were first given form. They all answered, 'Yes, we bear witness,' including you.

Allah : the Lord of all the Worlds and what is in them, including you. Allah has ninety-nine Names all of which are from and within the One, Allah. Allah, the supreme and mighty Name, indicates the One, the Existent, the Creator, the Worshipped, the Lord of the Universe. Allah is the First without beginning and the Last without end. He is the Outwardly Manifest and the Inwardly Hidden. There is no existent except Him and there is only Him in existence.

al-hamdulillahi wa shukrulillah : Praise to Allah and thanks to Allah.

'alim : a Muslim who has sound knowledge of the Qur'an and the Hadith, and accordingly of the Shari'ah and the Sunnah, and who puts what he knows into action.

amir : one who commands and makes the final decision; the source of authority in any given situation. When and wherever there is a group of Muslims it is the Sunnah to choose an Amir from amongst themselves.

aql : intellect, the faculty of reason. The noun derives from the verb which means 'to hobble a camel'.

arwah : the plural of ruh; spirits.

awliya : the plural of wali; the friends of Allah, and those who have the greatest knowledge of Allah, which is ma'rifa.

ayah : a phrase structure of the Qur'an, and also a sign, both in the linguistic and semiotic sense. There are ayat in the self and on the horizon.

ayat : the plural of ayah; signs.

baraka : blessing. A subtle energy which flows through everything, in some places more than others, most of all in the human being. Purity permits its flow, for it is purity itself, which is light. Density of perception blocks it. Since it is light, baraka is intimately connected with the ruh.

barzakh : an interspace between two realities which both separates and yet links them; commonly used to describe the interspace between the dunya and the akhira, which begins when death takes place, when the ruh leaves the body – and ends when the Last Day arrives, when the ruh and the body are reunited again; also used to describe the realm of the arwah in the Unseen, which is the abode of the ruh prior to its entering the unborn foetus in the womb after about sixteen weeks of pregnancy.

bayt al-mal : house of wealth; the treasury of the Muslims where income from zakat and other sources is gathered for redistribution.

Dajjal : the ultimate embodiment of kufr, manifesting as an individual, as a social and cultural phenomenon, and as an unseen force; sometimes called the AntiChrist, the Dajjal is the false Messiah whose appearance marks the imminent end of the world, the antithesis of Jesus. The science of recognising Dajjal is very intricate and carefully delineated. The manifestation will appear both as a person, and as a certain historical situation, and as a series of cosmic phenomena. The Dajjal will affect the masses and cause chaos.

Dar al-Harb : the abode of conflict, wherever the deen of Kufr is established.

Dar al-Islam : the abode of peace, wherever the deen of Islam is established.

deen : the life transaction, the way you live and behave towards Allah. It is submission and obedience to a particular system of rules and practices. Literally it means the debt or exchange situation between two parties, in this usage the Creator and the created, or as some say between the conditioned and the unconditioned, the limited and the limitless, or the many and the One. Allah says in the Qur'an that surely the deen with Allah is Islam.

dhikr : remembrance and invocation of Allah. All worship of Allah is dhikr. Its foundation is declaring the Unity of Allah, prostrating before Allah, fasting, giving to the needy, and doing the hajj, the pilgrimage to Makka. Recitation of the Qur'an is its heart, and invocation of the Single Name, Allah, is its end.

dinar : a 28 carat gold coin weighing approximately 4.25 grams.

dirham : a pure silver coin weighing approximately 3 grams.

du'a : making supplication to Allah.

dunya : the world as it is imagined, inwardly and outwardly. It has been compared to a bunch of grapes which appears to be in reach but which, when you stretch out for it, disappears.

fard : what is obligatory in the Shari'ah. This is divided into fard 'ayn, which is what is obligatory on every adult Muslim; and fard kifaya, which is what is obligatory on at least one of the adults in any particular Muslim community.

fasiqun : those who split and divide, either their selves inwardly, or existence outwardly.

fiqh : the formal study of knowledge, especially the practice of Islam. It is the science of the application of Shari'ah.

fitra : the first nature, the natural, primal condition of mankind in harmony with nature, with the self inwardly, and with existence outwardly.

fuqaha : the scholars of fiqh, who by virtue of their knowledge can give an authoritative legal opinion or judgement which is firmly based on what is in the Qur'an and the Hadith and which is in accordance with the Shari'ah and the Sunnah.

furqan : the faculty of being able to discriminate between what is halal and what is haram, between what is valuable and what is worthless, between what is fruitful and what is unfruitful, between what is good and what is bad, both for your self and for others. One of the names of the Qur'an is Al-Furqan. To embody the Sunnah and follow the Shari'ah is furqan.

Jibril : the angel Gabriel who was the means by which the Qur'an was revealed to the Prophet Muhammad, may the blessings and peace of Allah be on him.

ghayb : the Unseen.

ghusl : washing the entire body with water in accordance with the Sunnah of the Prophet Muhammad, may the blessings and peace of Allah be on him. It is necessary to have a ghusl on embracing Islam, after sexual intercourse or seminal emission, at the end of menstruation, and after child birth – and before being buried when your body is washed for you. It is necessary to be in ghusl and in wudu before you do the salat or hold a copy of the Qur'an. Ghusl is a purification both inwardly and outwardly.

hadith : the written record of what the Prophet Muhammad said or did, may the blessings and peace of Allah be on him, preserved intact from source, through a reliable chain of human transmission, person to person.

hadith qudsi : the written record of those words of Allah on the tongue of the Prophet Muhammad, may the blessings and peace of Allah be on him, which are not a part of the Revelation of the Qur'an, preserved intact from source, through a reliable chain of human transmission, person to person.

hajj : the greater pilgrimage to the Ka'ba, the House of Allah in Makka, and the performance of the rites of pilgrimage in the protected area which surrounds the Ka'ba. The hajj begins on the 8th of Dhu'l-Hijja, the twelfth lunar month of the Muslim calendar. The hajj is one of the pillars of Islam, and is a purification outwardly and inwardly.

hajrat al-aswad : the Black Stone, a stone, which some say fell from heaven, set into one corner of the Ka'ba in Makka by the Prophet Ibrahim, peace be on him, which the pilgrims in imitation of the Prophet Muhammad, may the blessings and peace of Allah be on him, kiss, so unifying all the Muslims throughout the ages in one place.

halal : what is permitted by the Shari'ah.

haram : what is forbidden by the Shari'ah. Also Haram: a protected area. There are two protected areas, known as the Haramayn, in which certain behaviour is forbidden and other behaviour necessary. These are the areas around the Ka'ba in Makka and around the Prophet's

Mosque in Madina, in which is his tomb, may the blessings and peace of Allah be on him.

hijra : to emigrate in the way of Allah to a place where it is possible to follow the way of Muhammad, may the blessings and peace of Allah be on him, and establish the deen of Islam as a social reality. Islam takes its dating from the first Hijra of the Prophet Muhammad, from Makka to Madina, in 622 AD.

hudud : the limits; the boundary limits which separate what is halal from what is haram, as defined by Allah.

'id : a festival. There are two main festivals of the Muslim year, on the first day of which 'id prayers are prayed.

'Id al-Adha : a four day festival at the time of the hajj. The 'id of the (greater) Sacrifice, it starts on the 10th day of Dhu'l-Hijjah, the day that the pilgrims sacrifice their animals, remembering the sacrifice which the Prophet Ibrahim, on him be peace, was prepared to make, and the sacrifice which he made instead.

'Id al-Fitr : a three day festival after the month of fasting, Ramadan.

idhn : permission or authority, either to teach, or to fight jihad in the way of Allah. Idhn is from Allah and His Messenger, may the blessings and peace of Allah be on him.

ihsan : the inward state of the mumin who is constantly aware of being in the Presence of Allah, and who acts accordingly. Ihsan is to worship Allah as though you see Him, knowing that although you do not see Him, He sees you.

ijtihad : exercising personal judgement; the faculty of deciding the best course of action in a situation, which is not expressly referred to in the Qur'an and the Hadith, and then choosing a course of action which is close to the Sunnah and in accord with the Shari'ah. Very useful when dealing with technology.

imam : the one who leads the communal prayers. In the first Muslim community of Madina al-Munawarra, the Amir was the Imam.

iman : trust in Allah and acceptance of His Messenger, may the blessings and peace of Allah be on him. Iman grows in the heart of the one who follows the way of Islam. Iman is to believe in Allah; His Angels; His Books; His Messengers; the Last Day and the Fire and the Garden;

and the Decree of what is good and what is evil. Thus iman is the inner knowledge and certainty in the heart which gives you taqwa and tawba and the yearning to know more.

insh'Allah : if Allah is willing; if Allah wants it.

Islam : the Prophetic guidance brought by the Prophet Muhammad, may the blessings and peace of Allah be on him, for this age for the people and jinn who desire Peace in this world, the Garden in the next world, and knowledge and worship of Allah in both worlds. The five pillars of Islam are the affirmation of the shahada; doing the salat; fasting Ramadan; paying the zakat; and doing the hajj if you are able. The peak of Islam is jihad. A person enters Islam by saying the shahada in front of at least two witnesses, and having a ghusl either directly before or after this.

isnad : the record, either memorised or recorded in writing, of the names of the people who form the chain of human transmission, person to person, by means of which a hadith is preserved – and accordingly these people themselves. One of the sciences of the Muslims which was developed after the Prophet Muhammad's death, may Allah bless him and grant him peace, is the science of assessing the authenticity of a hadith by assessing the reliability of its isnad.

'isra' : the Night Journey of the Prophet Muhammad, may the blessings and peace of Allah be on him, from Makka to Jerusalem and then through the realms of the seven heavens beyond the limit of forms, the sidrat al-muntaha, to within a bow-span's length or nearer to the Presence of the Real.

Israfil : the angel who will blow the Trumpet which heralds the Last Day.

Izrail : the angel who takes the ruh from the body at the moment of death.

Jabarut : the source world, the world of divine light and power. Shaykh 'Abd'al-Qadir al-Murabit writes, 'The kingdom of power. This is the kingdom of lights. Shaykh al-Akbar notes: "With Abu Talib it is the world of Immensity. With us it is the middle world." By this he indicates that the mulk is opposite the jabarut and it is precisely the realm of lights, the Divine Presence that creates the split between the two worlds on which creational reality is based. That means that Light is the barzakh, the inter-space between the visible and the invisible. In reality existence is one, the three kingdoms are one kingdom with one Lord. It is by the setting up of the limits and the barriers and the differences that the universal metagalactic existence is able to come into being. That which sets up barriers, and is the barriers, is none other than the One Reality in its sublime perfection unrelated to any form. The barriers are not realities in themselves yet without them nothing would be defined and no-one could define them.' (*Quranic Tawhid.* Diwan Press. 1981).

jahiliyya : the time of arrogance and ignorance which precedes the time when the way of Islam is established as a social reality. Anyone who does not have wisdom suffers from jahiliyya.

Jalal : Allah's Attribute of Majesty.

Jamal : Allah's Attribute of Beauty.

Jibril : the angel Gabriel, peace be on him.

jihad : the fight in the way of Allah against kufr. Inwardly, the greater jihad is the fight against the kufr in your own heart. Until your heart is purified, you are your own worst enemy. Outwardly, the lesser jihad is the fight against the kafir who attempts to subvert or destroy the practice of Islam.

Jinnah : the Garden, the final destination and resting place of the Muslims in the akhira, once the Day of Reckoning is past. Jinnah is accurately described in great detail in the Qur'an and in the Hadith.

jinn : beings made of smokeless fire who live in the Unseen. Some jinn are mumin, some are kafir, some are the followers of shaytan, and we seek refuge in Allah from the accursed shaytan.

jizya : the annual tax paid by all adult males of the ahlu'l-dhimma, who are guaranteed the protection of the Muslims in return.

Ka'ba : the House of Allah, in Makka, originally built by the Prophet Ibrahim, peace be on him, and rebuilt with the help of the Prophet Muhammad, may the blessings and peace of Allah be on him. The Ka'ba is the focal point which all Muslims face when doing the salat. This does not mean that Allah lives inside the Ka'ba, nor does it mean that the Muslims worship the Ka'ba. It is Allah whom the Muslims worship, and Allah is not contained or confined in any form or place or time or concept.

kafir: the one who denies the Existence of Allah and who rejects His Prophets and Messengers, and who accordingly has no peace or trust in this life, and a place in the Fire in the next life. Shaykh 'Abd'al-Qadir al-Murabit writes, 'Kufr means to cover up reality: kafir is one who does so. The kafir is the opposite of the mu'min. The point is that everyone knows 'how it is' – only it suits some people to deny it and pretend it is otherwise, to behave as if we were going to be here for ever. This is called kufr. The condition of the kafir is therefore one of neurosis, because of his inner knowing. He 'bites his hand in rage' but will not give in to his inevitable oncoming death.' (*Quranic Tawhid*. Diwan Press. 1981).

kafirun: the plural of kafir. The disbelievers.

khalif: one who stands in for someone else, in this case, the leader of the Muslim community. In the first Muslim community of Madina al-Munawarra, the Khalif was the Amir was the Imam.

kharaj: taxes imposed on revenue from land or the work of slaves.

khulafa ar-rashidun: the rightly guided Khalifs, Abu Bakr, 'Umar, 'Uthman and 'Ali, may Allah be pleased with them.

kitab: a book.

kufr: to cover up reality, to deny Allah, to reject His Messengers.

kutub: the plural of kitab; books, often meaning the Books revealed by Allah to His Messengers.

lubb: a core. This term is used in the Qur'an to indicate people who have great understanding in the core of their being, the heart. Those who have lubb are capable of worshipping Allah with deep knowledge and attaining ma'rifa.

Madina al-Munawarra: the city to which the Prophet Muhammad made Hijra, may the blessings and peace of Allah be on him, and where the revelation of the Qur'an was completed. The first Muslim community was established in Madina al-Munawarra, and Allah says in the Qur'an that this is the best community ever raised up from amongst mankind. Their hearts and actions were illuminated and enlightened, may Allah be pleased with all of them, by Allah and His Messenger; and Madina al-Munawarra is still illuminated by the presence of the arwah of those of them who are buried there, especially the Prophet Muhammad, may the blessings and peace of Allah be on him.

Mahdi : one who is rightly guided. The Prophet Muhammad, may the blessings and peace of Allah be on him, said that there would be a mahdi every hundred years who would revive the deen of Islam, and that the last of them would be the Mahdi who would fight the Dajjal until the Prophet Jesus, peace be on him, returned to this world and killed the Dajjal.

Makka : the city in which the Ka'ba stands, and in which the Prophet Muhammad was born, may Allah bless him and grant him peace, and where the revelation of the Qur'an commenced.

makruh : disapproved of without being forbidden.

mala'ika : the angels, who are made of light and glorify Allah unceasingly. They are neither male nor female. They do not need food or drink. They are incapable of wrong action and disobeying Allah and they do what Allah commands them to do. Everyone has two recording angels continually with them who write down their actions and none of this escapes the knowledge of Allah.

Malakut : the angelic world, the kingdom of Unseen forms. Shaykh 'Abd'al-Qadir al-Murabit writes, 'This is both the kingdom of the source-forms of the creational realities, crystals, atoms, organisms, and the kingdom of the spiritual realities, the Lote-tree, the Balance, the Throne and so on. It is the realm of vision as the mulk is the realm of event. As the characteristic of the mulk is fixity or apparent fixity so the characteristic of the malakut is flux and transformation or apparent flux. In fact one could say that the reality of the two worlds is opposite that, for indeed the solid forms are all in change, while the visions are all unfolding the fixed primal patterns on which all the visible world is based.' (*Qur'anic Tawhid*. Diwan Press. 1981).

mamnu'a : what is prohibited in acts of worship in the Shari'ah.

ma'rifa : gnosis, the highest knowledge of Allah possible to man or woman. It is to directly witness the Light of the Names and Attributes of Allah manifested in the heart. Shaykh 'Abd'al-Qadir al-Murabit writes, 'Gnosis, the central knowledge, for it is knowledge of the self, is a proof to the one who knows it and this is its glory and its supremacy over all others. By it its possessor knows the universe, how it is set up and its underlying laws in their action, their qualities and their essences. His knowledge of the Universe is his own self knowledge, while his knowledge of his own self is direct perception of his own original reality, the adamic identity. Everything he has comes from Allah. He never sees anything but he sees Allah in it, before it, after it. There is only Allah in his eyes as there is only Allah in his heart.' (*Qur'anic Tawhid*. Diwan Press. 1981).

ma'sha'Allah : it is the will of Allah; it is what Allah wants.

Masih ad-Dajjal : the false Messiah, the AntiChrist, the Dajjal.

Masih ibn Maryam : the Messiah, son of Mary – Jesus Christ, peace be on him.

Mikail : the angel in charge of the Garden.

mizan : balance, in life, inwardly and outwardly. Mizan is also used to indicate the means by which actions and intentions will be measured on the Last Day. Shaykh 'Abd'al-Qadir al-Murabit writes, 'Al-Mizan. Its meaning is the justice and harmony of all creation and therefore of time/space and therefore of us and events. It is the meaning of the Garden and the Fire, of the balance between the matrices, it is what was called in the ancient Tao-form of Islam in China, yin/yang. It is the secret of the contrary Names. It is what we are born and die on, and which turns our acts and intentions into realities to be weighed on the Day of the Balance.' (*Qur'anic Tawhid*. Diwan Press. 1981).

mudd : a measure of volume, one both hands cupped full, a double handed scoop.

mufsida : what invalidates acts of worship in the Shari'ah.

mufsidun : the mischief makers. Those who say they are putting everything right, when in fact they are only creating disorder.

muhsin : the Muslim who has ihsan, and who accordingly only gives reality to the Real, Allah. Only the muhsin really knows what Tawhid is. A wali of Allah, Shaykh 'Abd'al-Qadir al-Murabit, once said, 'The difference between the kafir and the muslim is vast. The difference between the muslim and the mumin is greater still. The difference between the mumin and the muhsin is immeasurable,' not only in inward state, but also in outward action.

Mulk : the phenomenal world, the universe. Shaykh 'Abd'al-Qadir al-Murabit writes, 'The visible realm. The mulk is what is experienced in the sensory (hiss) and in illusion (wahm). Of its nature mulk is both solid, sensory and pure-space, illusory. This is now confirmed by kafir science. The amazing interlocking substantiality of Mulk veils most people from the meaning-realm onto which it opens the intellect, thus it is designated kingdom for it is a realm of reality, seemingly complete in itself. It is not real, but it is made WITH THE REAL, in the language of Qur'an. Thus to understand it we must penetrate its imprisoning solidity.' (*Qur'anic Tawhid*. Diwan Press. 1981).

mumin : the Muslim who has iman, who trusts in Allah and accepts His Messenger, may the blessings and peace of Allah be on him, and for whom the next world is more real than this world. The mumin longs for the Garden so much, that this world seems like the Fire by comparison.

muminun : the plural of mumin; the believers.

munafiqun : the hypocrites. Those people who outwardly profess Islam on the tongue, but who inwardly reject Allah and His Messenger, may the blessings and peace of Allah be on him, and who side with the kafirun against the muminun. The deepest part of the Fire is reserved for the munafiqun.

Munkar and Nakir : the two angels who question the ruh in the grave after the dead body has been buried, asking, 'Who is your Lord?'; 'Who is your Prophet?'; 'What is your Book?'; 'What was your Deen?' The kafir will be confused. The mumin will have the best reply.

mushrikun : the idol worshippers, those who commit shirk.

muslim : one who follows the Way of Islam, doing what is obligatory and avoiding what is forbidden in the Shari'ah, keeping within the hudud of Allah, and embodying as much of the Sunnah as he or she is able, through study of the Qur'an and the Hadith followed by action. A Muslim is, by definition, one who is safe and sound, at peace in this world, and guaranteed the Garden in the next world.

mustahab : what is recommended, but not obligatory, in acts of worship in the Shari'ah.

mutafafifin : the cheaters; those who give short measure and demand more than a fair price.

nabi : a Prophet; a man rightly guided by Allah and sent by Allah to guide others. Altogether there have been one hundred and twenty-four thousand Prophets in the history of mankind. The last Prophet before the end of the world, the Seal of the Prophets, is the Prophet Muhammad, may the blessings and peace of Allah be on him.

nafs: the illusory experiencing self; you as you think you are. When the nafs is impure, it is an illusory solidification of events obscuring a light, the ruh. When it has been completely purified, the nafs is ruh.

Nar: the Fire of Jahannam, the final destination and place of torment of the kafirun and the munafiqun in the akhira, once the Day of Reckoning is past. Some of those Muslims who neglected what is fard in the Shari'ah and who did grave wrong action without making tawba will spend some time in the Fire before being allowed to enter the Garden, depending on the Forgiveness of Allah – Who forgives every wrong action except shirk if He wishes. Nar is accurately described in great detail in the Qur'an and in the Hadith.

nawafil: what is voluntary in acts of worship in the Shari'ah.

Nur: Light. Allah says in the Qur'an that Allah is the Light of the heavens and the earth.

Nuri Muhammad: the ruhani Light of Muhammad, may the blessings and peace of Allah be on him.

qadr: the Decree of Allah, which determines every sub-atomic particle in existence, and accordingly whatever appears to be in existence. One of Allah's Names is Al-Qadir, the Powerful, the One Who does whatever He wants. Again and again the Qur'an reminds us that Allah has power over everything and that Allah does what He wants.

qabr: the grave, experienced as a place of peace and light and space by the ruh of the mumin, who sees his or her place in the Garden in the morning and in the evening; and experienced as a place of torment and darkness and no space by the ruh of the kafir, who sees his or her place in the Fire in the morning and in the evening. After death there is a period of waiting in the grave for the ruh until the Last Day arrives, when everyone will be brought back to life, assembled together, and sent to the Garden or to the Fire. So do not have your body cremated.

qibla: direction. Everyone has a direction in life. The direction which the Muslims face when they do the prayer is towards the Ka'ba in Makka. This direction is what distinguishes the Muslims from everyone else, who have every direction except the qibla.

Qur'an : the 'Recitation', the last Revelation from Allah to mankind and the jinn before the end of the world, revealed to the Prophet Muhammad, may Allah bless him and grant him peace, through the angel Jibril, over a period of twenty-three years, the first thirteen of which were spent in Makka and the last ten of which were spent in Madina. The Qur'an amends, encompasses, expands, surpasses and abrogates all the earlier revelations revealed to the earlier Messengers, peace be on all of them. The Qur'an is by far the greatest of all the miracles given to the Prophet Muhammad by Allah, for he was illiterate and could neither read nor write. The Qur'an is the uncreated word of Allah. The Qur'an still exists today exactly as it was originally revealed, without any alteration or change or addition or deletion. Whoever recites the Qur'an with courtesy and sincerity receives knowledge and wisdom, for it is the well of wisdom in this age.

qutb : the Pole or axis of the Universe, the greatest living wali at any given point in time. Shaykh 'Abd'al-Qadir al-Murabit writes, 'This term is only understood by the one who has attained to it. An approximation would be to say that in him gnosis is complete inwardly so that outwardly his gnosis radiates as a sun over all the other gnostics. The proofs of the qutb are these: that he is surrounded by a circle of gnostics as a King is visibly recognisable by his Court, that the deen of Islam revives around him bringing life to the people, and thirdly that he names his successor before his death.' (*The Meaning of Man*. Diwan Press. 1977).

Ramadan : one of the pillars of Islam. It is the ninth lunar month of the Muslim calendar during which all adult Muslims who are in good health fast from dawn to sunset each day. During the first third of the fast you taste Allah's Mercy; during the second third of the fast you taste Allah's Forgiveness; and during the last third of the fast you taste freedom from the Fire. The Qur'an was first revealed in the month of Ramadan during the Night of Power, which is one of the nights in the last third of Ramadan. The fast of Ramadan is a purification outwardly and inwardly.

rasul : a Messenger, a Prophet who has been given a revealed Book by Allah. Every Messenger was a Prophet, but not every Prophet was a Messenger.

ruh : the spirit, formed of pure light, the Light of Allah.

ruhani : pertaining to the ruh.

rusul : the plural of rasul; the Messengers.

saʻ : hour; usually used to denote the Hour, that is the time when the world ends, and the yawm al-akhira begins.

saa : a measure of volume, equal to four mudds.

sadaqa : giving to the needy, in any form, including sharing wisdom, giving a helping hand, giving away clothing, food and money. Sadaqa is given voluntarily and willingly seeking only the pleasure of Allah.

sahih : healthy and sound with no defects.

salat : one of the pillars of Islam. It is the prayer which consists of fixed sets of standings, bowings, prostrations and sittings in worship to Allah. There are five prayers which are obligatory: subh which is done between dawn and sunrise; dhur which is done between mid-day and mid-afternoon; ʻasr which is done between mid-afternoon and sunset; maghrib which is done immediately after sunset; and ʻisha which is done between once it is dark and mid-night. The Muslim day begins at maghrib. It is necessary to be in ghusl and in wudu before you do the salat. Salat is a purification outwardly and inwardly.

salih : a developed man; by definition, one who is in the right place at the right time.

sayyedina : 'our master', a term of respect.

shahada : one of the pillars of Islam. It is to witness: 'La ilaha il'Allah, Muhammad ar-rasulu'llah,' that is, that: 'There is no god only Allah, Muhammad is the Messenger of Allah,' may the blessings and peace of Allah be on him. The shahada is the gateway to Islam in this world and the gateway to Jinnah in the next world. It is easy to say, but to act on it is a vast undertaking which has far-reaching consequences, both in inward awareness and in outward action, both in this world and in the next world. Affirming the shahada is a purification outwardly and inwardly.

shahid : a witness, a martyr in the way of Allah.

Shariʻah : a road; the Way of Islam, the Way of Muhammad, may the blessings and peace of Allah be on him, the road which leads to knowledge of Allah and the Garden. Shaykh ʻAbd'al-Qadir al-Murabit writes, 'It is the behaviour modality of a people based on the revelation of their Prophet. The last shari'ah in history has proved to be that of Islam. Its social modality abrogates all previous shara'i e.g. Navaho, Judaic, Vedic, Buddhic, etc. These shara'i however, continue until the arrival and confrontation takes place in that culture with the final and thus superior shari'ah – Islam. It is, being the last, therefore the easiest to follow, for it is applicable to the whole human race wherever they are.' (*Qur'anic Tawhid*. Diwan Press. 1981).

Shara'i : the plural of shari'ah; roads.

shaykh : an old man – an 'alim who has knowledge of Allah and His Messenger, may Allah bless him and grant him peace, and His deen – the one who guides you from knowledge of your self to knowledge of your Lord.

shaytan : a devil, particularly the Devil, Iblis (Satan), may Allah curse him, who is one of the jinn who was and is too proud to obey Allah, and who encourages everyone else to be likewise. Shaytan is part of the creation of Allah, and we seek refuge in Allah from the evil that He has created.

shirk : to associate anything or anyone as a partner with Allah, that is, to worship what is other than Allah, including your self, your country, your universe and anything it contains. Shirk is the opposite of Tawhid. Allah says in the Qur'an that He will forgive any wrong action except shirk. Shaykh 'Abd'al-Qadir al-Murabit writes, 'Idol-worship means giving delineation to the Real. Encasing it in an object, a concept, a ritual, or a myth. This is called shirk, or association. Avoidance of shirk is the most radical element in the approach to understanding existence in Islam. It soars free of these deep social restrictions and so posits such a profoundly revolutionary approach to existence that it constitutes – and has done for fourteen hundred years – the most radical rejection of the political version of idolatry, statism. It is very difficult for programmed literates in this society to cut through to the clear tenets of Islam, for the Judaic and Christian perversions stand so strongly in the way either as, rightly, anathema, or else as ideals. The whole approach to understanding reality has a quite different texture than that known and defined in European languages, thus a deep insight into the structure of the Arabic language itself would prove a better introduction to the metaphysic than a philosophical statement. The uncompromising tawhid that is affirmed does not add on any sort of 'god-concept'. Nor does it posit an infra-god, a grund-god, even an over-god. Christian philosophers were so frightened by this position that when they met it, to stop people discovering the fantasy element in their trinitarian mythology they decided to identify it with pantheism in the hope of discrediting it. That they succeeded in this deception is an indication of how far the whole viewpoint has been kept out of reach of the literate savage society. Let it suffice here to indicate that there is no 'problem' about the nature of Allah. Nor do we consider it possible even to speak of it. No how, who, or what or why. It is not hedging the matter in mystery. It is simply asking the wrong questions. The knowledge of Allah is specifically a personal quest in which the radical question that has to be asked is not even 'Who am I?' but 'Where then are you going?' (*Qur'anic Tawhid.* Diwan Press. 1981).

Sidrat al-Muntaha : 'the lote tree of the furthest limit', the place in the Unseen where form ends.

Sirat al-Mustaqim : the straight path, of Islam.

Sunnah : the form, the customary practice of a person or group of people. It has come to refer almost exclusively to the practice of the Messenger of Allah, Muhammad, may the blessings and peace of Allah be on him, but at the time that Imam Malik, may Allah be pleased with him, compiled *Al-Muwatta'*, meaning 'The Well-Trodden Path', there was no sense of setting the Sunnah of the Prophet apart from the Sunnah of Madina, so that the actions of its knowledgeable people were given even more weight than the behaviour of the Prophet related in isolated Hadith. The Sunnah of the Prophet Muhammad and the first Muslim community of Madina al-Munawarra is a complete behavioural science that has been systematically kept outside the learning framework of this society.

surah : a form, a large unit of the Qur'an linked by thematic content, composed of ayat. Every surah in the Qur'an has a particular form, and is named as such.

Surat'al-Fatiha : the form of both Opening and Victory. This is the opening surah of the Qur'an. Recitation of Surat'al-Fatiha is an integral and essential part of the salat, which means that every Muslim recites it at least twenty times a day. It is thus the most often daily repeated statement on the face of the earth today. Its translation in English is as follows:

In the Name of Allah, the Merciful, the Compassionate

Praise to Allah, Lord of the worlds, the Merciful, the Compassionate, King of the Day of the Life-Transaction. Only You we worship and only You we ask for help. Lead us on the Straight Path, the path of those whom You have blessed, not of those with whom You are angry, and not of those who are astray. Amin.

Surah Yunus : the form of the Prophet Jonah, on him be peace.

Surah Yusuf : the form of the Prophet Joseph, on him be peace.

takbir : the saying of 'Allahu Akbar' meaning 'Allah is Greatest'. Salat begins with a takbir.

taqlid : in reference to fiqh, it means the following of previous authorities and the avoidance of ijtihad.

taqwa : awe of Allah, which inspires a person to be on guard against wrong action and eager for actions which please Him.

taslim : giving the muslim greeting of 'As-Salaamu 'alaykum,' meaning 'Peace be on you'. Salat ends with a taslim.

tasawwuf : sufism. Shaykh 'Abd'al-Qadir al-Murabit writes, 'Its preferred etymology is that it derives from suf, wool. Shaykh Hassan al-Basra said, "I saw forty of the people of Badr and they all wore wool." This means that the sufi - tasawwafa - has put on the wool. This is distinct from those who confirm the way of Islam with the tongue and by book learning. It is taking the ancient way, the primordial path of direct experience of the Real. Junayd said, "The sufi is like the earth, filth is flung on it but roses grow from it." He also said, "The sufi is like the earth which supports the innocent and the guilty, like the sky which shades everything, like the rain which washes everything." The sufi is universal. He has reduced and then eliminated the marks of selfhood to allow a clear view of the cosmic reality. He has rolled up the cosmos in its turn and obliterated it. He has gone beyond. The sufi has said 'Allah' – until he has understood. All men and women play in the world like children. The sufi's task is to recognise the end in the beginning, accept the beginning in the end, arrive at the unified view. When the outward opposites are the same, and the instant is presence, and the heart is serene, empty and full, light on light, the one in the woollen cloak has been robed with the robe of honour and is complete. The Imam also said, "If I had known of any science greater than sufism, I would have gone to it, even on my hands and knees.'" (*Qur'anic Tawhid*. Diwan Press. 1981).

tawaf : circling the Ka'ba.

tawba : turning away from wrong action to Allah and asking His Forgiveness, returning to correct action after error, turning to face the Real whereas before one turned one's back. One of the greatest acts of tawba is to abandon the deen of kufr and to embrace the deen of Islam. Your turning to Him is in reality His turning to you.

Tawhid : Unity in its most profound sense. Allah is One in His Essence and His Attributes and His Acts. The whole universe and what it contains is One unified event which in itself has no lasting reality. Allah is Real. Shaykh 'Abd'al-Qadir al-Murabit writes, 'Our Imam said, "It is a meaning which obliterates the outlines and joins the knowledges. Allah is as He always was. Tawhid has five pillars: it consists of the raising of the veil on the contingent, to attribute endlessness to Allah alone, to abandon friends, to leave one's country, and to forget what one knows and what one does not know." His greatest statement on tawhid, which Shaykh al-Akbar has called the highest of what may be said on the subject is, "The colour of the water is the colour of the glass." Commenting on this Shaykh Ibn 'Ajiba said, "This means that the exalted Essence is subtle, hidden and luminous. It appears in the outlines and the forms, it takes on their colours. Admit this and understand it if you do not taste it." Tawhid is itself a definition whose meaning is not complete for the one who holds to it until he has abandoned it or rather exhausted its indications and abandoned it for complete absorption in the One.' (*Qur'anic Tawhid*. Diwan Press. 1981).

tayammum : purification for prayer with clean dust, earth or stone, when water for ghusl or wudu is either unavailable or would be detrimental to health. Tayammum is done by striking the earth with the palms of the hands and wiping the face and hands and forearms.

'ulama : the plural of 'alim; those who know. Allah says in the Qur'an that the 'ulama are those who fear Allah.

'umra : the lesser pilgrimage to the Ka'ba, the House of Allah in Makka, and the performance of its rites in the protected area which surrounds the Ka'ba. It can be done at any time of the year.

wajib : what is necessary, but not obligatory, in acts of worship in the Shariʻah.

wali : the friend of Allah; the one who has both inward knowledge and outward knowledge. The station of the wali is the station of knowledge of the Real by direct seeing. Inwardly the wali has gnosis of Allah. He or she has intimate knowledge of the Qurʻan and the Hadith, knowing their outward meanings and their inward meanings and their gnostic meanings, as much as Allah wills. Outwardly the wali embodies the Shariʻah of Islam and the Sunnah of the Prophet Muhammad, may the blessings and peace of Allah be on him. The greatest wali alive at any given point in time, the Qutb, is like a drop compared to the ocean of the Prophet Muhammad, may the blessings and peace of Allah be on him.

wudu : washing the hands, mouth, nostrils, face, forearms, head, ears, and feet, with water, in accordance with the Sunnah of the Prophet Muhammad, may the blessings and peace of Allah be on him, so as to be pure for prayer. You must already be in ghusl for wudu to be effective. You should ensure that your private parts and under-clothes are clean before doing wudu. Once you have done wudu, you remain in the state of wudu until it broken by: any of the conditions which make it necessary to have a ghusl; emission of impurities from the private parts – urine, faeces, wind, prostatic fluid, or other discharge; loss of consciousness by whatever means, usually by sleep or fainting; physical contact between man and woman where sexual pleasure is either intended or experienced; touching your penis with the inside of your hand or fingers; and leaving Islam. It is necessary to be in ghusl and in wudu to do the salat, and to hold the Qurʻan. Wudu is a purification both outwardly and inwardly.

yaqin : certainty. It has three stages:

ʻIlm al-yaqin, knowledge of certainty.
ʻAyn al-yaqin, source of certainty.
Haqq al-yaqin, truth of certainty.

The Raja of Mahmudabad defined them thus:

You are told – there is a fire in the forest.
You reach the fire in the forest and see it.
You are the fire in the forest.

Yawm al-Akhira : the Day After – the end of the world, and thus the Last Day, when everyone who has ever lived will be given life again, gathered together, their actions and intentions weighed in the Balance, and their place in either the Garden or the Fire confirmed. Yawm al-Akhira is also referred to in the Qur'an as Yawm ad-Deen, the Day of the Life Transaction; Yawm al-Ba'th, the Day of Rising from the grave; Yawm al-Hashr, the Day of Gathering; Yawm al-Qiyama, the Day of Standing; Yawm al-Mizan, the Day of the Balance; and Yawm al-Hisab, the Day of Reckoning. That Day will either be the best day or the worst day of your life, depending on who you are and where you are going. The Yawm al-Akhira is accurately described in great detail in the Qur'an and in the Hadith.

zakat : one of the pillars of Islam. It is an annual wealth tax paid only by Muslims, and not the ahlu'l-dhimma, usually in the form of one fortieth of surplus wealth which is more than a certain fixed minimum amount, which is called the nisab. Zakat is payable on: accumulated wealth; merchandise; certain crops; certain live-stock; and subterranean and mineral wealth. As soon as it is collected it is redistributed to those in need, as defined in the Qur'an and in the Hadith. Zakat is a purification both outwardly and inwardly.

zakat al-fitr : a small obligatory head-tax, one saa, of a local staple food, usually grain or dried fruit, which is collected from, or on behalf of, every single Muslim in the community at the end of Ramadan before the 'Id al-Fitr, and given to those in need, as defined in the Qur'an and in the Hadith. Zakat al-Fitr is a purification both outwardly and inwardly.

Zamzam : the well near the Ka'ba in Makka which provides the best water in the world.

○ ○ ○ ○ ○

Most of the definitions in this Glossary are taken directly or derive from the books listed in the Bibliography, which should all be read in order to arrive at an understanding which is far beyond the scope of this book.

○ ○ ○ ○ ○

Post Script

The world has changed a great deal since the first edition of *Dajjal* was written in the space of six weeks in 1980 and the revised edition completed in 1997. Suffice it to say that the tide and nature of events during the last 30 years have on the whole confirmed the original analysis and assessment – often more graphically than could have been imagined.

The opposites continue to polarise and what used to be disguised is now more apparent – and what Allah decrees will surely happen.

As during the twentieth century, the meaning of events in the Middle East can only be understood in the context of recognising what has to be done if the publicly proclaimed Zionist dream of establishing a Greater Eretz from the Nile to the Euphrates is to be realised.

Outwardly, the peoples of the world are faced with the choice of either being further enslaved by means of institutionalised usury and secular democracy, supported and masked by the doctrine of human rights – or of establishing governance in accordance with the Shari'ah of Islam, and implementing the abolition of usury and restoration of the gold dinar and silver dirham, supported and illuminated by worship of Allah.

Inwardly, the journey of knowledge for each of us continues – we are always free to stop at each and every step of the way – or to go on. As time passes and lives draw to their close, right now the choice is ours:

Furth, fortune and fill the fetters. – Say Allah! and go straight ahead!

> The angels descend on those who say,
> 'Our Lord is Allah,' and then go straight:
> 'Do not fear and do not grieve
> but rejoice in the Garden you have been promised.
> We are your protectors in the life of the dunya and the akhira.
> You will have there all that your selves could wish for.
> You will have there everything you demand.
> Hospitality from One Who is Ever-Forgiving, Most Merciful.'
> (*Qur'an: Surah Fussilat* – 41.29-31)

from a free spirit in a free world

Ahmad Thomson
Safar 1432 / February 2011

The Prophet's Mosque ﷺ, Madina

Bibliography

Qur'an, the uncreated word of Allah. Translations by Muhammad Pickthall, by Muhammad Yusuf Ali and by Shaykh Abdalhaqq & Aisha Bewley. Avoid gross mis-translations by non-muslims.

Al-Muwatta', of Imam Malik. Translated by 'A'isha 'Abdarahman at-Tarjumana and Ya'qub Johnson. Diwan Press. 1982.

Ar-Risala, of Imam Ibn Abi Zaid al-Qairwani. Translated by Alh. Bello Muhammad Daura. Northern Nigerian Publishing Co. Ltd. 1983.

Handbook on Islam, Iman, Ihsan, of Shaykh Uthman Dan Fodio. Translated by 'A'isha 'Abdar-Rahman Bewley. Diwan Press. 1978.

The Foundations of Islam, of Qadi 'Ayad. Translated by 'A'isha 'Abdarahman at-Tarjumana. Diwan al-Amir Publications. 1982.

The Shifa', of Qadi 'Ayad. Translated by 'A'isha 'Abdarahman at-Tarjumana. Madinah Press. 1991.

Life of Muhammad, of Ibn Ishaq. Translated by A. Guillaume. Oxford University Press. 1978.

Life of Muhammad, by Martin Lings. Allen and Unwin. 1983.

The Life of Muhammad, by Tahia Al-Ismail. Ta-Ha Publishers Ltd. 1988.

Sahih, of Imam Bukhari. Translated by Dr. Muhammad Muhsin Khan. Crescent Publishing House. 1974.

Sahih, of Imam Muslim. Translated by 'Abdal-Hamid Siddiqui. Nusrat Ali Nasri for Kitab Bhavan. 1987.

Sunan, of Imam Abu Da'ud. Translated by Ahmad Hasan. Sh. Muhammad Ashraf. 1984.

The Gardens of the Righteous, of Imam Nawawi. Translated by Zafrullah Khan.

Mishkat al-Masabih. Translated by Professor Robson. 1972.

Forty Hadith, of Imam Nawawi. Translated by Ezedin Ibrahim and Denys Johnson-Davies. The Holy Qur'an Publishing House. 1976.

Forty Hadith Qudsi, from Allah. Translated by Ezzedin Ibrahim and Denys Johnson-Davies. The Holy Qur'an Publishing House. 1980.

Kufr – an Islamic Critique, by Shaykh 'Abd'al-Qadir al-Murabit. Diwan Press. 1981.

Letter to an African Muslim, by Shaykh 'Abd'al-Qadir al-Murabit. Diwan Press. 1981.

Root Islamic Education, by Shaykh 'Abd'al-Qadir al-Murabit. Diwan al-Amir Publications. 1982.

The Sign of the Sword, by Shaykh 'Abd'al-Qadir al-Murabit. Medina Press. 1984.

The Book of Strangers, by Ian Dallas. Victor Gollancz. 1972.

The Way of Muhammad, by Shaykh 'Abd'al-Qadir al-Murabit. Diwan Press. 1974.

Diwans of the Darqawa. Translated by 'A'isha 'Abdarahman at-Tarjumana. Diwan Press 1980.

The Darqawi Way, of Shaykh Mawlay al-'Arabi ad-Darqawi. Translated by 'A'isha 'Abdarahman at-Tarjumana. Diwan Press. 1979.

The Meaning of Man, by Shaykh 'Ali al-Jamal. Translated by 'A'isha 'Abdarahman at-Tarjumana. Diwan Press. 1978.

Qur'anic Tawhid, by Shaykh 'Abd'al-Qadir al-Murabit. Diwan Press. 1981.

Indications from Signs, by Shaykh 'Abd'al-Qadir al-Murabit. Diwan Press. 1982.

Jesus, Prophet of Islam – Revised Edition, by Muhammad Ata'ur-Rahim and Ahmad Thomson. Ta-Ha Publishers Ltd. 1996.

Jesus in the Qur'an – Revised Edition, by Ahmad Thomson and Muhammad Ata'ur-Rahim. Ta-Ha Publishers Ltd. 2012.

For Christ's Sake and *Islam in Andalus* (the Revised Edition of *Blood on the Cross*), by Ahmad Thomson and Muhammad Ata'ur-Rahim. Ta-Ha Publishers Ltd. 1996.

Making History, by Ahmad Thomson. Ta-Ha Publishers Ltd. 1997.

The Bible, the Qur'an and Science, by Maurice Bucaille. 4th Edition.

The Holy Bible, by various authors. King James and New International Versions. Hodder and Stoughton. 1979.

The Gospel of Barnabas. Edited and translated from the Italian Ms. in the Imperial Library at Vienna, by Laura and Lonsdale Ragg. Aisha Bawany Waqf. 1977.

The Protocols of the Elders of Zion. Translated by Victor E. Marsden. British Patriot Publications. 1978.

The Thirteenth Tribe, by A. Koestler. Hutchinson & Co. (Publishers) Ltd. 1976.

The History of the Jewish Khazars, by D.M. Dunlop. Princeton University Press. 1954.

The Controversy of Zion, by Douglas Reed. Veritas Publishing Company (Pty) Ltd. 1985.

Last Days of the Romanoffs, by Robert Wilton. Thornton Butterworth. 1920.

History and Destiny of the Jews, by Josef Kastein (alias Julius Katzenstein). Translated by Huntley Paterson. John Lane. 1933.

False Inheritance, by Michael Rice. Kegan Paul International. 1994.

For the Coming Man, by Shaykh 'Abd'al-Qadir al-Murabit. Murabitun Press. 1988.

The End of Economics, by 'Umar Ibrahim Vadillo. Madinah Press. 1991.

Islam against Economics, by 'Umar Ibrahim Vadillo. Murabitun Publications. 1991.

Fatwa on Paper-Money, by 'Umar Ibrahim Vadillo. Madinah Press. 1991.

The Workers have been Told a Lie about Their Own Situation, by 'Umar Ibrahim Vadillo. Murabitun Publications. 1992.

Jewish Foundations of the New World Order, by Leo Jung. Herald Square Press, Inc. 1949.

The Signs before the Day of Judgement, of Ibn Kathir. Translated by Huda Khattab. Dar Al-Taqwa Ltd. 1991.

✥   ✥   ✥   ✥   ✥

Many of the books on Ezra Pound and the Nuremberg Trials in the British Library – and many others, here, there and everywhere.

About the author

Ahmad Thomson was born in Chipata, Zambia, and was educated principally in Zimbabwe and in England, obtaining a Bachelor of Laws Degree with Honours at the University of Exeter, and a Diploma in Law at the City University of London. He was called to the Bar by the Honourable Society of Gray's Inn in 1979. As well as being the author or co-author of several books and practising as a barrister, the author has worked as a bus conductor, accountant, potter, publisher, oriental carpet warehouseman, delivery van driver, hospital cleaner, theatre porter and editor. The author embraced Islam on the 13th August 1973 at the hand of the Raja of Mahmudabad, *alayhi rahma*, and has travelled widely in the Muslim world in search of knowledge, including England, Spain, Morocco, Algeria, Tunisia, Egypt, Sudan, Saudi Arabia, Jordan, Syria, Turkey, Iran, Pakistan, India, Thailand, Malaysia, Singapore and Indonesia. Since knowledge is infinite, the search continues, and if you want what Allah wants then there is no confusion as what Allah wants happens.

By the same author

The Last Prophet
may the blessings and peace of Allah be on him
and on his family and on his companions and followers
The Wives of the Prophet
Fatima az-Zahra
Asma bint Abi Bakr
The Journey of Ahmad and Layla
The Moghuls
The Difficult Journey
The Way Back
The Next World Order
Making History

As co-author with Muhammad Ata'ur-Rahim

Jesus, Prophet of Islam – Revised Edition
Jesus in the Qur'an – Revised Edition
For Christ's Sake – Part One of the Revised Edition of Blood on the Cross
Islam in Andalus – Part Two of the Revised Edition of Blood on the Cross

As co-author with Abdal-Haqq and A'i'sha Bewley

The Islamic Will